# The Monadic Age

T0272160

# The Monadic Age

## Notes on the Coming Social Order

**Ingo Niermann**

*Sternberg Press*

The thirty-three essays in this book are grouped thematically into seven topics as major as life can get: identity, games, home, death, freedom, anxiety, and love. Differing in year of origin and point of view, all of the essays aim to fathom fundamental change in the Western world. They complement each other while persisting well enough on their own. In doing so, they correspond to the coming social order they unfold— the Monadic Age.

# Contents

# A Brief Introduction to the Monadic Age

Fifteen hundred words give a glimpse into the playbook
of the post-liberal mindset, recall the great disappointments
of the Liberal Age, define how the monad is about to replace
the individual, trace the beginnings of the Monadic Age, and
sketch the future manifestations of this new social order.

Recently, I caught up with a friend, freshly divorced after ten years of marriage. Being over an increasingly toxic relationship, she was ready to open herself up to the world again and find new love. But the world wasn't the same. Now in her early forties, men hadn't lost interest in her. She looked stunning, pursued an enthralling art career, and had two loving children. Most reasonable men of her age were taken, but she also attracted younger men.

My friend had no problem with the prospect of a younger partner. It was just that she couldn't wrap her head around the available men in their twenties and early thirties. Many were invested in gardening, but she couldn't take their return to nature too seriously. Was a garden nature at all? During sex, she missed the intensity of touch. It felt more as if the men were looking at an image from the outside—like taking a selfie. Many said they were nonbinary and polysexual—but why did they need to contain the overcoming of gender stereotypes in new, normative terms? Many were into poly-amory but not intense romance. Rather, they seemed to be taking the passion out of their relationships—hedging them like another kind of garden.

What my friend told me about her recent intimate encounters sounded as though it were taken straight from the playbook of the post-liberal mindset. It's not just that liberal institutions such as representative democracy, privacy, or freedom of speech are eroding. A new social paradigm, which I call *monadism*, forces a radical reinvention of all social parameters.

Liberal society promised to let everyone realize their full potential: there wouldn't be different classes, only different aspirations. Despite the institutionalization of certain basic rights and the unleashing of an enormous production of goods, it didn't work out so well. The rich ripped off the poor, and together they took from other states and the environment. To avoid revolution, liberal states reinvented themselves as welfare states, making massive efforts to redistribute wealth and opportunity. Still, success was only possible due to continued exploitation of other countries and the environment; as soon as these bucked significantly, the tensions within and between welfare states heated up.

Developments in intimate life were similarly limited. The bourgeois marriage only allowed for a heterosexual binarism. Husbands might have pursued outlandish ambitions—in jobs, politics, hobbies, or affairs—while wives were largely confined to housework and motherhood. Emancipation and sexual liberation allowed for different forms of relationships. But as people overcame the constraints of the bourgeois marriage, they were confronted with fierce competition—much like the global marketplace.

Today, two major post-liberal dispositions are unfolding. On the one hand, people envision a harmonious community of all human and nonhuman beings (multispecies kinship, a rainbow of identities). On the other hand, people isolate themselves within their own identities and belongings (filter bubbles, safe spaces, gated communities, charter cities, prepping).

Monadism recognizes that these two seemingly contradictory dispositions stem from a similar understanding of the world: one is more optimistic, the other more pessimistic, but ultimately, they're interdependent. Changing from aggressive parasites to benevolent participants in the global ecosystem is an uncertain and risky maneuver. Before seeking harmony, we humans, a highly dominant species, must first of all restrain ourselves from coercive interactions with our environment. And to protect ourselves sufficiently from our environment, we must minimize its abuse. Monadism is the synthesis of these two dispositions.

While the individual is defined ex negativo as something that can't be divided, the monad (Greek for "unity") implies self-fulfillment. In Gnosticism, the word *monad* has been used as a synonym for the supreme, all-encompassing God, as employed in Gottfried Wilhelm Leibniz's *La monadologie* (*The Monadology*, 1714) as a synonym for souls that coexist according to a divine predetermination. I don't expect us or our descendants to evolve into largely autarchic, autotrophic beings in perfect harmony with each other, but I do expect us and our descendants to be increasingly shaped by that ambition.

Technical progress has been the driving force behind this social change. The Liberal Age has been propelled by industrialization (mass production, mass media), allowing for an immense amplification of human labor and power. Its major political challenge has been how to effectively generate and fairly distribute the produced wealth. The Monadic Age is propelled by computations (automation, interactive media) that will eventually be able to directly manipulate anything on Earth—without human help or understanding (AGI, the "singularity"). Against the background of the destructive forces that have already been unfolding through industrialization, now the major political challenge is how to constrain the potentials of these computations usefully.

| | | |
|--:|:-:|:--|
| individual | ▶ | monad |
| self-realization | ▶ | self-sufficiency |
| self-discipline | ▶ | self-drill |
| tolerance | ▶ | consent |
| autonomy | ▶ | autarchy |
| narcissism | ▶ | autoeroticism |
| autofiction | ▶ | autofantasy |
| fanaticism | ▶ | co-op fantasy |
| novel | ▶ | game |
| vandalism | ▶ | self-infliction |
| agency | ▶ | reversibility |
| majority rule | ▶ | consociationalism |
| humanism | ▶ | environmentalism |
| global village | ▶ | global kinship |
| universal rights | ▶ | universal liability |
| globalization | ▶ | harmonization |
| mechanization | ▶ | automation |
| milieu | ▶ | voluntary tribe |
| family | ▶ | ego tribe |
| nationalism | ▶ | segregationism |
| prosthesis | ▶ | extra organ |
| dignity | ▶ | safe space |
| saving | ▶ | prepping |
| civility | ▶ | intimate correctness |

From Individualism to Monadism

Arguably, the Monadic Age already begins with the Nuclear Age. The detonation of nuclear bombs confronts humanity with its enormously destructive power, unique in visibility and immediacy. Governments seek to protect their people in bunkers and to tame nuclear energy in painstakingly sealed power plants. At the same time, the possession of nuclear bombs acts as a shield against aggressions from other countries, and nuclear power promises energy independence. But instead of nuclear weapons protecting countries in an egalitarian way, an oligarchy of a few nuclear powers has gained unprecedented imperialist potency. And the use of nuclear energy has led to long-lasting radioactive waste and the risk of a catastrophic meltdown.

With digitalization, it's the other way around: at first digitalization acts as a catalyst of the Liberal Age, because it leads to the internet—a ubiquitous network of machines and people through which globalization can unfold without limits. But the internet is also being used for devastating global manipulations of both computers (hacks, distributed denial-of-service attacks) and minds (fake news, clickbait, echo chambers, mindfucks). Now, computers are more in demand to secure people's privacy and autonomy, and computers that run important programs are protected from humans and each other like monads.

As a monad, the only thing that you can lay claim to is yourself—that is, your mind as an inseparable part of your body. "You" isn't a distinct manifestation like a soul or a self, it's all of your holobiont and cyborg body. You're more like your own tribe—*ego tribe*—in constant change and exchange but nonetheless single and singular. Whereas aristocratic societies are based on the enslavement of others and bourgeois societies on the enslavement of yourself, monadic societies are based on the re-creation of yourself as distinctly unique.

Monadism is easily confused with egocentrism. As a monad, you're reluctant to interact with the world, less because you mainly care about yourself than because you don't want to impose a solidarity that predetermines others' needs. Interacting with the world, you can't take anything for granted.

To interact safely with consent and care, monads tend to segregate in communities of like-minded people—*voluntary tribes*. These can be in constant flux or solidify as largely autonomous, if not autarchic, substates—independent of international supply chains, each more or less automatically producing most of its own food, energy, and machines. For monads, states are just another cluster within an immense agglomeration of mutual agreements. Citizenship takes on the character of a membership or a share rather than that of a birthright. The democratic claim of reversibility shifts from your government and law to your own commitment: as in games, everybody must always have the option to exit as well as an abundance of other possibilities to enter.

Even when living as crowded urbanites, monads avoid the implicit violence of random encounters. Robots pamper, transport, maintain, and satisfy, and communication and entertainment are mostly virtual. However small, your home can be an office, factory, farm, school, hospital, or prison. Even when you go out on the street in person, you don't have to meet anyone. You don't even have to pay attention to the actual street. Before sharing your home and territory, you take them with you, or at least create them virtually wherever you go. Before starting a family, you extend your ego tribe with entities like pets, robots, avatars, or tattoos that are easy to care for or can be exchanged without worries. Further implemented into a monadic *body with more organs*, you feel these adoptions as part of yourself.

*The Monadic Age* unfolds in thirty-three autonomous—monadic—essays that I've written on topics as diverse as environmentalism, terrorism, geopolitics, housing, the metaverse, AI, nonbinarism, language, charity, euthanasia, identity politics, tattoos, ableism, birthrates, war, religion, sex, and art. As the corpus took shape, I rewrote parts, particularly to synchronize terminology. Nevertheless, each essay is explicitly rooted in the circumstances of its initial draft: the Islamic State, the European refugee crisis, Donald Trump's presidency, my mother's death, the COVID-19 pandemic, and the Russia-Ukraine war, among others. Although I believe that the trajectory of the human species continues to follow grand narratives, I doubt that any one person can grasp them properly while they're happening. *The Monadic Age* is meant to be a stopover in describing what is possibly the last manifestation of humans as an Earth-dominating species. Whether human efforts *to reconcile with the world*, if not *to reconcile the world*, will work out, or whether they will end just as disastrously as the efforts to conquer and subdue it, only history will tell.

Glossary

**autoeroticism.** Autoeroticism seeks erotic self-fulfillment and is not to be confused with narcissism—the obsessive need for appreciation. Autoerotic pratices are at the forefront of a general shift from the liberal ambition of expansive self-realization to the monadic ambition of less invasive self-sufficiency within an **ego tribe** or a **body with more organs.**

**autotrophy.** Biotechnical progress will eventually allow monadic self-sufficiency to be deployed on processes such as metabolism and thermoregulation. Ideally, you become autotrophic as a primary producer and also as a self-decomposer—not even consuming inorganic material. All you require is the occasional intake of sunlight.

**augmented virtuality.** Just as augmented reality extends the physical environment with virtual elements, augmented virtuality spices up virtuality with physical elements.

**autofantasy.**    While the Liberal Age is preoccupied with finding yourself, the Monadic Age is about overcoming yourself. Virtual games are a main inspiration. Acting camp, your fantastic personas remain in a state of **augmented virtuality**.

**body with more organs.**    The liberal deterritorialization as an imagined "body without organs" with an endless variety of exchangeable protheses is followed by a monadic reterritorialization of the body with a potentially endless number of extra organs that you identify with. Your empathy is limited and often misleading, but when it comes to your own organs, you just feel them.

**co-op fantasy.**    A fantasy in which other characters are embodied by independent entities, either sentient people or non-player characters. Co-op fantasies can be self-fulfilling (e.g., cryptocurrencies).

**ego tribe.**    Rather than being egocentric, as a **monadist** you deny that an "ego" even exists and perceive yourself as an ever-changing variety, an ego tribe. You can extend your ego tribe with easy-to-care-for entities like pets, robots, avatars, or tattoos. Further implemented into a **body with more organs**, you feel these adoptions as part of yourself.

**exorcism.**    The adoption of a virtual identity doesn't stop the moment you unplug. Exorcist practices such as cleansing rituals, debriefings, or hypnosis to get rid of expendable identities are required in relation to **inorcism**.

**inorcism.**    An advanced hybrid reality—addressing all your senses—that allows you to experience yourself unlike your physical manifestation. Different from analog immersive techniques like reading, watching, hypnosis, or lucid dreaming, you don't have to focus but are beset—at your own request. What happens is the opposite of **exorcism**: a deliberate and reversible act of inorcism.

**intimate correctness.**    Intimate correctness completes political correctness by making feelings part of your etiquette—like words and gestures—and overcoming discriminating patterns of attraction. Just as you can work on yourself to become more attractive, you can drill yourself (self-drill) to be attracted to people whom you tend to overlook or avoid.

itsie.    Someone who condemns gendered pronouns as human exceptionalism and uses the pronouns *it/it/its* (singular) and *they/them/their* (plural) for all things and beings.

monad/monadism.    While the individual is defined ex negativo as something that can't be divided, the monad (Greek for "unity") implies self-fulfillment. Liberalism understands individuals as free atoms that are allowed to move every which way, as long as they avoid direct collisions; in monadism, individuals shouldn't interact with one another, unless they do so with consent and care (autoeroticism, autotrophy, museal native).

museal native.    As modernization gains speed, ever-larger parts of the world are put under protection. In the world, as in a museum, individual humans find their place as collectors, guards, conservators, visitors, or their very own museum (ego tribe). As members of Indigenous tribes take on the role of ecological natives, modern societies generate museal natives.

obit.    An autofiction running backward from an anticipated death by choice. Everything that you do is legitimized as leading toward that end and as better than already dying now—for yourself, society, and the environment. Obit is the Latin word for perished (as in "obituary").

orc/orcie/orcism.    Inorcism and exorcism are summarized as orcism. The respective verb is *to orc*; the noun, *orc*, or, cuter, *orcie*. These terms also refer to Orcus, the Latin name for the god of the underworld, and to the orcs, a species of monsters in the fantasy writings of J. R. R. Tolkien.

**self-drill.** The multiplicity of the ego tribe regards gaming as its main paradigm and shifts focus from introspective, "mindful" self-realization to repetitive, automatized play. You self-condition (i.e., drill yourself) into various characters (autofantasy). You can also drill yourself to make great personal challenges like death more bearable, if not enjoyable (obit), or to exert intimate correctness.

**tardie.** The opposite of an early adopter, a tardie delays the implementation of novelties not out of conservative beliefs, but following a pragmatic calculus: in times of accelerating change, you'd better reserve your elasticity for when change becomes substantial.

**voluntary tribe.** To interact safely with consent and care, monads segregate in communities of like-minded people—voluntary tribes—that can be in constant flux or solidify as largely autonomous, if not autarchic, substates. Voluntary tribes don't necessarily demand exclusivity in membership or in territory. An enormous multiplicity of voluntary tribes coexists and competes.

# I.   REBIRTH OF THE SUBJECT

The expansive liberal individual eats itself and is challenged
by the self-sufficient monad.

Words for the Monadic Age
2022

A. Tardies

**In their quest for immortality, writers—myself included—have been skeptical about neologisms. Wondering to what extent this conservative bias has limited my speculative reach, I set out to invent at least one significant new term.**

I've always been late. When I was born, my parents initially thought I was deaf because it took me weeks to respond to any sound. I was also a late talker, and late in puberty. More importantly, I wanted to be late, if develop at all. I didn't want to grow older or get bigger. The taller you are, the smaller everything else appears, and I didn't like that. I loved hanging out on the floor, but in modern Western culture, it was a space reserved for kids. Only kids were allowed to move under tables, in between grown-ups' legs. Kids had so much more fun. As a kid, if you gave me a sheet of paper and a pen, I would draw a different world—I was able to see it all, even though I wasn't particularly good at drawing. If you gave me a few toy cars, or Lego bricks, or even just sticks and stones, I could create a different world and stay there for hours.

　　Grown-ups had to work, and even in their free time, they didn't seem to do anything that really entertained them—unless they drank alcohol. Alcohol would make them laugh about things that were barely even funny to me. When they drank a lot, they even forgot how to speak and walk, and fell asleep at the table. Alcohol was the drug that made them young again, and it didn't work very well. It made them laugh so loud that it hurt my ears. It made them stick to their chairs, not jump, run, or roll around. It made them eat so much that their bellies became huge and they moved even less. I promised myself to never stop being playful and to never get drunk.

But I wasn't an Oskar Matzerath, the boy in Günter Grass's novel *The Tin Drum* (1959) who stops growing by force of will. My body grew automatically, and so did my mind. Paradoxically, the reason I had so much more fun than adults was that I was inclined to learn. This made me explorative, curious, and creative. Being a child was like being a butterfly—only to then turn into a grub.

In kindergarten, I dreamed of becoming a truck driver or a crane operator. Steering these machines would be like playing, just bigger and more real. I expected the thrills of these jobs to compensate for the general tedium of being an adult. But when it became undeniable that my toys were losing their magical powers, I realized that it was only a matter of time until these jobs would become just as boring as playing with toys.

The only thing that could prevent me from being as boring and bored as grown-ups would be to never stop learning. In secondary school, learning was more of an effort and less playful than when I was a little kid, which is why it took me quite a while to realize that learning was all that was left to never grow up and to continue to get truly overwhelmed and excited. Every fundamentally new thought I encountered or came up with sent chills down my spine and a sweet sensation in my penis. Still, I was almost too late by the time I decided to obtain higher education.•

I studied what appeared to me to be the greatest possible challenge: philosophy. My ambition was to come up with no less than a theory of everything (reading popular science books on general relativity, quantum theory, and string theory gave me the impression that physics alone wouldn't cut it). It was highly unlikely that I would succeed in this challenge, but if I did, I anticipated the greatest possible joy. This wouldn't be some prophetic mock-up; this would be the one true revelation. Any time my motivation would wane, I would feel ready to die like the protagonist of Johann Wolfgang von Goethe's epic play *Faust* (part 1, 1808; part 2, 1832) after he exclaims: "Beautiful moment! Do not pass away!"

I was very aware that my search for absolute knowledge was already obsolete. Not only was I highly unlikely to succeed, I was also highly unlikely to find any support, sympathy, or companionship in my quest. Rather, my professors and fellow students would ridicule or ignore me. From the beginning, I was a lost cause.

But from my understanding, my professors and classmates were lost causes too. How could you seriously study philosophy in such a mature and sedate way? I couldn't imagine anyone else at our institute waking up at night, alarmed at being basically clueless. No wonder philosophy had lost all relevance.

When I escaped into literature, it was a bit easier to play the freak. Thanks to my huge round head, I still looked pretty much like a child, even in my late twenties. This gave my rigorousness a cute touch. But my ambition to understand everything, now on a more concrete level, felt just as displaced. Not only had the world of literature mostly given up on trying to gain a new overall understanding of the world but even the few who stuck with it wouldn't take me seriously, since my writing came without any apparent novelties in style, grammar, or vocabulary. Just the opposite: I sought to get as much irritation and revelation as possible out of a linear story with a few characters talking and doing things at a few unspecific places, using common words. Still, most of my readers would give up trying to understand my novel after a single page. It was just too arduous to figure out if my writing was any good.

I traveled the world but was struggling to buy a new pair of trousers, a sweater, or a bike. Just as I didn't come up

Real Estate Porn •

• Intimate Correctness

with new words, I would never have a kid or buy a house.• Rearrangements would have to suffice. There were no final answers, only never-ending struggles to find them.

I stretched my mode of investigation and came up with a whole book series of megalomaniac solutions to solve world problems. The Solution Series, published by Sternberg Press since 2008. My solutions included the biggest human-made building on the planet—a collective tomb for many millions of people—for which I installed a prominent jury to devise a master plan. I developed plans for the reunification of Korea and presented them in Seoul. I founded an Army of Love for a need-oriented redistribution of encompassing love, and gathered experts from different fields to perform dozens of trainings to explore the practical challenges of such a redistribution.• But all my projects remained exploratory; they were too outlandish for others to take over and properly implement. I gained some international recognition for my social designs, mostly in the role of stimulatory pranks (this saved me from being disturbed by the independent existence and eventual death of my ideas).

When I turned forty, I experienced how K-HOLE, a collective of millennials based in New York, came up with a series of highly trenchant trend reports. What started more as a work of fan fiction led to commissions by major brands, culminating in 2013 with the use of a portmanteau that went viral: *normcore*. Blending the words *normal* and *hardcore*, K-HOLE used the term to describe people like me who, despite being receptive to the world of fashion, go for an undistinguished personal style. They told me that I had served as one of the inspirations for coining that anti-trend.

The media and fashion brands got it all wrong and tried to turn normcore into a proper trend with collections and looks, but to me the term came as a revelation: a single new word was able to describe a major aspect of my way of life (i.e., not paying any particular attention to that which wasn't essential for my quest). As I was completely on my own, no monk's cowl awaited me. Anything that made me stick out would create unnecessary frictions. I was what writer Ernst Jünger had called an "anarch" (a renegade in disguise), but in a merely aesthetic sense.

Could there be more of those words? To really grasp a new understanding of the world, isn't it crucial to mark it with a new vocabulary?

In general, literary writers are reluctant to coin words. Many are generally quite conservative (as any new media further reduces the attention they get) or their artistry allows them to nail down things, processes, and characteristics with existing words. (They don't need the cake mix; they can bake with the basic ingredients.)

But there is also a striking calculus behind our conservatism toward words: establishing a neologism is very much trial and error, and the risk of failing is extremely high, even more so when you place the words in a book or magazine that probably won't have more than a few hundred or a few thousand readers. The texts that you publish as a progressive writer are meant to stay significant and readable for decades, if not centuries, so why spoil them with obvious failures? The same goes for new words and conventions of speech coined by others, unless they reflect the parlance of their protagonists.

For people active on social media—from actual and aspiring influencers to very occasional or only-for-friends posters—the calculus is completely different: everything gets forgotten, unless you break through with a powerful meme (a look, a movement, a gesture, a word).

Not that many people care about who first came up with a meme. And so far, it's not possible to copyright single looks, movements, gestures, or words. It wasn't K-HOLE who came up with the term normcore, but a cartoonist named Ryan Estrada (who as of today is still without a Wikipedia entry). Estrada invented the word in 2008 for what he later described as an "unfunny and forgettable" webcomic; the following year, the term entered the *Urban Dictionary* without giving him credit.

Turning GIFs and social media posts into NFTs is a

way to retroactively authorize, monetize, and immortalize some of those volatile but impactful cultural microinventions. Theoretically, it also becomes possible for the public (and also private) use of any registered new meme to lead to the automatic transaction of microroyalties.* But so far, words aren't at the forefront of the digital *copyrightification* (not my invention; there is a YouTube account of the same name, which currently has one subscriber). The popular use of the term *meme* is limited to cartoons consisting of one or a few images combined with a minimal punch line. Words aren't enough.

There aren't many incentives for literary writers to come up with new words instead of new novels. Even though only a few people—and even fewer people of substantial cultural influence—read non-genre fiction, at least publishing novels allows you to apply for scholarships, win prizes, and secure a teaching position in creative writing. In this teaching position, you might, like me, give your students the task of coming up with a new word that's missing. In my case, this has led to remarkable inventions. But we didn't work on giving these words a chance to go viral, and all of us probably forgot about them.

Now, I would like to invent a significant new word myself. It's not that I've kept totally clear of that ambition in the past. In German, I came up with two compound words as titles for nonfiction books—rather bulky words with up to six syllables: *Minusvisionen* (Minus visions, 2003) and *Umbauland* (Reconstruction country, 2006). These words were camp takes on the possibility in German to create compound words of a crackjaw length, not words meant to alter the common perception of the world. I also came up with some names for imaginary movements and forms of terror when writing an alternate reality about a segregation of White men, *Deutsch Süd-Ost* (German southeast, 2020). My video series *Deutsch Süd-Ost*, 2020, was commissioned by steirischer herbst '20. Most were redefinitions of existing words, but I came up with one catchy neologism, *Walder* (forest-er), that refers to actually existing White supremacist deep ecologists. Still, they would regard

Society of Games •
Automatic Privacy

my views on them as too critical to adopt the term, and for the rest of the world, they were too fringe to care about how to compellingly name them.

As a student, I adored German sociologist Niklas Luhmann. He had brought Talcott Parsons's systems theory to a new level and turned the prevalent, socially engaged form of sociology on its head. He had done this with practically no new terms, only by—often drastically—redefining existing ones. But there was one exception. In the 1970s he stumbled across the neologism *autopoiesis* (self-creation) coined by the biologists Humberto Maturana and Francisco Varela in an effort to look at biological processes from the viewpoint of cybernetics—the basis of the more complex systems theory. The term didn't transmit any new biological knowledge, but it hit Luhmann as a revelation. It took him years to reformulate every aspect of his theory accordingly.

Writing about the times we're in and where we're headed, I came up with a number of catchy phrases (*comic purgatory*, *middle-class warriors*, *corona tribes*, *ego tribes*, *intimate correctness*, *abnormcore*) that you can find in this book. But the more I got a sense of what was utterly new and not just post-something, the more I felt that I was missing some words. Maybe even just a single word that would unlock a fundamentally new understanding of our times.

## B. Itsies

Common approaches for creating gender-appropriate language both complicate our existing language and support human speciesism. A focus on overcoming words and morphemes solely for humans is more inclusive than adding new ones.

Before I start my search for an important new word, I must withstand serious doubts. Therefore, I revisit my previous examples:

Autopoiesis has exactly the same meaning as self-creation. The only reason Niklas Luhmann got so excited about that new term is that he wrote in German. In German, there are two words for creation, and both come with serious problems. One, *Schöpfung*, is mainly used in a metaphysical sense. The other, more secular one, *Bildung*, also means education. The word *Selbstbildung* would make most people think of self-education, not self-creation. Autopoiesis worked as a loanword with classical, strictly intellectual connotations. Though it risks appearing a bit pretentious, especially in an Anglo-Saxon context, autopoiesis was Luhmann's poetic concession within an otherwise rather technical vocabulary. The term was probably a factor in my becoming a fan of his systems theory, but it also made me doubt if his approach was really that bulletproof.

The first time that I encountered normcore (avant la lettre) was in the novel *American Psycho* (1991) by Bret Easton Ellis. The protagonist, a New York investment banker and serial killer, dedicates lengthy praise to mainstream pop albums by Phil Collins and Whitney Houston. He obviously isn't just a conformist *yuppie* (back then a popular term to describe a young consumer with a fashionable, high-income job and deferred family commitments), he's a yuppie with a camp attitude—and he overdoes capitalist egoism by committing sadistic murders. White male supremacy allows him to get away with his crimes. Twenty years later, our camp conformism was pauperized; it wasn't geared toward a cohort of investment bankers but toward an average middle class. Our look as such wasn't a signifier of privilege. In late neoliberalism, every class, race, and gender was allowed, if not encouraged, to buy their clothes from mainstream brands like Gap or Uniqlo. Our privilege as White males was rather that we could dress so cheaply and effortlessly in the context of the creative class and not fear degradation. Another decade later, the declaration of this lazy exploitation of race and gender privilege as edgy feels as dated as the perception of the protagonist of *American Psycho* as cool.

For a change, I look at some neologisms that don't just mark vanguard thinking but the urge for the emancipation of the unnamed. Words that fight for substantial equal rights. Words that might be a matter of life and death:

In the 1860s, gay German lawyer Karl Heinrich Ulrichs was wondering how to describe his sexual orientation without defaming it. He came up with *Urning* (Uranian) for a man who desires men, *Urningin* for a woman who desires women, *Dioning* (Dionian) for a man who desires women, and *Dioningin* for a woman who desires men. These words were derived from two Greek myths about how Aphrodite was born: according to Hesiod, in a parthenogenesis from the foam of Uranus's genitals; according to Homer, from Zeus impregnating Dione. The classical derivation of Ulrichs's neologisms came with the price of confusing sexual reproduction with sexual orientation. Even though Ulrichs seems to have been the first gay activist, *Urning/-in* and *Dioning/-in* were pushed aside by Austrian writer Karl Maria Kertbeny's more technical neologisms *homosexual* and *heterosexual*, derived from the Latin words *homo* (similar) and *hetero* (different).

Soon, the terms homosexual and heterosexual became academic standards. But even a hundred years later, my parents avoided them. It was unthinkable that they would call themselves heterosexual. They were the normal ones, and the homosexuals were the others, those *vom anderen Ufer* (from the other side of the river). Getting a bit more raunchy, my father would call homosexuals *warme Brüder* (warm brothers)—men who don't stay cool around their bros. This expression was related to the German equivalent of the word gay, *schwul*, which was an old expression for sticky, sultry weather (later evolving into *schwül*). My parents would have never used schwul; they would have considered it to be too vulgar.

It wasn't until I made my first gay friends as a teenager that I heard people making use of the term. As they called themselves schwul, the word also became part of my vocabulary. Not much later, it became a common colloquial term, just as gay did in the Anglo-Saxon world. Quickly, the common use freed schwul from sleazy connotations. A successful case of reclamation. Homophobic people, kids in particular, started to use schwul as a general synonym for bad. But this has nothing to do with the old negative connotations of schwul; these people would have made the same "joke" with Urning if it had been the common expression for gay.

This doesn't mean that the word *Urning* wasn't an important invention. At that time, there was no gay community and coming out as gay was almost suicidal. Only classical references could legitimize a life beyond bourgeois norms. Even more importantly, Ulrichs not only invented noble names for being gay or lesbian—he also named those who loved the opposite gender and those who did both. This paved the way for the trio *homosexual*, *heterosexual*, and *bisexual*. Once this was established, gays could be freed from pseudo-academic stigmatization as *pederasts*, *pedophiles*, or *sodomites*.

German is a strongly gendered language. First, nouns have a gendered article, either male (*der*, *ein*), female (*die*, *eine*), or neutral (*das*, *ein*). Second, many nouns that characterize humans have a gender inflection. Often, the female inflection entails adding the suffix -*in* to the male version: *Bauer/Bäuerin* (male and female peasant), *König/Königin* (king and queen), etc. Ulrichs was following the same principle with *Urning/Urningin*. Many people would even say *Lesbierin* for lesbian instead of *Lesbe*.

When female emancipation led to women entering professions that had been previously reserved to men, this speech code resulted in two apparent injustices. Firstly, for many professions, only a male version existed, and people still had to get used to the female inflection. Secondly, and more importantly, the male versions of human characterizations were also used when the gender of the respective person was undefined or mixed. Referring to the equally gendered French, feminist writer Monique Wittig concludes: "The result is to deny them [women] any claim to the abstract, philosophical, political discourses that give shape to the social body." Monique Wittig, "The Mark of Gender," *Feminist Issues* 5 (1985).

In the late 1970s, German feminist linguists started wondering what to do about this sexist disparity, most famously Luise F. Pusch. In her essay collection *Das Deutsche als Männersprache* (*German as a Language of Men*, 1984), she sets forth two scenarios. The first one is to get rid of the feminine morpheme -*in* altogether. In return, any characterization of humans of undefined or mixed gender would get a neutral instead of a male article. Depending on the person's gender, you would speak of *der Professor*, *die Professor*, or *das Professor*—making use of the lucky fact that the German gendering isn't binary, like Spanish or French, but allows for male, female, and neutral nouns. Not only is this solution simple and elegant but also the gender inflection -*in* comes with a historical burden. Originally, it hadn't been used to describe women as occupying certain positions but as *the wives of men* occupying those positions. *-In* had marked women as an appendage of men. Still, Pusch argues that the de-gendering of the German language would be too radical and opts for a second, more intricate scenario: whenever the gender of the described person is undefined or mixed, any characterization would need both versions, male and female.

Over the years, Pusch, a very charismatic and hands-on intellectual, turned out to be pretty successful with her insistence on the general visibility of the female inflection. Only the spelling of her proposal remained in a state of flux. More cautious people would put the female suffix in parentheses: *Professor(in)*. Others would use a slash: *Professor/in*. Pusch herself merged the male and female versions into one, putting the beginning of the female suffix in camel case to give it extra importance: *ProfessorIn*.

Language traditionalists, literary writers in particular, were reluctant to write words that included parentheses, a slash, or camel case. Some pedants would also point to the fact that German adjectives (as opposed to French or Spanish ones) don't get gendered. Therefore, they would remain male unless you also wrote *professor(in)al*, *professor/inal*, or *professorInal* instead of *professoral* (professorial). But it seemed like these reactionary forces were fighting a losing battle.

That is, until the growing nonbinary community claimed visibility too. As their gender identity was situated somewhere in between men and women, they asked for a placeholder in between the male basic form and the female suffix, either in the form of an underscore (_), a colon (:), or an asterisk, in this case known as a gender star (*). When pronouncing these placeholders, you would have to mark them with a glottal stop, the "gender pause"—a micromoment of silence for those overlooked by gender binarism. Again, the demand of the nonbinary community seemed plausible. Soon, gender star and gender pause became part of the language regime of major media outlets and governmental offices.

Pusch wasn't too happy about this development. She had just barely secured visibility for the female half of the population, when a rather small minority pushed into the middle. The basic male form gained independence, while the female suffix was left as a loose adjunct.

Of course, the multiple gender inflection is meant to hurt. Twisting our tongues, we're reminded that the language we're speaking has been invented by and preserved for men. The multiple gender inflection is no newspeak that purifies our language, it rather shines a light on how dirty it is. Still, it's an elitist practice—particularly against non-native speakers.

Just as water always makes its way, several avoidance maneuvers have come into play. The most popular one is to replace a gendered noun with an according participial construction: *der\*die Student\*in* (the student) becomes *der\*die Studierende* (the studying person). But this only works when there is a verb that corresponds to the noun. Another maneuver is to use the plural whenever possible, as in that case, male and female share the same female article *die*. Or to switch to the cumbersome passive. Or finally, as in my case, to pretty much give up on formal German communication and switch to the more gender-neutral English.

In the long run, Pusch's efforts to make the female inflection more visible might have had the opposite effect, instead seeming to propel its extinction—or the extinction of German as a written language altogether. In retrospect, you might wonder if *der/die/das Professor* would have been such a radical solution. True equality demands the same amount of syllables for all genders.

An even easier solution would be for German speakers to give up on the gendering of nouns altogether and switch to a general neuter: *das Professor*, *das Baum*, *das Tisch*, and so on. In case this feels too enforced, you could abrade the indefinite articles *ein* and *eine* to a general *e* and the definite articles *der*, *die*, *das* to a *d* or *de*—exactly what happened when English lost its gender inflections. Abrasion could also lead the way for languages that lack a neutral gender, like Spanish and French.

The general neuter would also tackle another problem of gendered nouns: arbitrary gender assignments to everything that's nonhuman. While for humans there is a basic male form and a female inflection (similar to the biblical creation of Adam and Eve), most animals and all plants and things are stigmatized by a single linguistic gender. For instance, in German, the sun is female (*die Sonne*), the moon is masculine (*der Mond*), flowers are female (*die Blumen*), and most animals are male, but turtles, spiders, snails, and many insects are female.

If you're serious about a multiple gender inflection, how can you limit it to humans and not speak of *Löw*innen* (lions), *Vögel*innen* (birds), and *Schildkröt*innen* (turtles)? And what to do about the few privileged animals for which German has reserved different words for the male and the female? To be gender-correct, we would have to stop speaking of a gender-undefined cat as *die Katze*, but say *die*der Katze*Kater* or, to save at least one syllable, *die*der Katz*Kater*.

Finally, when claiming the same rights for all genders, why should we make such an effort to always distinguish between them? Imagine if in English you were obliged to always add the gender when talking about someone's profession: *female professor, male professor, fe*male professor*, etc. Or when discussing class, age, height ... This would be perceived as a source of discrimination, not a remedy against it.

Gender discriminations still in place need to be addressed. Gender differentiation might also be needed to foster affirmative action.* But the default setting of an inclusive language needs to be de-gendered, just as it needs to be de-raced. The same goes for passports. (Biometry doesn't need to know your gender.)

In English, gender neutrality isn't complete either. Just as in German and all other European languages that I know of, in English the third-person pronouns for a gender-undefined human used to always be male: *he/him/his*.

Different practices have been developed to cope with this sexism. Some people have switched to a default *she/her* whenever the gender is undefined; some have alternated between *he/him* and *she/her*; and some have tried to fuse *he/him* and *she/her* in one way or another. Again, things got more complex when the nonbinary community also sought to claim visibility. A number of neologisms like *xe* or *zie* have been proposed, but *they* became the most common one—it hints at their identity not being single. At the same time, the use of *they* as a singular pronoun isn't utterly new but can be traced back to the fourteenth century—rewind to the personal pronoun *you* that was first used for the second-person singular and then also for the second-person plural. This allowed *they* to also quickly gain popularity as a gender-neutral singular pronoun that refers to antecedents of undefined gender. *They* solves two problems at once—without even being a new word. This is a solution I can get behind. As soon as I realized that the singular use of *they* was a serious option, I made consequent use of it and felt ashamed for ever having used *he*.

Still, from a posthumanist perspective, the English triad of *he/she/they* is also problematic, as it continues to distinguish between gendered humans and mostly ungendered animals, plants, and things. In German all nouns are gendered: *er* (he) and *sie* (she), just like *es* (it), can refer to anything in the world, albeit in an arbitrary manner. By contrast, in English there is a big divide between a mostly human *he/she* and a nonhuman *it*. The use of *they* as a singular person pronoun reserved to humans solidifies that divide. It's like expanding the estates of the realm instead of declaring a republic.

Environmental biologist Robin Wall Kimmerer, member of the Native American Citizen Potawatomi Nation, proposes *ki*, derived from the Potawatomi word *aaki* for land, as a gender-neutral personal pronoun "to signify a being of the living earth. Not *he* or *she*, but *ki*. [...] *Ki* is a parallel spelling of *chi*—the word for the inherent life energy that flows through everything. It finds harmony with *qui* or 'who' in Latinate languages. I've been told it is the name of a Sumerian Earth goddess and the root of Turkic words for *tree*. Could *ki* be a key to unlocking a new way of thinking, or remembering an ancient one?" Robin Wall Kimmerer, "Speaking of Nature," *Orion*

*Magazine* 36, no. 2 (March/April 2017). For the plural form of *ki*, Kimmerer proposes the existing word *kin*: "Our words can be an antidote to human exceptionalism, to unthinking exploitation, an antidote to loneliness, an opening to kinship."

But what counts as living, and what doesn't? Kimmerer points out that "in my language, the wind is understood as animate." In a Shinto context, stones are too. In that sense, what does *not* count as living—things made by humans? Or all things made by animals—nests too? Wherever you draw the line, it creates new divisions.

What is even so special about the living that they deserve a special pronoun? Isn't it more important whether something is conscious and thereby able to feel? But we don't even know what consciousness is or how to test it. Any special pronoun for a certain group of antecedents fosters speciesism.

The only just solution is also the simplest: to take Wittig's claim in "The Mark of Gender" that "gender then must be destroyed" seriously—get rid of *he*, *she*, and all new personal pronouns altogether and only use *it* (singular) and *they* (plural). Trans people, just like slaves, have been defamed as *it*. In German, girls (*Mädchen*) and women, in a more vulgar sense (*Weiber*), are also referred to as *it*. But from a posthumanist perspective, these groups can reclaim these denigrations as an honor.

Some trans and nonbinary people are already asking to be referred to as *it*. Feminist women could do the same. Donna Haraway's famous essay "A Cyborg Manifesto" (1985) argues that the liberation of women and the liberation of nonhumans—animals and cyborgs—go hand in hand. You can't separate human from nonhuman discriminations.

The last line of defense for a diversity of personal pronouns is that without them, complex, referential sentences become more cumbersome. But sentences are trending toward getting shorter and shorter anyway. Languages like Turkish or Korean that already forego gendered pronouns come instead with a multiplicity of appellations, particularly to express hierarchical relations—for instance *Abla* in Turkish for "older sister." In a similar, though nonhierarchical manner, some nonbinary people insist on not being referred to by personal pronouns at all, but instead always by their name of choice. In a next step, we could all have individual pronouns based on the initial letter of our first name or, in formal contexts, on the initial letter of our last name. In case we're referring to two people with the same initial letter, we could switch to the first two letters.

Today, we're communicating with more people than ever. Instead of long letters, we write or speak quick successions of replies. Short and simple rules. We're receptive to new words, but they shouldn't have more than one or two syllables, which should be easy to pronounce. Only for traditional autocrats is lengthy communication a virtue in itself—to exercise and indicate power over their bored audience.

Around the year 2000, I was part of the short-lived rationalist collective Redesigndeutschland. In our ambition to simplify every aspect of life, I came up with a German grammar without any conjugations, declinations, or articles. See "Rede-deutsch," in my book *Solution 1–10: Umbauland* (Berlin: Sternberg Press, 2008). Our aim was to make the German language more competitive. We didn't pay much attention to inclusive language; our ambition was the inclusive use of language. We presented our new grammar a few times and translated parts of Goethe's *Faust* to prove how well our grammar dealt with sophisticated poetry. But people were laughing at us.

Current German efforts for a gender-appropriate language prove that it's possible to substantially change habits of speaking within the span of years. But it goes in the direction of more circuity, not less. And thereby imposes power, instead of dismantling it.

This doesn't mean that our rationalist approach at Redesigndeutschland was any better. When I talk with students about my repulsions for camel case and special characters, they hardly get me. Why be so stiff, and rant against efforts to stick out a bit by breaking the rules? In fact, the standardization of German orthography was a nationalist-bourgeois endeavor right after the foundation of the German Empire in 1871. Up to that point, many words were written in different ways. Some people used camel case to identify the single parts of compound words. Even the Bible had them. To give God additional importance, Martin Luther went for a double uppercase: *GOtt* (GOd).

The ambition to write texts that don't become outdated is like wanting a tattoo with the guarantee of no regrets.* The effort to avoid any blunder can only lead to (as in my case) no tattoo at all. What characterizes a good tattoo is its inherent boldness. The same goes for a good text. Unlike not having tattoos (like me), we can't practically avoid writing or speaking. We can't completely hide doing so either. In principle, everything that we've written or spoken can show up anytime, anywhere.

Thanks to AI's ability to work, write, read, speak, and listen, there is no need for our language to be too efficient, steady, or universal. Any language dogmatism will eat its own tail: what today appears to be inclusive might tomorrow appear to be discriminatory. What today appears to be funny might tomorrow sound like a bad joke.

There is no perpetual minimalism that we can escape to. It's as atavistic as trying to create a painting of eternal beauty. But giving it a try can nonetheless lead to impressive results. Particularly when this is what you learned to be good at, which is why I still avoid special characters and emojis in my texts and instead focus on getting as far as possible with what conventional language has to offer. Except for maybe that one new word.

C. Orcies

Trans and nonbinary people could be the revolutionary subjects of a new—monadic—age. Their intensified sensual relationships with themselves are at the forefront of a paradigm shift from expansive self-realization to less invasive self-sufficiency. Virtual environments will make us love the other not just like ourselves but *as* ourselves.

At the beginning of this essay, I described myself as late. This has had two diametric effects: on the one hand, I'm reluctant to change (and to use new words), and on the other hand, unfinished as I am, I keep up with new developments. I hardly implement them, but I could do so eventually.

In general, there is nothing special about my unwillingness to turn into a proper grown-up. My cohort, Generation X—kids in the 1970s, teenagers in the 1980s—grew up with the mantra of "life as continuous self-reinvention." It was fashionable to appear *androgynous* and to be *bisexual* (predecessors of *nonbinary* and *queer*). Later on, in the 1990s, it was fashionable for creative practices and lives to be *hybrid* (predecessor of *fluid*) and for relationships to be *open* (predecessor of *polyamorous*). On the downside, the urge to not define life too rigidly made it difficult for us to take on challenges. We suffered from *undecidedness* (predecessor of *FOMO*) and *slacking* (predecessor of *goblin mode*).

Still, in the Western world, we're experiencing fundamental changes between my generation and subsequent ones that make me feel rather aligned with the younger folks. These changes aren't a matter of radicality in general sociopolitical subjects, as is still the case with previous generation gaps. Specific post-labor concerns of millennials and Generation Z, including the environment, gender, and racial justice—often summarized as issues of *wokeness*—have been crucial topics of progressive political debates since the 1970s.°

What many members of my generation find difficult to understand is the way *wokies* fight with such sensitivity and rigidity against what they perceive to be minor discriminations. Why put so much energy into defining an adequate language or creating safe spaces in the relatively protected context of universities? Why care so much about White supremacy when the rise of Asia is already teaching us a grim lesson?

The common explanation for what has been defamed as "Generation Snowflake" (its members are deemed unique and fragile, like snowflakes) sounds similar to previous accusations that have been lodged against younger generations by older ones: They're spoiled. They don't acknowledge our groundwork. They, basically full, start playing with the food instead of sharing with those who really need it. And in doing so, they provoke a right-wing backlash that questions the liberal and egalitarian core values of Western democracy—with nationalists and supremacists also playing the identity card.°

Following that argument, my generation could blame its own pamperedness in the first place. We were the ones who ranted against neoliberalism and zero tolerance but didn't really do anything about it and rather enjoyed the associated comforts. As long as you were White and middle class, you would have to make quite an effort to leave your safe space. Pretty much wherever in the world you ended up drifting, your safe space was already waiting for you. But for the younger ones, the global progression of neoliberalism rubs off the privileges of the White middle class.

It's not that wokies didn't try to revive traditional, hands-on social democracy and socialism. In large numbers, they supported Bernie Sanders in the US, Podemos in Spain, Syriza in Greece, etc., whereas my generation just let the wealth and income gap widen; rents, education, and health care become unaffordable; and our environment undergo further destruction. It was my generation and the boomers who gave up on the fight for collective justice to focus on selfish self-realization.

All of this is why we get easily annoyed when we're told that we don't acknowledge the rights and vulnerabilities of minorities. Wasn't this acknowledgment the one thing we've been rather good at? But then again, why not push our concerns a bit further?

I feel aligned with wokies in regarding the humanistic project as fundamentally flawed. We strive for a world that goes beyond being *post*humanist and no longer depends on humanism as a point of reference. Everybody has the right to exist according to their very own condition, not only humans and not only according to an assumed humanness.°

While already during my humanities studies there was ontologically no way around multiple forms of constructivism (systems theory, post-structuralism, deconstructionism, actor-network theory), for my generation, questioning humanist "universalism" (i.e., human speciesism) has been and is still very much a taboo. To suggest otherwise would prompt accusations of opening the door to moral relativism. And indeed today, when people speak up about their identity, they reformulate the aristocratic idea of assigned privileges—not based on unique traits but on unique loss and pain. Instead of attacking social injustice on a fundamental level, they follow the logic of reversal—as Pusch did with her proposal of a gender-appropriate language.° It's no surprise that identity politics has been quickly appropriated by right-wing extremists.

The woke objective is to tackle identity politics on an intersectional level and provide an apparatus for the sensitive and peaceful coexistence of multiple identities and even species. How is that possible? How do we weigh the interests of different forms of life or consciousness? Any decision-making process is necessarily unjust. All that's left is to aim at an impossible ideal. No matter whether we—or nonhuman agents like AI, pets, and husbandry—reform, revolt, compete, or complement, we don't just "stay with the trouble," as Haraway claims, but inevitably create new dilemmas.

In politics and other efforts to improve the world, you always have to set priorities, make sacrifices, deal with uncertainties, and become corrupt. But aspiring to a just world inclusive of all species and identities, respecting all ambitions and vulnerabilities—it's not even possible to formulate such an ideal. All you can do is facilitate processes that allow as many creatures as possible, who are as different as possible, to utter and satisfy their particular preferences, thereby making the fallacy fragmented and diverse. An expanded humanism that to some degree tries to include some nonhuman creatures comes as a biased compromise.

Even more, wokies fail as revolutionary subjects for a new social contract. The underprivileged are too invested in particular identity politics; the descendants of the White middle class hang on to their remaining privileges and are intimidated by guilt. Wokies might be in control of the humanities departments and the academic arts, but this control comes at the cost of a rapid loss in popularity, influence, and funding. Many wokies are trapped in a dogmatic radicalization similar to that of Western Maoist and Leninist activists in the 1970s. Woke concerns slosh into the mainstream but might lack the force to fundamentally change society.

For revolutionary subjects to be successful, they don't need to be numerous. The fewer you are, the more you can act and feel like the elite. Others identify with you without daring to be too much like you. You're their radical alter ego. A permanent reminder that they could do better.

Lesbians, for instance, acted as revolutionary subjects within the feminist movement of the 1970s. They had an insurmountable advantage in overcoming the dependency on men and in the separation of sexual pleasure and reproduction. Similar to White middle-class wokies today, heterosexual women were stuck in complicity, while lesbians were exercising a way out. Their existence increased the guilty conscience of heterosexual female feminists. Whatever they were enduring, it wasn't fate. They could decide against it and give up on romantic involvement with men. Lesbians raised the bar. And the fact that most heterosexual female feminists missed it gave lesbians extra authority.

Among wokies there is also a hierarchy—based on the degree of your oppression. Even more, what counts is less your personal oppression and more the oppression that's assigned to the identity cluster you're born in. The dignity of suffering is inscribed in every hero narrative. Not only were lesbians' intimate lives unpolluted by men, they had to pay for it with social discrimination. But identity politics gives you less choice in becoming a hero than in the Middle Ages. It's fatalism petrified as divisive determinism: either you're born oppressed or not. A heterosexual woman can live in celibacy or become a political lesbian, but a White wokie can't become a wokie of color. An abled wokie can disable themselves—but a chosen disability wouldn't count as a handicap.

There is only one exception to not being able to make yourself an identity hero: you can transition, or at least identify as nonbinary. Even women who transition to men are considered drastically more oppressed than they were before. Men can transition to women, keeping their "superior" height* while counting as more oppressed than women. TERFs (trans-exclusionary radical feminists) who have animosities against trans people for playing unfair* can be defamed as transphobic.

Why does identity politics allow you to change your gender but not your race? The common explanation goes that human races don't actually exist, only racism does, which makes the effort to change your race an act of racism. But then again, what is gender? From a woke perspective, your gender can't be reduced to your physical sex: a vagina doesn't make you a woman, and a penis doesn't make you a man. When you simultaneously oppose any fixed gender roles, what remains to make you identify as a woman, man, both, or in between?

Identifying as nonbinary or trans or changing your physical sex is the golden ticket of identity politics. As with race, you can be discriminated against because of a gender that from your own understanding doesn't even exist. But in that case, your gender attribution would be only a social given; you couldn't choose it. The fact that many wokies think of gender as a choice *and* are sympathetic with the urge to align sex and gender to some degree reveals a rather conservative notion of gender roles* that resembles an effort to merely extend, not overcome, humanism. Genderism, no better than racism?

I'm heterosexual, not *heterogenderal*. I feel a general attraction to the features of the female body but not to feminine appearances. I'm not *homogenderal* either. I'm attracted to certain feminine behaviors (in particular, dressing up) and I'm appalled by others (in particular, affirmative smiling), just as I'm attracted to certain masculine behaviors (in particular, rigidness) and appalled by others (in particular, being domineering). I regard myself as heterosexual but somewhere between *agenderal* and *bigenderal*—as opposed to most heterosexual men, who are also or mainly heterogenderal. It's remarkable that with all the discourse about the difference between sex and gender, the words hetero-, homo-, bi-, and agenderal are hardly in use. (I actually just came up with them myself, only to then find some queer online discussions about whether someone might be homosexual but heterogenderal.)

When it comes to our own sexual and gender identity, the woke discourse has moved in the opposite direction: gender overshadows sex. Even people who change their sex are referred to as transgender, rather than transsexual. Those who feel in line with their sex are called cisgender, rather than cissexual. There is no specific term for being fine with your sex but not with your gender. If that's the case, you fall under the vague category nonbinary.

But again, I regard myself as cissexual, not as cisgender. When I came into puberty, I wondered if I was OK with having a penis and a rather straight body, or if I would have preferred a vagina, curves, and a uterus. I reached the conclusion that all in all I was quite happy with having a male body. This was mostly because I wasn't fond of the idea of having children and thought it would be hard to have a body that would constantly remind me—and several days a month, painfully—of the ability to bear them. Aesthetically, I could have gone without a penis, but as an extraordinary tool of joy, I could live with it.

My attitude toward my own gender has been pretty similar to the way I approach my heterogenderality. I like my physical strength, but since puberty I've avoided any overt signaling of masculinity (manspreading, a chesty voice, weight training, predatory behavior, growing a beard). This avoidance often resulted in people in my heteronormative environment thinking I was gay. Later, I found myself in an artistic environment where my behavior didn't feel too deviant.

The attitude of most cisgender people I know toward their own body appears to me to be quite pragmatic. They deal with what they're given, emphasizing some aspects, hiding and suppressing others. In contexts like sports there is still a lot of "body patriotism," but this is obviously a trained behavior.• Initiations into specifically masculine and feminine ethics are waning. Which is why, when asked about my sexual identity, I would feel like a fraud if I, a normcore-looking man who doesn't have to fear being harassed at night on most streets in the world, were to call myself nonbinary.

Though I find it punctilious to come up with all sorts of terminological boxes for various degrees of living outside the box, I wonder if we're still not being specific enough—also regarding being trans. As long as sex-reassignment procedures weren't widely available, the difference between being transsexual and being transgender wasn't significant. Today, transgender and transsexual can mean very different things. You can be transgender while being fine with your existing body, or cisgender but appalled by your sex.

What makes people not just go against gender expectations but rework their sex? It's a complex procedure that requires ongoing, potentially carcinogenic hormone therapy, and must, to some degree, remain incomplete. In particular, reassignment therapy impairs your abilities for sexual intercourse and obstructs natural procreation. Changing your sex, you might be a traditionalist who doesn't want to pursue a certain gender role without the according sex. But the complications of transitioning make this explanation less plausible. A different line of reasoning is that transsexuality seeks autoerotic fulfillment. As trans writer Andrea Long Chu puts it: "The truth is I have never been able to differentiate liking women from wanting to be like them." Andrea Long Chu, "On Liking Women," *n+1*, no. 30 (Winter 2018).

Sexologist Ray Blanchard even controversially argues that many cases of male-to-female transsexuality are exclusively driven by "autogynephilia," the sexual arousal of men perceiving themselves as women: a heterosexual "erotic target location error," which in moderate forms leads to cross-dressing and can culminate in a sort of cross-bodying. Blanchard has been accused of "sexualizing" female trans identities (while overlooking "autoandrophilia" in trans men) and fueling anti-woke resentments of transgender people as basically being mentally deranged narcissists. In fact, Blanchard observed extensive autogynephilic practices particularly in trans people who had not yet started reassignment therapy. These practices could therefore be easily explained as a coping mechanism to mitigate gender dysphoria. However, the eligible critique of Blanchard's hypothesis overlooks that being trans is first of all a sensual relationship with yourself. Encountering yourself as a person that you want to be with and keep on choosing every day makes it similar to an ongoing romantic encounter.

Autoeroticism has a utopian quality. Not just in the sense of libidinous self-sufficiency in these times of intimacy's rigorous commodification, but in enabling yourself to magnanimously love other creatures—not out of the need to be accepted and loved in return. For love to flourish and not to strangle you and the other(s), it needs that dialectical twist—which can be traced back to the Talmudic and biblical command to "love your neighbor as yourself" (Lev. 19:18). But Christianity separated platonic charity (i.e., pity) from sensual love *; as a consequence, legitimate self-love was reduced to self-pity, while autoeroticism was defamed as perverted.

Since the rise of psychoanalysis, autoeroticism has been pathologized as narcissistic: the result of an incomplete or regressive personality development. Narcissism is a vague term for being preoccupied with oneself that confuses autoeroticism with an obsessive need for appreciation—the love of oneself is equated with the urge to make oneself loved. Being self-content is equated with ruthless egoism. Even as Christian prudery is waning, autoeroticism continues to be stigmatized—also in relation to being transgender. Again, Chu's take in "On Liking Women": "The primary function of gender identity as a political concept—and, increasingly, a legal one—is to bracket, if not to totally deny, the role of desire in the thing we call gender."

In individualistic societies, narcissism becomes ubiquitous. We're no longer born into a fixed social order but constantly compete for recognition. Except for those who gain prominence, people continue to gain most of others' attention and affection from relationships that function as long-term barters. Despite the growing number of possibilities for fifteen minutes of fame, even more futile and distant interactions—as on social media—are largely based on an informal give and take. But what has drastically changed is that while in traditional societies most people only court during adolescence, in individualistic societies people might engage in the preludes to relationships (flirting, sexting, hooking up, casual sex, dating) throughout their lives. As rising single and sinking sex rates indicate, more and more people are shifting their focus in life from being in relationships to evaluating potential relationships.* They might find this phase more promising, more rewarding, more protected from bad experiences. But it also makes them more insecure about their actual social value and more desperate for appreciation. In other words, more narcissistic.

Autoeroticism promises to free your self-esteem from relying on the recognition of others. Instead of seeking someone else's or several others' exclusive love, in your relationships with others you can focus on concrete social needs like companionship, exchange, sex, or infatuation.

The more the social acceptance of transitioning grows and the medical tools for transitioning improve, the more heterosexuals will be intrigued about transitioning into their own love interests. Cissexuals who are preoccupied with their own appearance might also claim to be driven by—homosexual—self-love. But no matter how much effort they put into appearing seductive—even while perhaps having little or no sex at all—they might be driven by the desire to delight or intimidate others. Cissexuals can't contend with transsexuals as the pacemakers of social change. The role of transsexuals as revolutionary subjects of an autoerotic turn could resemble that of lesbians for feminism.

Anti-wokies rightfully sense an ethical imperative of transsexuals: not being at ease with your given body. Transsexuals don't just fight for equal rights and visibility, but inherently claim the cultural-political dominance at the dawn of a truly individualistic age.

Just as narcissism gets confused with autoeroticism, individualism often gets confused with egoism. In fact, people who are very invested in self-realization tend toward libertarianism and social Darwinism: whether you're suffering from cancer or unemployment, it's supposed to be your own fault. But unless you believe in a strict mind/body divide that allows you to be "trapped in the wrong body," transsexuality is less about realizing yourself and more about overcoming yourself and what has long been considered humans' key mission in life: natural procreation.

Transsexuals and autoeroticists are at the forefront of a general shift from an expansive self-realization to a less invasive self-sufficiency. More and more, aggression is directed inward, replacing vandalism and violence with self-inflicted harm and suicide. The scruples grow about giving birth to children with potentially unhappy or harmful lives—without their or the environment's consent.* Biotechnical progress will eventually allow metabolism and thermoregulation to become self-sufficient processes. Ideally, you become auto-trophic as a primary producer and also as a self-decomposer—not even consuming inorganic material. All you require is the occasional intake of sunlight. Human autotrophy was first pro-posed by the cosmists in the early twentieth century, in particular by geochemist Vladimir Vernadsky—though what they had in mind wasn't the transformation of humans themselves into autotrophic beings but synthetic food production on an industrial scale, utilizing the energy of the sun.

The urge for self-sufficiency leads to what my termino-logical efforts make me call the *Monadic Age*. While the indi-vidual is defined ex negativo as something that can't be di-vided, the monad (Greek for "unity") implies self-fulfillment. In Gnosticism, the word *monad* has been used as a synonym for the supreme, all-encompassing God, as employed in Gottfried Wilhelm Leibniz's *La monadologie* (*The Monadology*, 1714) as a synonym for souls that coexist according to a divine predetermination. I don't expect us or our descendants to evolve into largely autarchic, autotrophic beings in perfect harmony with each other, but I do expect us and our descen-dants to be increasingly shaped by that ambition. While liber-alism understands individuals as free atoms that are allowed to move every which way, as long as they avoid direct colli-sions, in *monadism* individuals shouldn't interact with one another, unless they do so with consent and care.

In a previous secular appropriation, psychoanalyst Béla Grunberger (1903–2005) used the term monad to describe the symbiotic unity of a fetus with its mother. For Grunberger, this state of effortless and complete satisfaction is what humans try to reconstitute for the rest of their lives. The healthy devel-opment of a child requires buffering it from the frustrations of reality and sheltering it with ersatz-monads—first the breast-feeding mother, then the family and the surrounding culture. Concepts like those of an almighty God, paradise, or utopia serve as projections of prenatal bliss. Later, philosopher Peter Sloterdijk built up his *Sphären* (*Spheres*) trilogy (1998–2004) on humanity's cultural history as a manifold foam of individual bubbles, like love and family, and collective globes, like religion and nation, and took Grunberger's concept of the ersatz-monad and fused it with biologist Jakob Johannes von Uexküll's topology of *Umwelten* (ecospheres). But from an ecological understanding, Grunberger's use of the term monad is misleading. Just like the modern family, organization, or state, a womb is a highly dependent entity—and mothers aren't self-sustaining either. By contrast, monadism aims at emotional *and* metabolic independence.

Today, two major sociopolitical dispositions are unfolding. On the one hand, people envision a harmonious community of all human and nonhuman beings (multispecies kinship, a rainbow of identities). On the other hand, people isolate themselves within their own identities and belongings (filter bubbles, safe spaces, gated communities, charter cities, prepping). Monadism recognizes that these two seemingly contradictory dispositions stem from a similar understanding of the world: one is more optimistic, the other more pessimistic, but ultimately, they're interdependent. Changing from aggressive parasites to benevolent participants in the global ecosystem is an uncertain and risky maneuver. Before seeking harmony, we humans, a highly dominant species, must first of all restrain ourselves from coercive interactions with our environment. And to protect ourselves sufficiently from our environment, we must minimize its abuse. Monadism is the synthesis of these two dispositions.

On a socio-territorial level, with technological progress, both the exploitation of our environment and our dependency on it have grown in size and intensity. Now, monadic states and communities will have to regain the ability of tribes to be largely self-sufficient—independent of international supply chains, with each more or less automatically producing most of its own food, energy, and machines.*

On an individual level, a substantial initial change for creatures of the Monadic Age could be to shrink in size, except for their heads—the brain, eyes, ears, and nose could be equipped with neuron enhancements. This would save our descendants a lot of energy and also make them look cuter. Another initial adaptation could be to grow fur. Our naked skin costs us a lot of energy, whether for heating or cooling. With veganism becoming the norm, the naked skin will be perceived as an unpleasant reminder of the origins of humans as cruel predators who, equipped with the unique ability to sweat, outran much faster prey during hunts that were agonizing tests of endurance.

Our descendants could look a bit like the Wombles— a species of roundish, furry herbivores conceived by British children's author Elisabeth Beresford in the 1960s. They inhabit burrows but spend most of their time outside in parks, have a life expectancy of several hundred years, are communal but with strong individual characters, and are very keen on recycling. Their key motto "Make Good Use of Bad Rubbish" is also phrased as "wombling free." I grew up with an animated series of the Wombles that started in 1973, two years after the foundation of Greenpeace, and they became my ecological role models. Emulating them, I hoarded whatever sorts of used materials I could get ahold of and tried to dig burrows (or at least covered trenches) to live in.

In "A Cyborg Manifesto," Haraway claims that women, animals, and cyborgs could together be beneficial for a blurring of the humanist dichotomies of human/nature and mind/body. But while ecofeminism has made patriarchalism responsible for that divide, at the same time the popular feminist discourse has portrayed women as the more civilized human sex and men as instinct-driven animals who lack human ethics and consideration. Biohacking aims at liberating the mind from spatial and bodily limitations, thereby rather

Still from *The Wombles*, 1973–75, TV series

reaffirming the mind/body and human/nature divides. Bio-hackers often believe that a human mind can be transferred to any data processor as long as it's big enough and fast enough.[*] For biohackers, nature and body become replaceable—our nature could also be terraformed on Mars; our body could be a machine. By artificially replacing body or nature, biohackers exacerbate their exploitation. Our extropist descendants might no longer dominate the whole of Earth but instead only certain parts even more radically.

By contrast, as a monad the only thing that you can lay claim to is yourself, that is, your mind as an inseparable part of your body. "You" isn't a distinct manifestation like a (meta-physical) soul or a (secular) self, it's all of your holobiont body. You're in constant change and exchange, but you're single and singular. See Max Stirner, *Der Einzige und sein Eigentum* [The unique and its property] (Leipzig: Otto Wigand, 1844). The pamphlet is an early effort to overcome humanism in favor of an anarchic egoism. Maybe in the future it will be possible to convert different complex sentient individuals into one, but for now humans and post-humans persist as units. Maybe, as a cyborg, you consist of parts that have been artificially attached and that don't be-long to you in the legal sense (they might be leased or impose certain terms of use), making the claim to yourself—and your-self only—less trivial.

Humanism already acknowledges the individual as the crucial social reference whose needs legitimize all social entities. But despite declaring the "freedom of the individual," humanist notions are pretty much fixed.[*] When you don't ful-fill a certain degree of "human" sameness, for instance by being non-White, non-male, or disabled, your rights can be limited. When you openly intend not to live anymore, you can be incarcerated just as you can when you openly intend to kill others.

Gradually extending its notions of what counts as human, humanism gets more and more diluted—to finally be replaced by monadism. Rather than being egocentric, as a monadist you deny that an "ego" even exists and perceive yourself as an ever-changing variety, an *ego tribe*.* You're reluctant to interact with the world not because you mainly care about yourself but because you don't want to impose a solidarity that predetermines others' needs. Just like your gender(s), your deficiencies are individually defined.

Wokies have been criticized for being oversensitive. In fact, the woke concept of "trigger warning" is derived from therapy work with people suffering from trauma—as is the fashionable effort to be "mindful." Being highly attentive inhibits us in everyday life. Still, fully acknowledging people's individuality means there is no way back to liberal norms of what counts as acceptable behavior.* We can train ourselves to be more tolerant, but we can't impose our own level of tolerance on others. The result could be to systematically segregate in communities of like-minded people—*voluntary tribes*—that can be in constant flux or solidify as largely autonomous, if not autarchic, substates.* The broad overcoming of assigned gender identities could be a substantial first step in self-declared identities superseding all assigned ones.

Anti-wokies might object that this is exactly what has already been happening in liberal societies. Not only do they allow you to change class according to your merits, they also allow for the widest range of self-expression ever. When class mobility wanes in liberal post-labor societies, being an artist becomes the defining mode of existence—with your own body as both the most available and the most daring artistic material.* Transitioning falls in line with a rapidly growing regime of visible body modifications, ranging from workouts, tattoos, and plastic surgery to gender-reaffirming hormone treatments. These modifications also have strong autoerotic aspects. But they can all be understood as supplementing the existing body rather than questioning it—just as artists, even as unsteady bohemians and provocative enfants terribles, have been supplementing humanism and the bourgeois order.*

Anti-wokies rant against granting importance to something as marginal as the gender binarism of toilets, personal pronouns, and passport details, but at least trans and nonbinary

(margin notes) • Ego Tribes • Intimate Correctness • Middle-Class Warriors • Expanded Sex Work • Consensual Gift Economy

activists are persistently questioning *something*. And even if for now, nonbinary and trans people are mainly perceived as a middle-class phenomenon, they exist in all classes—unlike the previous revolutionary subjects, yuppies and nerds, who were predominantly male and middle class.

Yuppies have acted as the revolutionary subjects of neoliberalism; nerds have been the revolutionary subjects of cyber libertarianism. Both share the ambition to rejuvenate and accelerate male-dominated reckless capitalism. Their rise went hand in hand with the demise of lesbians as the revolutionary subjects of feminism and the demise of hippies as the revolutionary subjects of communitarian libertarianism.

Once unisex (respectively unigender) toilets, passports, and personal pronouns are implemented, what comes next? Will the trans and nonbinary communities exhaust themselves as revolutionary subjects and seek to adapt? Instead, they could use their momentum to impose nonbinarism and transitioning not just on our gender identity but also on our species identity—an even greater biological and cultural prison—and join forces with the dispersed communities of otherkins. Otherkins identify themselves as nonhuman to some degree—be it as an animal (therians), a plant (plantkin), a machine (robotkin), a fantasy character (fictionkin, for instance elves or furries), an abstract entity (conceptkin, for instance elementkin, nightkin, forestkin, oceankin, spacekin, shadowkin, weatherkin), or as otherworldly (celestialkin, angelkin, godkin). Combinations and shifts are likely.

Just as many premodern societies allowed humans to obtain gender identities beyond the male-female binary, they also allowed certain nonhuman identities to be obtained. As in assumed shapeshifters, the distinction between humans and nonhumans often wasn't that clear. In modern society, shapeshifting is contained in the realm of fantasy.• Otherwise, it's regarded as a psychotic condition.•

In fact, there aren't yet any tools available to biologically transform a human into a nonhuman creature or vice versa. But while sex reassignment surgery and hormone replace-

• Abnormcore

• Society of Games

ment therapy have existed for about a hundred years, there are also not yet any medical tools available to turn biological men into child-birthing women or biological women into semen-ejaculating men.

Trans and nonbinary people have been attacked and ridiculed for the biological "incompleteness" of their identities. Their well-developed rhetoric against gender essentialism can serve as a blueprint to also question species essentialism. After the gay and lesbian communities integrated more and more varied sexual and gender identities into what is currently the LGBTQIA+ Recently, efforts have been made to expand the acronym to include premodern deviations from cis-heterosexuality. So far, these efforts have been limited to addressing Native American forms of nonbinarism under the neologism *Two-Spirit* (2S). Moreover, there is still no agreement on whether it's better to put "2S" at the beginning or at the end of the acronym. community, the trans and nonbinary communities could again integrate a growing variety of nonhuman or transhuman identities. Furries often identify as trans or nonbinary anyhow. Emphasizing such intersections, species dysphoria could be depathologized and depoliticized analogously to gender dysphoria.

Expanding beyond the species barrier, trans and nonbinary communities wouldn't just question why a heterosexual man should impose his male toxicity on women instead of becoming a woman, or why a heterosexual woman should submit to toxic masculinity instead of becoming a (better) man. They would also question why a pet owner or a conservationist should exert paternalistic power over their beloved animals instead of becoming an animal (to some degree).

Intellectual approaches exist that align trans studies and animal studies in their stance against humanism, for instance gender scholars Eva Hayward and Jami Weinstein's concept of *tranimalities*. See Eva Hayward and Jami Weinstein, "Introduction: Tranimalities in the Age of Trans⁺ Life," in "Tranimalities," ed. Eva Hayward and Jami Weinstein, special issue, *TSQ: Transgender Studies Quarterly* 2, no. 2 (May 2015). But turning an expanded, posthuman understanding of being trans or nonbinary into a comprehensive revolutionary force requires an incisive practice, facilitated by new technical tools. No yuppies without computer trading, no nerd economy without IT, no overall trans without mixed reality. While in the foreseeable future the biomedical tools for sex- and species-transitioning remain limited, soon a mixed reality, addressing all our senses, will make it easy to experience ourselves as fantastical beings of our choosing or as the very creature right in front of us.

Different from analog immersive techniques like reading, watching, hypnosis, or lucid dreaming, we won't have to focus but will be beset—at our own request. What happens is the opposite of exorcism: a deliberate and reversible act of *inorcism* (a word that currently has just a few thousand hits on Google, and for which there is no lexical entry except in the *Urban Dictionary*). The adoption of a virtual identity doesn't stop the moment we unplug. Inorcism will require exorcist practices like cleansing rituals, debriefings, or hypnosis to get rid of expendable identities. Just as we summarize the acts of emigration and immigration as migration, we might summarize inorcism and exorcism as *orcism*. The respective verb could be *to orc*, the noun, *orc*, or, cuter, *orcie*. The fact that these terms also refer to Orcus, the Latin name for the god of the underworld, and to the orcs, a species of monsters in the fantasy writings of J. R. R. Tolkien, fits all too well.

As a narcissist you'll orc to be loved as other creatures, while as an autoeroticist you'll turn into creatures that you love. In the former case you'll likely replace yourself with more-abled creatures, superior in features like looks, strength, flexibility, speed, or intelligence. In the latter case you might also prefer features superior to your own, but first and foremost they must intrigue you—erotically, intellectually, or politically. Instead of just loving these creatures like yourself, you now love them *as* yourself.[*]

If they're existing animals, we're likely to start with pets, as we're already used to loving them intensely since childhood—cats in particular. While dogs are very steady in their love and service, cats don't have much practical use (besides hunting rats and mice) and are only partly domesticated. They're able to change homes independently or even survive in the wild. This sense of independence makes them promising candidates for autoerotic fulfillment. In the analog realm, the popular cosplay character of the catboy already gives an idea of how a transgender or nonbinary identity can incorporate that of a cat. Often the catboy is wearing a maid costume, emphasizing the domesticity of the cat and supplementing its sense of independence with radical servility—toward its own demands.

A monadic society divides along the lines of those with whom we mainly identify. An enormous multiplicity of representations and alliances coexists and competes. Meanwhile, the prevailing monadic effort is to stay autarchic unless consent is granted to interact.

> This meandering essay didn't result in me coming up with a new word in the strict sense, but I find orc, orcie, and orcing too promising to keep on searching. Meanwhile, in an effort to give this rather long essay some shape, I came up with similarly catchy terms for its first two parts: (A) easy enough, I find myself well characterized as a tardie, and (B) for people like me who would like to get rid of any gendered, respectively human pronouns, I came up with the term itsie (as in "itsy-bitsy"). Perhaps most importantly, I mustered the courage to appropriate the beautiful and widely forgotten two-syllable word monad.

Ego Tribes
2017

Since the 1990s, personal tattoos have gained rapidly in popularity. Tattoos anticipated social media, and as your unconditional companions they define a tribe that is only you.

In 1908, architect Adolf Loos famously declared: "The modern man who tattoos himself is a criminal or a degenerate. There are prisons in which 80 percent of the inmates are tattooed. The tattooed who are not behind bars are latent criminals or degenerate aristocrats. If someone who is tattooed dies in freedom, then he does so a few years before he would have committed murder." Adolf Loos, "Ornament und Verbrechen" [Ornament and crime], a lecture held in 1908 and first published in German in *Frankfurter Zeitung* in 1929. My translation. As a protagonist of functionalism, Loos believed that "cultural evolution is equivalent to the removal of the ornament from articles of daily use." Apparently, he also understood the body as an article of daily use. Today, the glory days of functionalism are over, but the way objects of utility are designed—even luxury ones like cars—is still rather plain. Meanwhile, the fact that so many people are getting tattoos indicates a prevalent understanding of the body as a work of art.° Loos was right: "The herd must distinguish themselves through the use of various colors, modern man uses his clothes like a mask. His individuality is so strong that he no longer needs to express it with his clothing." But as the religious pressure to hide your body (even from yourself) weakens, there is an increasing social (Darwinistic) pressure to expose its shape and parts of the skin, as much as the weather allows. This pressure increases the more intimate you get with people.

Being tattooed used to carry the stigma of being an outcast or criminal for the simple reason that most jobs and venues prohibited the display of tattoos on the grounds of obscenity. Only outcasts and criminals wouldn't have much to lose by being tattooed. Today, evolved individualism—what I call *monadism*—pleads for full sovereignty over your own body; this includes the right to kill yourself, mutilate yourself, cosmetically modify yourself, transition from one gender to another, or abort. Meanwhile, monadism also comes with increased respect for others. Not only are physical violence and abuse banned but also mental violence and abuse are increasingly problematized. Every statement is scrutinized for traces of hate, triggers of trauma, or misinformation. You're not supposed to express yourself freely in front of others without their explicit consent—unless the expression is a permanent part of your body. Body modifications appeal as the synthesis of two diametrical practices of self-assurance: self-infliction and narcissism.* A tattoo is the body modification with the lowest threshold: it requires relatively little effort and can be—to start off—quite tiny or hidden.

The Western popularity of tattoos was preceded by that of graffiti, a highly visible and often monumental art form. In an increasingly individualistic environment, graffiti had allowed young people to express themselves artistically even if they were bare of the means and patience to study, get a studio, and pursue a career. When graffiti became strictly prosecuted, the public surface that you could still paint on was consenting people's skin. But the tattoo designer and the tattooist are often not the same person, and the act of tattooing itself must refrain from creative spontaneity. Meanwhile, it's the tattooed who endures the pain of the production, who decides on when and where to show the work, and who might even have come up with the tattoo's design. With graffiti, the sprayer is the hero, whereas with tattoos, it's the tattooed. By commissioning and accumulating different motives, the tattoo customer is a collector, curator, work, museum, and maybe artist in one—a perfect example of monadic autarchy and dedifferentation.[*]

Individual tattoos anticipated social media but only became ubiquitous once social media was established. Both act in between public and private. Like toggling privacy settings on and off, you can hide or reveal tattoos by putting on or removing clothes, though you can't be sure that information, once revealed, won't spread in uncontrolled ways. Once you've reached a certain level of intimacy, hiding becomes impossible. The fundamental difference between tattoos and social media is that with tattoos, space is limited, both posting and deleting are made dot by dot by hand, and the process costs a decent and visible amount of time, money, and pain—today's three most vital currencies. (Imagine a social media profile limited to a certain number of pixels for the rest of your life and for which each pixel must be individually programmed.) Even more, tattoos age and depart with you. They're not subject to the terms of use of some tech corporation and can't even be inherited. They're only yours.

Today it's rare that people—partners, best friends, family members—get matching tattoos. A tattoo might show your commitment to a certain community, but unless you're part of a rigid gang, it's you who decides if, how, and where to put it. Tattoos used to indicate that you belonged to a tribe; now they indicate a tribe that is only you. Through your different intellectual phases, intimate partners, social roles, avatars, styles, and cosmetic enhancements, you turn into a multitude of (often contradicting) personas, but your tattoos always stay with you—uniting all these personas as the one and only monad that is you. The other way of uniting them, though in retrospect, is to write a memoir or, more concise, an auto-fiction. At least playing with that idea became ubiquitous. Again, writing a book is a serious investment—in terms of time and mental pain.

Different from elements of style (clothes, hair, makeup, phrases), tattoos not only reveal your current fashions but also those of your past. The earlier you started getting tattoos, the more relatable you are—and at the same time unique. However generic your tattoos might be, the more of them you get over time, the less likely it becomes that someone else will have a similar pattern. As with emojis, it's not the single image but the sequence and context that give personal meaning. While tattoos mostly resonate with social media as a medium, their semantics mostly resonate with emojis—derivates of the smiley icon* that promise to encapsulate all states of mind in a generally positive take on life. But just as emojis have evoked anti-emojis that abound in negativity, like Pepe the Frog and Wojak, it remains possible to tattoo doubtless horror.

With tattoos, you're never completely naked and lonely. Fashions, homes, and friendships change; experiences fade away; but tattoos stay with you, no matter what. You don't have to feed them like pets, water them like plants, or dust them off like furniture. Tattoos are your unconditional companions in a semi-nomadic digital life. Tattoos promise to make you both less materialistic and less socially dependent. Tattoos aren't just assets to show off—the moment you look at them or see them in the mirror, they make you less emotionally dependent on others, in line with technically refined masturbation gadgets and autoerotic body modifications.*

With every day, a tattoo becomes a bit blurrier and it becomes a bit more likely that you'll get fed up with it. While fashion, cosmetics, and cosmetic surgery promise and burden you with permanent renewal*—only to sooner or later age and die anyway—tattoos compensate as fatal acts. You might regret them, but at least you did something that's worth regretting—in moderate terms. Unlike other acts of carpe diem (YOLO), tattoos are completely harmless to your health and your environment. In that sense, a tattoo excels not only a fashion statement (Would there have been something like normcore without tattoos?), partner, or pet but also drugs. Furthermore, there is hope that tattoo removal will become an easy procedure before you get fed up with yours. In that sense, tattoos anticipate a future in which we won't live just one but multiple life spans, and console us about that future's not-yet-existence. Getting a tattoo is like living a day as though it were your last while already knowing it's quite likely more days will come.

A secular worldview doesn't allow for definite answers and therefore worships goods and procedures that increase contingencies: money, recycling, health, education.* Irreversible processes like aging and death are perceived as horrendous flaws.* In this context, marking yourself for life is an outrageous act that's usually outbalanced by the ambiguity of the tattoo's meaning—in particular, to which extent you would even identify with the eventual meaning. Therefore, most tattoos show rather than say something. When they do say something, it's often written in a stylized way that's hardly decipherable from a distance. Even more, most tattoos follow a camp aesthetic—overdoing it in a sympathetic way, somewhere between serious and ironic. You could even argue that today, tattoos are intrinsically camp: you just can't be totally serious about them (it's impossible that they could fully represent you for the rest of your life)—but they also can't be just a joke (which you would have to carry with you for the rest of your life). Individual tattoos are the apotheosis of camp.

The future promises more and more ways to enhance ourselves as cyborgs and transhumans. Against that background, getting

Comic Purgatory •

Comic Purgatory
• Society of Games

ink tattooed into the skin serves as a future-atavistic (the opposite of retro-futuristic) ritual of giving up on the skin as an ever-blank canvas. There is no neutrality in the way that we were born. We're written by code (genes, family, milieu, etc.) and we're on the cusp of rewriting that code in radical ways. Therefore, as with social, technological, and personal progress in general (computer updates, urban planning, scientific progress, archiving, cult of awareness), the overall approach isn't one of overwriting; it's one of adding and recontextualizing, while carefully restoring all previous phases, as done in natural parks, cultural heritage sites, libraries, collections, emulations, recordings, or memories. But while the storage capacity of computers is still growing at an exponential speed, the strictly limited space on our skin is similar to that of the limited space on Earth or our limited capacities for attention.•

Getting a tattoo is both modest and invasive. Modest in the sense that tattoos don't expand over the limited space and time that our own body "naturally" occupies. Since the percentage of people who opt to be mummified or frozen is still very low, almost all tattoos are destined to disappear again. Invasive in the sense that while you yourself might get so used to your tattoos that you hardly notice them, strangers can't overlook them. A new lover can't not ask you about the meaning of your tattoos. With clothing, makeup, and perfume we express—but even more so, hide—ourselves: our naked body, our own odor, our wrinkles and pimples. It's unclear whether a person's decisions in that regard are driven by their own preferences or rather by the need to just put on something. Not so with tattoos: instead of hiding certain parts of your skin, tattoos highlight them.

While the Enlightenment was all about creating a universal public sphere—strictly divided from the private—identity politics, social media, and individual tattoos expand subjective speech and expression into the public realm (without having to address the public in person). Identity politics claims a mutual community; social media is about your very own community; with individual tattoos, the community is just you. Following the 1970s diagnosis of late-capitalistic consumer society as generally inclined toward narcissism, individual tattoos and social media mark another climax in "the tyrannies of intimacy" See Richard Sennett, *The Fall of Public Man* (New York: Alfred A. Knopf, 1977). and the decline of a general public sphere.• But since ancient Greek democracy, this Western public sphere has only ever been dominated by a White male elite. In contrast, social media and individual tattoos give voice to everyone. While social media is under cooperative algorithmic control, tattoos—for now—resist capitalist monopolization and serve as <u>a naive tool of giving voice in the most direct way</u>. They oppose the world that we live in as not real enough (too mediated by digital technologies) or still too real (not fantastic and playful enough).

Since the belief in modern utopias is fading, fears and hopes about <u>a retribalization of society</u> have become virulent. Moderate scenarios expect the world to fall apart in slick and affluent city-states and a barbarian hinterland•; more drastic ones expect a complete postapocalyptic relapse into nomadic hordes of hunters and gatherers. Today, tattoos mainly cater to your *ego tribe*. But it's only a matter of time until pattern recognition and global, fully automated tattoo chains will turn tattoos into another corporation- and state-controlled commodity. However cryptically and illusively you operate, deep learning will easily decode your intentions. To stand up against manipulation, people will have to unite—leading to a renaissance of tribes and associated tattoos on a voluntary basis.• Previous movements and subcultures have been easy to wipe out or instrumentalize, as they lacked the inner strength of a tribe. Gangs were the only exception—being held together by their illegality and sometimes also by a tattoo (or even a completely irreversible branding). But a tribe could also be installed the other way around: a community starting with the inking of a common tattoo. Later, it might extend to a common genetic modification. The basic logic is set: instead of tediously following a code, you inscribe it directly onto yourself.

# Abnormcore
2014

Today's common beauty ideals still follow social Darwinist
assumptions that were coined during industrialization.
Published in 1989, Katherine Dunn's novel *Geek Love* foresees
an automatized future in which limbs become atavistic and
all that you seek is attention through deviation.

In war, what counts are the soldiers killed. The injured are of
secondary concern; one hardly bothers to distinguish between
those who have suffered only a laceration and those who remain permanently injured. Casualty figures for toes, fingers,
hands, feet, arms, legs, eyes, and ears remain uncertain.

As a child of the 1970s, the sight of men with their pant
leg(s) or jacket arm(s) tied off is still very familiar to me. Three
decades after Germany lost World War II, the fallen and the
exterminated haunted one's dreams, but the amputees were
wandering monuments to guilt and shame. Shouldn't they be
glad just to be alive at all? And who knew if their tragic stories
were true, or if they hadn't just exploded a hand grenade when
lazily fishing? Anyone who collected for the war-blinded wearing a Jewish-star-yellow bandage (Why only for the blind?)
was suspected of being a malingerer.

The Nazi ideal of the toned giant, bursting with strength
and health, came from a time when cities like Berlin and

Munich were full of people impaired by war and industrialization. Still, even in today's affluent Western society, now that most of the war-disabled have died and automation has replaced most physically demanding labor, tall continues to take precedence over short,• and strong over lanky. Or, as Michel Houellebecq writes in the novel *La possibilité d'une île* (*The Possibility of an Island*, 2005), "Youth, beauty, strength: the criteria for physical love are exactly the same as those of Nazism."

Even if we had that kind of genetic makeup, it wouldn't be reason enough to submit to it. Ideals of beauty have changed radically time and again, and many people today would find Lucas Cranach the Elder's *The Three Graces* (1531) with their puffy bellies, fine hair, and low-set buttocks rather ugly. But there are good reasons to look for baldness, short legs, sagging breasts, and drooping shoulders when choosing a partner: short people consume fewer calories, weak people are more cautious, and less attractive people aren't as likely to be wooed away by rivals.

Traditionally, special demonic and magical abilities were even attributed to particularly abnormal people. Only social Darwinism, which misunderstands evolution as a teleology striving toward a single ideal, declares them to be inferior and, at best, pitiable deformities. And it is, of all things, the growing prominence of individualization that keeps increasing the pressure to optimize oneself physically and thus also to conform—until at some point boredom sets in and we can't stand it any longer. People are already inking their perfectly trimmed and surgically modified bodies with weird tattoos.•

Isn't it about time to take it to the next level and look for new attractive body shapes? Who still needs long legs when prostheses make you walk much faster and can be removed comfortably in a tight airplane seat?• The true "prosthetic god" not only uses glasses to see better, as described by Freud, it completely replaces its eyes and elevates itself from a defective to a torso being.

The most vivid view of this new aesthetic order to date

Heightism

Posthuman Test Grounds • Ego Tribes

is provided by boxing reporter Katherine Dunn's circus novel *Geek Love*, published in 1989. As early as 1952, author Bernard Wolfe published the postapocalyptic science-fiction novel *Limbo '90*, in which, in order to never go to war again, the men of the Western world have their arms and legs amputated and either have them replaced with nuclear-powered prostheses or, in the fundamentalist version, place themselves entirely in the care of their wives. However, the novel's particularly obnoxious misogyny and lengthy philosophical omissions are hard to take. *Geek Love*, on the other hand, became a bestseller and, in its inversion of normal and abnormal, had a lasting impact on the grunge scene and beyond. Kurt Cobain and Courtney Love counted it among their favorite books, it inspired stunt performer Jim Rose to create a circus of crass acts that toured with Nine Inch Nails and Marilyn Manson, and it anticipated the MTV series *Jackass* (2000–2002). Wes Anderson's *The Royal Tenenbaums* (2001) seems like a sugary rip-off compared to *Geek Love*. Later, the yearning to be radically different is kitsched up in the boom of vampire movies and series.

*Geek Love* is about a circus family, the Binewskis, who run a freak show. In North America, the geek is a voodoo-inspired curiosity who bites the heads off living chickens. Mother Binewski, a girl from a good family, became such a geek after her dream of becoming a trapeze artist was dashed.

The modern circus was developed in nineteenth-century England and France. Over the course of industrialization, it trimmed sensations from a wide variety of contexts into spectacles lasting just a few minutes. Amusements previously reserved for the aristocracy, such as horse training, were made accessible to the masses and radicalized, for example, as lion training. Meanwhile, the shock and surprise effects of magic, pantomime, fortune-telling, and freak shows had their origins in animistic rituals. In *Geek Love*, the cross-milieu fascination that draws Mother Binewski to the ring is losing steam. On the one hand, the circus must now compete with cinema and television, and on the other hand, it has prompted accusations of cruelty to animals and humans. It is only to experience a renaissance with Cirque du Soleil, an acrobatic musical free of sawdust, smelly animals, and false magic.

The Binewskis take another course and set out to breed some particularly outlandish freaks. Mother Binewski administers insecticides, radium, and various drugs during her pregnancies in order to induce the most blatant mutations possible in her children, and becomes virtually blind as a result. At best, the Binewskis can market their six stillbirths in a trailer named Museum of Nature's Innovative Art. But a few times they get lucky: "Aqua Boy" Arturo grows fins instead of arms, Elly and Iphy are born as Siamese twins, and their son Chick develops telekinetic powers. Only the first-person narrator, Olympia, a hunchbacked and bald albino dwarf, isn't really good for anything. But instead of blaming her parents for making her a human experiment, she longs to be even more outlandish.

At one point, Olympia participates in a topless casting at a nightclub. She overcomes her shame, wiggles her hump, and proudly exposes breasts that hang to her knees. Yes, she's deformed, but can still feel a thousand times superior to a normal guy, no matter how attractive or healthy. When a rich heiress offers Olympia's daughter a pile of money for a makeover to turn her into a normal-looking woman, Olympia doesn't shy away from murder. Olympia is abnormcore.

Dunn describes in detail the jealousies between the Binewski offspring. As the eldest, Arturo keeps a strict watch to make sure no one disputes his rank as the family's biggest star, and when he learns of Chick's telekinetic powers, he tries to kill him. The girls surrender to Arturo, and the twins fight over who gets to cut the meat for the armless man. The parents pretend not to notice anything; for them the children remain their "dreamlets."

Arturo's whole ambition is to inspire awe. He chops off a horse's feet to make it an attraction with a stump dance, and when a footless man offers him a masturbation machine made from a converted record player and a hose, he tells him that no one who proudly shows off their stumps needs such a thing: "Wear silver sequin pads and dance on a lit stage where they can see you. [...] They want those things hidden away, disguised, forgotten, because they know how much power those stumps could have."

In his shows, Arturo lets the audience tell him what moves them. The fact that he openly displays his deformity makes them trust him. They pour their hearts out to him, in an effort to somehow make up for his heavy blow of fate. Arturo takes a chance and begins to act as an oracle. He leads the fair back to its spiritual origins and rises to become the savior of a new religion, since both are based on wonder, horror, and hope. As he puts it: "O.K., a carnival works because people pay to feel amazed and scared. They can nibble around a midway getting amazed here and scared there, or both. And do you know what else? Hope. Hope they'll win a prize, break the jackpot, meet a girl, hit a bull's-eye in front of their buddies. [...] Religion works the same way. The only difference is that it's more amazing [...] And it's a whole lot scarier [...] This scare stuff laps over into the hope department too. The hope you get from religion is a three-ring, all-star hope because the risk is outrageous. Bad!"

To make his audience literally tremble, Arturo has his voice piped directly into the pews. He has a system built that allows him to speak underwater. All he still needs is a gripping message of salvation—until twenty-two-year-old Alma speaks up during a performance. Her hair is thin and colorless and she's obese, but nowhere near big enough to pass for an attraction in this age of overeating. When she starts crying, Arturo gives the usual therapy blah about lack of self-love, but when asked rhetorically what she really wants, Alma replies, "I want to be like you."

The Aqua Boy goes for it and as a test has Alma amputate all her toes. When that still isn't enough for her, he has her amputate her arms and legs as well. And indeed, she's finally rid of the "weight of rot," loses some kilos, gains color, and feels great in her body.

Alma's example establishes the Arturo sect: others also have their limbs amputated and travel behind the circus in their own caravans. The more limbs the followers have amputated, the further forward they move on the grandstand, which now holds ten thousand spectators. The completely limbless lie prone in the sawdust, directly in front of the dolphinarium. The still non-operated novices care for the amputees, and Arturo has to grapple with questions such as whether breasts count as part of the torso or should be amputated, whether he also admits people who are already missing limbs, and whether the several step-by-step operations shouldn't instead be consolidated into a single complete shrinking.

Arturo's sect isn't driven by body integrity dysphoria but by the ambition to reach the next stage of civilization: "Consider the bound feet of the Mandarin maiden ... and the Manchu scholar who jams his hands into lacquered boxes so his fingernails grow like curling death. Even the Mexican welder sports one long polished nail on his smallest finger which declares to the world, 'My life allows superfluity. I have this whole finger to spare, unnecessary to my labor and unscathed by it.'"

While the usual transhumanism focuses on expanding human capabilities and thus follows the baroque logic of the superhero,* Arturo extends the modern principle of reduction not only to furniture, clothes, and houses but also to humans themselves: less is more.

As it is with totalitarian concepts: it's hard to find the point where enough is enough, and radicalization unfolds an unstoppable dynamic. When the Siamese twins' following grows and they begin to do sex work with the slogan "The Exquisite Convenience of Two Women with One Cunt," Arturo has one of the sisters lobotomized, which promptly gives him the idea that to continue the shrinkage on a spiritual level, his followers should all be lobotomized too.

Incest, immaculate conception, a journalist who sells maggots fattened with amputated limbs as a side hustle—Dunn leaves nothing out. But she manages to make you so familiar with the Binewskis and their topsy-turvy value system that nothing really shocks.

In recent years, films celebrating people with disabilities as everyday heroes have proliferated: Ben Lewin's *The Sessions* (2012) is about a man paralyzed from the neck down who, in his early forties, finally masters his deflowering. Olivier Nakache and Éric Toledano's *Intouchables* (2011) is about a paraplegic man who integrates a Black migrant into French society and has a lot of fun in the process. These heroes follow the pattern of David Lynch's deformed *Elephant Man* (1980) and Barry Levinson's autistic *Rain Man* (1988), who prove themselves to be at least as endearing as people without disabilities, if not more so.

The freak show is also currently experiencing a renaissance. People no longer go to the circus for this but watch television offerings that range from countless documentaries presenting the most bizarre physical abnormalities, from *Girl with Eight Limbs* (2008) and *The Man with the 10-Stone Testicles* (2013) to the reality TV series *The Undateables* (since 2012) and *Britain's Missing Top Model* (2008), which feature people with disabilities. Officially, these shows claim to help boost the self-confidence of people with disabilities and society's acceptance of them, but guardians of public morals accuse the shows of exhibiting people with disabilities all the more shamelessly.

The protagonists of such broadcasts have agreed to participate voluntarily. If you want to acknowledge people with disabilities as full members of society, you must concede to them the right to let themselves be used for sensational stupidities. You can't only be proud of how pretty but also how bizarre and ugly you're perceived to be. Effectively, the freak show is more honest and emancipatory than an empowerment that reduces freaks to "We're humans too." Especially when they organize the show themselves.

Mother Binewski says, "What greater gift could you offer your children than an inherent ability to earn a living just by being themselves?" Her effort to give her children a particularly extravagant genotype is the neoliberal alternative to a guaranteed basic income. Thanks to social media and technical surveillance, we're each in the ring every day, vying for attention. The crucial question, as with the Binewskis, is how many people are watching us.

> **The war on doping is harmful and vain, like the war on drugs. As there aren't and never have been "natural" sports, it would be beneficial to redefine sports as the test grounds of the posthuman condition.**

Doping is as old as competitive sports. In the ancient Olympics, common performance-enhancing nostrums included extracts of horsetail plants, animal hearts and testicles, ground hooves, bread with opium, and wine. Doping was perceived as unfair and uncouth but not as effective as black magic, bribery, or foul play (and therefore not as illegal).

With the revival of the Olympic Games in the late nineteenth century, new potent drugs like strychnine, cocaine, and amphetamines came into play. Even though officially prohibited since the 1930s, doping was largely tolerated throughout the twentieth century. The Cold War made any interference in international sporting events an extremely delicate political affair.

Since the fall of the Iron Curtain, the fight against doping has become more rigorous. The list of substances and methods banned by the World Anti-Doping Agency, established in 1999, numbers in the hundreds. Professional athletes are not only tested at competitions but at any time. Still, it's a game of cat and mouse. Besides bribing and cheating, new drugs and techniques are constantly being introduced to circumvent existing prohibitions.

What is all this effort about? Different from ancient times, the emphasis is less on doping being unfair than on it being dangerous to your body. The war on doping comes with a moral litany about professional athletes as "clean" role models. They're supposed to exemplify what is possible with just willpower and good genes.

In 2016, I ghostwrote the memoir of Nils Schumann, the German winner of the 800-meter Olympic gold in 2000. Nils Schumann, with me and Erik Niedling, *Lebenstempo: In Alltag und Sport den eigenen Rhythmus finden* [Pace of life: Finding your own rhythm in everyday life and sports] (Freiburg: Herder, 2016). After his unexpected triumph, Nils struggled to repeat his success. He lost years due to severe injuries, and when he finally gave up on his career, it coincided with personal insolvency. I worked on the book together with artist Erik Niedling, and in the process, we couldn't stop wondering: Had Nils done *it*? In fact, he had been in contact with a dubious physician and one of his trainers had been convicted of the possession of illegal substances.

Nils gave a disarming answer: he would have probably been doping, if only he could have afforded it. At the time of his career, an undetectable "therapy" was supposed to cost around 100,000 euros per year. Due to his series of losses and injuries, Nils simply didn't have that kind of money—"and the bank won't give you a loan for it either."

Nils wouldn't have been concerned about harmful side effects, just the opposite: "As a competitive athlete, you train and fight in the unhealthy red zone all the time and can't avoid taking food supplements such as L-carnitine, glutamine, or creatine. These can also endanger your health. Yes, doping can even be healthy for a competitive athlete, at least relatively speaking. For those who dope have to work less hard to achieve the same results. The fact that I stumbled from one injury to the next was not due to bad luck, but due to overwork."

Competitive athletes are under permanent medical observation. In contrast, the laity enhance the effectiveness of their training unsupervised, taking unregulated amounts of unverified growth hormones, testosterone, and anabolic steroids and combining them with stimulants like speed and crystal meth. Several studies show that in Germany around one-fourth of all men and one-tenth of all women who go to the gym dope. See, for instance, Carsten Boos and Karen Petry, *Medikamentenmißbrauch im Freizeitsport* [Medication abuse in recreational sports] (Lübeck: Medizinische Universität Lübeck, Klinik für Orthopädie, 2000). They risk high blood pressure, heart attack, kidney failure, impotence, and depression. Before competitions, half of recreational long-distance runners tend to take painkillers. Kay Brune et al., "Analgetikamissbrauch bei Marathonläufern" [Analgesic abuse in marathon runners], *MMW—Fortschritte der Medizin* 151, no. 40 (2009). Muting the warning signals of the body increases the risk of serious injury. Physical loading multiplies the dangers of any medication.

The futility and noxiousness of the war on drugs is well known. Most Western countries are in the process of legalizing or tolerating the consumption of popular drugs. But the war on doping still goes undisputed. Crack athletes serve as the guinea pigs for radical surveillance. They give up on their right to privacy to qualify for a *Truman Show* of Sports. Soon they might have to agree on implementing a chip that monitors their metabolism 24/7—only to have to make even greater efforts to trick the system. Clean athletes who break one world record after another are the secular equivalent of celibate priests: role models of outrageous hypocrisy.

It would be more rewarding to transform elite sports into test grounds of the posthuman condition where extraordinary heroes experiment with whatever performance-enhancing technique is available. Life science and tech companies could sponsor them to test and promote their latest inventions.

Parasports, which allow prostheses that can, in some cases, make you perform better than with natural limbs, might be a promising example for evolving in that direction.* Future elite sports could allow artificial webbing, gills, wings; gene editing; performance-enhancing substances. Meanwhile, traditional elite sports could subsist as the last stronghold of a human revanchism, with athletes naked and barefoot just like in Ancient Greece, divided into two "natural" sexes.

In June 2023, lawyer and entrepreneur Aron D'Souza unveiled plans for the "Enhanced Games"—an alternative to the Olympics where doping is allowed—using a line of argument similar to that of this essay.

Body with More Organs
2020

> The legal protection of nature, pioneered in the 1970s,
> follows paternalistic assumptions. To let nature speak for
> itself, we must equip ourselves with additional organs
> that allow us to sense other beings as we sense ourselves.

Western environmentalism understands humanity as the
ungrateful child of generous Mother Earth. This narrative
resonates with the biblical parable of the prodigal son who
squanders his inherited fortune. Once he has used up all his
resources, the son returns home and begs for forgiveness
from his loving father.

To extend this allegory, the Enlightenment can be read
as the attempt of the son to overcome his father and the
biblical parable altogether by making himself into his own
father; environmentalism reestablishes the parable with a
gender switch and turns it against itself. Now the father is in
the position of the vain son whose patriarchalism appears as
a futile rebellion against Mother Earth. This narrative has
made feminism and environmentalism obvious allies and
explains the skepticism toward both by otherwise progressive
forces. How to overcome the dichotomy between the Enlight-

enment's sense of triumph and environmentalism's sense of repentance?

In 1972, Christopher D. Stone, professor of law at the University of Southern California, published his seminal article "Should Trees Have Standing?—Toward Legal Rights for Natural Objects." Christopher D. Stone, "Should Trees Have Standing?—Toward Legal Rights for Natural Objects," *Southern California Law Review* 45 (1972). Stone argued that law has progressed over time to confer rights upon creatures that society had previously considered incapable or unworthy of having rights: children, the enslaved, women, minorities, noncitizens, people with mental disabilities, fetuses, and even endangered species. With environmental exploitation on the rise, it seemed to Stone high time we expand these protections and legal statuses to natural objects.

Speaking within the terms of the allegory: Mother Earth's prodigal son humanity wouldn't return home to her, but would give her a place in his new home. As an equal member of the family, or as a cherished retiree? As natural entities can't represent themselves, Stone proposed that we should protect the rights of natural entities as we would those "of legal incompetents—human beings who have become vegetable."

"Should Trees Have Standing?" was published at a turning point in Western civilization. The previous year, Greenpeace had been founded and the Club of Rome presented its study on the self-destructive environmental effects of unchecked economic expansion, which led to the oft-cited report *The Limits to Growth*. Only days after Stone's article was published, William O. Douglas, associate justice of the US Supreme Court, referred to it in adjudicating an environmental organization's lawsuit against the Disney development of a ski resort in the Sierra Nevada mountains. Douglas, too, suggested that natural objects should be granted legal personhood.

Stone's then-novel approach has since become common practice. In 2008, chapter 7 of the constitution of Ecuador included the rights of nature "to exist, persist, maintain and regenerate its vital cycles." Bolivia changed its constitution accordingly in 2009. The first case of two humans acting as legal guardians of a natural entity—the Vilcabamba River in Ecuador—was successfully argued and won in 2011. Since then, numerous countries have passed similar treaties, laws, and judicial decisions. The UN has been discussing the rights of nature in a series of "Harmony with Nature" dialogues by the General Assembly, and has started an initiative for a "Universal Declaration of the Rights of Nature."

Stone's article is strikingly Eurocentric, though. From the get-go, it cleaves to Charles Darwin's assumption in *The Descent of Man* (1871) of a gradual extension of humans' compassion, from prehistoric tribes to global humanism and beyond: "As man gradually advanced in intellectual power, and was enabled to trace the more remote consequences of his actions [...] so would the standard of his morality rise higher and higher." Stone ignores that for Indigenous communities in particular, it has always been a common practice to attribute personhood to natural entities—not as "incompetents" but as beings that articulate themselves in ways that humans can understand.

Stone concedes that monotheism introduced the concept of a dominion of "man" over all other creatures and things, and that it was precisely Darwin's theory of the survival of the fittest "that gave moral approbation to struggle, conquest, and domination." But Stone doesn't believe that "a changed environmental consciousness will in and of itself" be able to stop "an increasing number of humans, with increasing wants, and [...] an increasing technology to satisfy them at 'cost' to the rest of nature. [...] Notwithstanding the vaunted 'harmony' between the American Plains Indians and Nature, once they had equipped themselves with rifles their pursuit of the buffalo expanded to fill the technological potential."

For Stone, it's legal instruments that propel change, and he might be right. Still, the juridification of nature didn't turn out as the linear Western project that he had imagined. So far, the states that recognize environmental personhood all have strong Indigenous communities and often explicitly refer to them as guardians of nature. For instance, in New Zealand it's only in the frame of treaties with different Maori communities that rivers, forests, and mountains are acknowledged as entities with rights.

Colombian anthropologist Astrid Ulloa coined the term "ecological natives" to describe Indigenous people who act as "political-ecological agents": "The problem is that 'we'—the modern, capitalist West—need ecological natives. We need them to be uncontaminated by capitalist markets. We need them to be engaged with us as our subjects, subalterns, opponents, or as our colonized, underdeveloped, or oppressed others. [...] They have to be 'our' Utopian reality [...] while we are comfortable, secure, well-paid and safe in our houses, offices, universities, libraries, meetings, seminars or resorts talking, thinking and picturing them." Astrid Ulloa, *The Ecological Native: Indigenous Peoples' Movements and Eco-governmentality in Colombia* (New York: Routledge, 2005). The concept of the ecological native perpetuates patronizing idealizations of the "noble savage." These idealizations have been temporarily mirrored by White urbanite Greta Thunberg—diagnosed with Asperger's syndrome, OCD, and selective mutism, and thereby regarded as a particularly innocent child—as an advocate of innocent nature.* Because of their assumed naturalness, the protection of Indigenous peoples has been seen within a continuum of ecological conservation.*

Stone argued that basically everybody could act as the guardian of environmental persons: "Natural objects can communicate their wants (needs) to us, and in ways that are not terribly ambiguous. I am sure I can judge with more certainty and meaningfulness whether and when my lawn wants (needs) water, than the Attorney General can judge whether and when the US wants (needs) to take an appeal from an adverse judgment by a lower court."

What Stone implies with "want" or "need" is "to preserve the natural object as close as possible to its condition at the time the environment was made a rights-holder." Not in the sense of freezing evolution at its current state, or liberating nature from human interference: neither would be practical, as long as our civilizations continue to keep a hold over earthly life. Whenever "the costs of making [the object] whole somewhere else, in some other way" accrue, these benefits should be paid into a trust fund on behalf of that object.

Stone's proposal disregards the actual feelings of nonhuman entities: "Given the conjectural nature of the 'estimates' in all events, and the roughness of the 'balance of conveniences' procedure where that is involved, the practice would be of more interest from the socio-psychic point of view [...] than from the legal-operational." Indeed, human rights don't include the right to happiness either. Rather, they're meant to cater to the conditions for humans to take care of themselves while in "pursuit of happiness." This is somewhat undefined: it's up to each individual whether their preference is in fact to be happy or not.

Still, we make a fundamental distinction between objects that we assume have feelings and agency and ones that we believe lack them. We can wish for the latter to continue to exist because of their beauty, their practical function, or as someone's property or creation. But secular societies can't express pity for these objects, fear their revenge, or assess their relative intrinsic worth. Beyond our own personal preferences, we can't reliably differentiate the value of a mountain, a car, a shred of trash, or the bacteria in someone's gut.

Maybe even more significant is that to grant basic rights to natural "objects" implies not caring about individual, mortal lives, but about whole habitats and species that can potentially thrive forever. As we can't take care of all creatures on Earth—or even just manage to leave them alone—the whole ecological movement has been following this approach, and deep ecology, as formulated in 1973 by the philosopher Arne Næss, also applies these ethics to the human species. The extreme position is that in order to protect nature from our destructive drive, our own self-extinction is required, with the exception of maybe a few exemplary individuals.

Humans couldn't even be pitied for their pettiness. Our habitual assumption that we feel more because our brains are especially large isn't backed by any substantial research on how consciousness actually works. Recently, Alex Jordan, a marine biologist at the Max Planck Institute of Animal Behavior in Konstanz, Germany, proved that the cleaner wrasse, a fish around ten centimeters long, passes the mirror self-recognition test. And it's not necessary to know who one is to feel excruciating pain. There is solid evidence that fruit flies dream. How might they suffer? Plants too?

To find special legitimation for our own Western existence, it wouldn't suffice to merely refrain from harming our environment. We would actually have to do good, and according to the 2010 Universal Declaration of the Rights of Mother Earth "play [our] role in Mother Earth for her harmonious functioning." What is harmonious about infanticides, rapes, droughts, famines, or plagues? We can't even manage to reeducate ourselves, and we have no right to punish nature for not knowing better while we consciously commit even greater crimes knowing all too well. But we could prevent the worst from happening, at the very least.

Soon one will look back at our time as the last years of an unbelievable ignorance, not just about human-inflicted harm against nature, but within nature too. To promote empathy with our environment, we shield ourselves from its cruelty—even though the evidence of it is accumulating exponentially. In the wake of the miniaturization of information technology in the 1960s, biologists started to equip animals with small radio tags to track their movements. Later came cameras, GPS, and electronic sensors. As a result of those observations we know, for instance, that cats eat only 30 percent of their brutally killed prey. So, shouldn't we breed cats that are less bloodthirsty? And do the same with wild animals, as a result of similar findings?

Breeding, mass surveillance, genetic engineering—humans have always been more keen to apply new technologies to nonhumans than to themselves. Soon it will be possible to automatically equip all kinds of creatures—down to microbes—with information technology, process the input, and control behavior accordingly. We—or rather our machines—won't just be able to listen and talk to these creatures, but to read and rewrite their minds and nervous systems as well. With the Internet of Things comes the Internet of Beings. The question won't be whether to alter our environment or not, but how to hinder the algorithms from acting in an all-too-patronizing manner. In other words: our next challenge will be not just to understand nonhuman creatures and take care of them, but also to let them participate in our decision-making processes.

The realm of information technology is guided by the ineradicable belief that with greater and greater streams of information we'll finally be able to reach a godlike level of certainty about our world. Mechanism design will guide us to the best-case scenario for everybody. It's a belief that goes back to Vladimir Vernadsky's and Pierre Teilhard de Chardin's ideas of the "noosphere" in the 1920s, rooted in Plotinus's prophecy of the world soul, itself rooted in Platonic idealism. All three have in common that they separate a pure sphere of reason from an impure world of matter. This already went wrong once—big time—with the ordinary internet. Exponential computational powers go hand in hand with exponential means of manipulation.

When Taiwan's digital minister Audrey Tang asks for "a form of democracy that includes rivers, mountains, animals and other nonhumans, giving these agents a political voice via an avatar," it won't be enough, as she optimistically proposes, for "people [to] start to devise their own games that are win-win for everyone involved. If they detect a win-lose dynamic, people will simply turn it into a game, working together to develop a better mechanism instead of focusing their energy on making other people lose so that they can win." Joanna Pope with Audrey Tang, "After Zero-Sum: Serenity for Democracy," *Arts of the Working Class*, no. 120, "The New Serenity" (2020). Why should they? As long as some enjoy it when others lose, or prefer not just to win but to win ever more, one would have to exchange these people with ideal game participants. And who would be in charge of such a transformation? •

To avoid ever-greater concentrations of power, we must create a democracy that allows nonhumans to actually have a say. Prior to the 2012 edition of documenta, its artistic director, Carolyn Christov-Bakargiev, asked: "What would a world be if the bees were voting, and how could the bees vote? Or a strawberry, how can a strawberry vote?" Carolyn Christov-Bakargiev, quoted at the 2012 Creative Time Summit, New York. Back then, her remarks were widely ridiculed, seen as a hilarious, if not ludicrous, provocation. And indeed, when I asked her how this could work, her ideas were very much in line with Stone's "How Trees Could Have Standing?": to have humans act as proxies.

On which basis would these people judge, for instance, if a strawberry prefers to be eaten or rot in the bush? Probably the strawberry itself doesn't know, and is unable to choose between different options (not just in the sense of flourishing or not, but in having an understanding of itself). So how could we make the strawberry eligible, without basically replacing it with something completely new? Maybe by equipping it with wheels or an exoskeleton, as imagined by cognitive scientist Joscha Bach. See Joscha Bach, "How to Build an Artificially Intelligent Plant," March 11, 2016, http://bach.ai/how-to-build-an-ai-plant/.

No false modesty here: whatever we turn natural entities into, they will be our fabrication, just as we already domesticated and cultivated and transformed most natural entities that surround us. Rather than declaring these things independent beings, it would be more "natural" to acknowledge them as part of us. Instead of us belonging to our environment as something bigger than us, or our environment belonging to us as property, we would be something bigger than us. The liberal deterritorialization as an imagined "body without organs" with an endless variety of exchangeable protheses would be followed by a reterritorialization of the body with a potentially endless number of extra organs. The terms *body without organs, deterritorialization*, and *reterritorialization* refer to concepts developed by philosophers Gilles Deleuze and Félix

Guattari in *Capitalisme et schizophrénie* [Capitalism and schizophrenia], 2 vols. (Paris: Les Éditions de Minuit, 1972–80). Or to speak again in the parable of the prodigal son: Mother Earth wouldn't become an "incompetent" one of our kind, she would become one with us.

Stone recognized that empathy is a limited mechanism. We can misinterpret others or completely ignore them, but when it comes to our own organs, their signals shoot straight to our brain. We don't feel empathy with our organs, we just feel them.

Our body representation is malleable, allowing us to perceive outside entities as our own. Synchronous brush-strokes on a concealed hand and a visible fake hand can give the impression of touch and ownership of the fake hand. Mirror-touch synesthetes replicate the perceived sensations in other beings—some also in nonhuman animals or objects— as sensations of their own body.

The Internet of Beings will allow us to send data generated from entities all around the world right to our limbic system. We could decide by ourselves which ones become our additional organs, and how their signals transform into feelings. These organs could be part of our own legal property, or someone else's. Everybody would have the right to feel everything.

Some might prefer masochistic scenarios that give them pleasure whenever their entities of choice are harmed. Some might find relief in self-destruction. But most would likely go for entities that they're able to identify with, and that they want to be all right.[*] Most might identify with obviously attractive choices (such as dolphins or trees); some might challenge themselves and go for entities that used to make them feel uncomfortable (like jellyfish or mold). Our choices and settings would be full of anthropocentric biases. Our environment would still be misrepresented. But at least we would get in line with our needs and wishes for it.

• Orcies

Monadic life is defined by the reversible excitements of recreational games.

The internet and virtual reality turn gaming into society's main paradigm. Everyday routines are gamified to keep us motivated. The parameters of gaming question the limits of the liberal order. Common-good games promise solace.

Franz Kafka's unfinished novel *Der Verschollene* (*The Man Who Disappeared*, 1911–14) tells the story of the enforced and unsuccessful emigration of a sixteen-year-old European to the US. In the last fragment, the stranded protagonist sees a poster that says: "The great Theater of Oklahoma is calling you! It's calling only today, only once! Whoever misses the opportunity now, misses it forever! Those who think of their future belong with us! All welcome! Whoever wants to be an artist, step forward! We are the theater that has a place for everyone, everyone in his place!"

Karl is uncertain if he should take the offer seriously: How can they accept everyone? And what about the payment? But he doesn't have much to lose and so gives it a try. The audition that awaits him is megalomaniacal. The applicants have to walk over a stage filled with hundreds of women costumed as angels who stand on pedestals and blast from elongated trumpets. A highly subdivided recruitment committee asks the aspirants about their skills and previous professions and categorizes them accordingly. But the committee doesn't require any evidence; in fact, it accepts everyone. Before the applicants travel to Oklahoma, they're invited to a lush meal during which photographs of the theater are handed around. The only one Karl can get hold of shows the US president's grandiosely lit loge, itself the size of a theater.

The novel aborts without revealing what this theater is all about. In one version of the text, it's called a "nature theater." Does this imply that it's situated outside? Did Kafka envision a Gesamtkunstwerk that happens in real life and in which the actors play themselves? Was the Theater of Oklahoma meant as an allegory on the afterlife with Karl being already—unknowingly—dead? Or was it a satirical utopia of the New World, characterized by full employment and the absence of money? Kafka's work on *Der Verschollene* ended with the First World War.

Almost sixty years later, in 1970, at the peak of the Vietnam War and the Western student protests against the US intervention, the media theorist Marshall McLuhan further developed his theory of the electrified world as a global village into that of a global theater. In the global village, everyone can know about everyone else, without delay and as though present. The global theater is characterized by satellites that observe the world from above, as well as the new art form of the happening, which lacks a strict division between actors and audience and isn't properly scripted: "Sputnik and the moon shots brought about, in effect, the institution of a new kind of global theater, in which all men become actors and there are few spectators. The population of the world is both the cast and content of this new theater. The repertory of the theater consists of a perpetual happening, which can include the retrieval or replay of any previous happenings that men choose to experience." Marshall McLuhan and Barrington Nevitt, *Take Today: The Executive as Dropout* (New York: Harcourt Brace Jovanovich, 1972).

In the early 1970s, the resolution of satellite cameras didn't yet allow for the observation of individual people. If down on Earth everybody turned into actors, who would be the audience watching from above? Would it be the secret service, or the computers that would take the position of the new gods? And what exactly distinguishes our normal life from a play if the latter lacks a script? Aren't humans always role-playing anyhow?

Again, McLuhan's notes on the global theater remained rudimentary and ambiguous. He stopped exploring the idea—all in all, a few repetitive paragraphs scattered over several publications—in 1973, when the US withdrew from Vietnam and the oil crisis set in. Now the Western world was no longer divided between the authoritarian dickheads and the hippies fighting any fixed order, but between the masses fearing unemployment and inflation and the neoliberal elite making even more money off that fear.

With virtual reality, the idea of life as a theater gained new plausibility—at least whenever we go online. There, it's easy to adopt a new identity and to place ourselves in every imaginable scenario. We can meet with others, or we can each have it all for ourselves. We can move at enormous speed, or not budge and let everything that we want come straight to us. As in theater, in virtual reality our character or environment can completely change from one moment to the next. Only this change isn't predetermined—it can be spontaneous. We can speak languages that we don't know. We can sing even if we can't sing, and dance even if we can't dance. We can fly without wings. And we can sense it all as much as if we were daydreaming. In virtual reality, everything is fake, unless certified as true.

Why all the fuss about virtual reality when brain stimulation technology will allow us to daydream at any time and for as long as we want? Because in virtual reality we can meet others and experience what they've created. We don't have to come up with what we want all by ourselves. We're not in an *autofantasy* in which only we embody the characters but in a *co-op fantasy* in which other characters are embodied by independent entities, either sentient people or non-player characters. We or others can program and select these entities to meet our expectations, or we can opt for levels of surprise and friction. We can satisfy our wants to such a degree that we don't even have to make the effort to formulate them, or we can challenge and train our taste in ever-new ways.

Our biggest problem in the virtual world is what to choose. Different from gods, we can sense and process only so much at a time, which is why the virtual world makes it easy for corporations and gurus to lure us into their extremely restricted scenarios and terms—even easier than it is with social media.*

Those who are particularly successful in locking people into their virtual reality must face the same challenges as dealers of extremely addictive psychoactive drugs: users might neglect their real lives to a degree that makes them wither away. Eventually, machines might feed us, keep us fit and clean, and protect us against heat, cold, and other dangers. But getting back to Karl's main concern when applying for the Theater of Oklahoma: What about the money?

Users who still have property can give it away for a certain number of carefree years. Or, to keep a bit of a challenge, the number of carefree years could depend on their performance. And the rest of the population? Today, we get "paid" with the free use of social media for giving away our personal data and exposing ourselves to advertisements. But the less we own and earn, the less our data and attention are worth. Science fiction has fantasized about humans being harvested for their organs, vital energies, or natural resources, but with the advances in AI and cultured meat, these scenarios—however dystopian they were meant to be—appear as wishful thinking.

In case there isn't a socialist revolution, the urge to gamble will be the remaining monetary pull toward a life predominantly led in virtual reality. To incentivize the use of social media, it's enough to pay people in others' attention (which can be monetized only by a small elite of influencers). Social media makes you compete for likes and followers—gamifying your social interactions. When playing an actual game with others, however, you already have their attention. As in theater, you can aspire for additional spectators and applause, but since it's quite a time commitment to watch others play a game, attention is even more focused on a few actors than it is in social media.

Offering everybody opportunities to win money, virtual games can generate even greater profits than social media: people spend more time playing, and the chance to win money makes them willing to spend even more money. Gaming companies can offer incentives to keep the gains in the game. Some create substitute currencies that can't be exchanged back into real money. But the more real the earnings feel, the more we're willing to invest. We're willing to buy shoes that make us walk faster, even though we could fly; or to buy land and build a home, even though we don't need shelter.

As a result, not just recreational games but also more and more services—online and offline—are framed as gambles. Learning a language, you win or lose coins with every right or wrong answer, with every skipped challenge or accepted hint. Driving within the speed limit prompts a thumbs-up on a big screen and participation in a lottery funded by speeding fines.

Games are popular because following a manageable set of rules provides for a reliable rate of excitements and successes. Games are setups of an ideal world, which is why religions tend to explain life as a game: there is a manageable set of commandments, there are regular gratifications and penalizations, there are random interventions—either by a deity or by people's free will—to mix things up a bit, and the victorious end of the game (death) is marked as paradise or reincarnation. Paradise tends to appear as a very pleasant but rather boring place, which is why in most religions the dead continue to interfere in worldly affairs. Reincarnation comes with a new game level.

Pre-liberal societies have also been codifying important

interactions with uncertain outcomes—like dating, elections, and war—as games. Or is it the other way around, with games being playful copies of those strictly codified, suspenseful interactions? In any case, flippancy is what distinguishes actual games from those gamelike events: you're free to join games and you can leave them at any time without fearing serious consequences.

In liberal societies, strictly codified interactions only exist as nostalgic residue from the past. This also affects the role of games. Children still have the ability to get completely lost in games, as they help them learn to cope with the world in a sort of safe space (in terms of both danger and frustration). Most grown-ups, unless drugged, stay very conscious of a game being just a game, which tends to make them more relaxed when playing, and also more bored.•

But the internet, virtual reality, and AI are making gaming radically more attractive, also to grown-ups, because they allow for:

- <u>experiences addressing all our senses</u>—at any time, together with an optional number of people from all over the world. We don't just immerse ourselves in divergent environments but adopt divergent identities. What happens is the opposite of exorcism: a deliberate and reversible act of *inorcism*. The adoption of a virtual identity doesn't just stop the moment we unplug. Inorcism also requires exorcist practices such as cleansing rituals, debriefings, or hypnosis to get rid of unpleasant or expendable identities. Just as we summarize the acts of emigration and immigration as migration, we might summarize inorcism and exorcism as *orcism*. The respective verb could be *to orc*, the noun, *orc*, or, cuter, *orcie*. (The fact that the word also refers to Orcus, the Latin name for the god of the underworld, and to the orcs, a species of monsters in the fantasy writings of J. R. R. Tolkien, fits all too well.)•

- <u>experiences that promptly adapt to our current needs.</u> While AI enables social media to offer a personalized selection of content, in games AI personalizes the content itself. The game gets quieter or louder, slower or faster, easier or more

• Tardies

• Orcies

challenging, depending on our mood and condition. As narcissists our struggles are rewarded with endless attention; as nostalgists we're placed in a scenario from the past; as underground lovers we discover glitches and cheat modes. We can experience ourselves as fantastical beings, as a stranger that we're curious about, or as highly familiar. We can game within a clearly virtual reality, a bizarrely mixed reality (our normal environment, but with a fantastical body; our normal body, but in a fantastical environment), or a discreetly augmented reality. Autofiction—a poorly animated, tedious tweak of yourself—gets supplanted by *autofantasies* and *co-op fantasies*: maximalist wish fulfillments. As a fan, you befriend your heroes or turn into them; as an extremist, you annihilate all your political enemies; as an environmentalist, you interact with or as endangered nonhumans.

   - <u>endless grades of gambling</u>. In physical space, gambling is often forbidden or only allowed in certain places, under distinct rules. The moment you enter those establishments, you feel stigmatized as a gambling addict. Online, you gamble anonymously and without restrictions. Governmental requirements can be easily sidestepped by changing your VPN. In physical space, gambling usually comes with a minimum monetary stake, while online gambling allows you to start off playing for free and with only symbolic gains. Once you're hooked on a game, it might gradually turn into a financial undertaking. Rather than offering a zero-sum game where the winners take the money from the losers, P2E (play to earn) games let only the winners win and rather let the participants pay to enhance their chances (pay to earn). The use of game bots is banned, just as doping is in sports. Besides, the internet grants access to an abundance of highly speculative products that are classified as financial investments but are basically bets (i.e., gambles).

Gaming becoming the main paradigm of recreational online activities also impacts our offline interactions. Virtual games are adapted for physical spaces, as with paintball and escape rooms, while classic analog entertainment like card and board games are experiencing a revival. And even without being explicitly gamified, all aspects of life are conditioned by games.

Cultural artifacts have always shaped our view of the world. The associated dangers have been widely described, at least since the invention of the romantic novel.* Later on, visual mass media led to the assumption that, as media theorist Jean Baudrillard put it, we've become unable to encounter things in real life and instead always perceive them through their medial "simulacra," which are more rewarding or easier to grasp.

Virtual games don't just appear to be a better or more exciting reality—we can enter and participate in that simulation. On the one hand, this distracts us even more from "reality" (not that "reality" would ever be accessible to us as something other than our own fabrication), but on the other hand, it makes it easier for us to adapt our expectations from the virtual into the real: The following categories show certain similarities with those of established game theories, for instance, by sociologist Roger Callois in his book *Les jeux et les hommes* [Man, play, and games] (Paris: Gallimard, 1958). But in the context of online gaming, these traditional categories often feel insufficient.

- contingency. Liberal societies are uncomfortable about irrevocable processes. Humans make mistakes, and what is good for you now won't necessarily be good for you in the future. That's why people can get divorced; prisoners are rehabilitated; monuments, landscapes, and endangered species are protected; and violence must be avoided. Still, liberal societies agree on certain irrevocable rules: constitutions, human rights, morals, manners. They believe in the universal and lasting potency of knowledge and money, while frowning upon the body for its decay and eventual death. By contrast, the virtual world offers potentially endless opportunities and dimensions. There is no entropy, speed limit, or gravity in place unless you preset it. You can jump in space and time and between as many worlds as you like. You have infinite power and can create, correct, or destroy anything at any moment.

Everything can be right next to anything, something, or nothing. Each game comes with specific irrevocable rules and assets—you can interrupt, leave, or change at any time to start completely over, often even with a new avatar (i.e., body). Real life is increasingly expected to be just as contingent: people declare themselves gender fluid to be able to switch back and forth between different grades of different genders. Cryptocurrencies are created out of the blue, and just by limiting the total amount of tokens, they might turn into the new gold. Money and objects of symbolic value used to be the subjects of a collective hypnosis that we were born into. With cryptocurrencies, however, we're fully aware of participating in a self-fulfilling co-op fantasy. Worldviews and identities are considered a matter of choice, not of conviction (metaphorically speaking, they depend on how you pill yourself). Some people alternate between two diametrical worldviews or identities, as if playing good cop/bad cop or chess against themselves. Citizenship is regarded as a membership or a share rather than something acquired at birth. The democratic claim of reversibility shifts from your government and law to your own commitment: everybody must always have the option to exit as well as an abundance of other possibilities to enter.* What you (still) can't overcome is death. But at least you can choose the moment and orchestrate the circumstances of your ultimate exit yourself.* Liberal societies pathologize, if not criminalize, suicide for being absolutely irrevocable. Even more, life is regarded as a gift from God, parents, or evolution that you're not supposed to waste. From a gaming perspective, your life is only yours—and death is your ultimate joker. Maybe you'll get frozen and hope for a respawn.

- transgression. Liberal societies are driven by the urge for personal satisfaction. It's you, first and foremost, who must enjoy what you're doing. Depending on your personal preferences, you make friends, marry, have children, and/or pursue your career. Still, in liberal societies your decisions are largely shaped by the morals, tastes, and expectations of your family and peers. In games you can leave all favors behind.

• Middle-Class Warriors
Pre-AGI Democracy

• Comic Purgatory •

Your avatars are limited by certain characteristics, but which one you choose is up to you. In a game you can't just fight for what you want, you can *be* what you want. Maybe not right away, so that the game doesn't get too boring, but eventually, after mastering a number of levels, you obtain superpowers and spectacular looks. For now, the limited immersive possibilities of virtual games make you keenly aware that your avatar isn't you. Hence the particular popularity of games in which you don't fully identify with your character but at most sympathize with it in a camp way (i.e., in an ostentatiously playful mode), and allow it to do things that you'd never permit yourself to do. Many cosplay—that is, replicate the looks of existing game, saga, or comic characters in real life.° Supremacist women transform into hyperfeminine bimbos or sportive Amazons, supremacist men into ripped, fully shaved Greek statues or trimmed medieval knights. Accursed politicians are perceived as literal lizards, favorable politicians as time lords or space travelers that rescue the chosen ones from a doomed planet Earth. Environmentalists claim to communicate with nature and hear its complaints and cries. Being trans or nonbinary isn't just a matter of sexual identity but of emulating a transhuman control over yourself. Pulling down the gender barrier is a launchpad for testing the species barrier and performing various otherkins (animals, fairies, elves, goddesses, etc.) in various combinations.° The autofantasies are often so beyond plausible that they could be taken for goofy satire or dumb lunacy. But the ridiculousness of these choices also prevents them from being taken seriously. With ubiquitous surveillance and an infinite range of choices, it has become increasingly difficult to make solid decisions.° Acting camp, your fantastic personas remain in a state of *augmented virtuality*.° Artists act as self-proclaimed healers or shamans,° and influencers initiate magical rituals—like repeatedly "scripting" or "manifesting" your wishes—that are similar to solving a simple task in a game. For all this to be more than a fad, it's important that, from time to time, some people make a seriously life-wrecking choice and fully transgress. A benchmark

• Sweetness

• Church of Lots  • Orcies
• Expanded Sex Work

Mixed Zones •

is highly sanctioned physical violence: trolls nonchalantly threaten force or death, or maybe even turn into mass shooters, terrorists, or guerillas who orchestrate their lethal attacks like shooter games and supplement them with game plans.*

- drill. Liberal societies' esteem of the individual has caused a historically unique interest in psychological complexities. These usually arise from the frictions between the expectations and capacities of the family and the milieu you're born into, on the one hand, and your own expectations and capacities, on the other hand. The realist novel—arguably the prime cultural artifact of liberal societies—is less about what physically happens than about how it's motivated and perceived through the thoughts and emotions of a few, if not a single, main character(s). Talk therapy allows everybody, even without writing, to access their own life as a novel that continues to write and rewrite itself. Then again, novel writing is very much autofiction—eventually turning the artist's troubled character into the actual piece of art. In games, your character is solely your own choice—unless you put yourself under social pressure by playing publicly. Your personal background might influence what game you play and how you play it, but it's not part of the game. In comparison to realistic novels, the backstories of game characters are relatively schematic: they often fit in a paragraph. Your frictions as a player with the character's set traits aren't usually worth telling, since the character is your choice, and you can drop it for another at any time. Taking a game character for granted isn't a matter of introspective, "mindful" self-realization but of repetitive, automatized play. You self-condition (i.e., drill yourself) into the character. See my publication *Choose Drill / Drill dich*, 100 Notes—100 Thoughts / 100 Notizen—100 Gedanken, no. 34 (Kassel: dOCUMENTA (13); Ostfildern: Hatje Cantz, 2012). The simpler the character, the easier it is to internalize it. In the era of the realistic novel, characters are meant to be unraveled; in games, the quest awaits you in the challenges of play. The stories of sagas and comics unfold in a similar way, and many games explicitly refer to them. Games and gamers are often regarded as reactionary, desperately longing for the pre-psychological dualities of good or bad, win or lose. But your game character being simple and superficial is what allows it to work as your alter ego and to overcome the limits of your own character. Different from novels and other passive media, games don't require just passive identification, but you acting as that character. Still, you yourself don't disappear—you yourself never being singular anyhow.* With virtual reality catering to all your senses, the avatar not only adds more traits to your character but also more organs to your body.*

- <u>reward</u>. Liberal societies don't exactly force you to work. Still, most people work primarily to make a living— most of the days for most of the time that they're awake. While a lazy approach to work might put your job at risk and an eager one might eventually lead to a bonus or promotion, jobs don't usually compensate good performance in real time. When you work on a commission basis or run your own business, your income might be more related to your specific performance, but there is often a long delay between work and payment. By contrast, games pamper you with distinct, frequent, and consistent rewards. Besides gambling or P2E, these rewards are only symbolic. Even more, you're showered in them: you score with every task that you solve, and in particularly addictive virtual games, this can happen more than once a second. Often, every loss or gain is accentuated by specific noises, the mastering of greater challenges with fanfare and a little clip. In addition, you might compete against other players or your own personal best. To avert boredom, after mastering a certain number of challenges, you enter a new level where things are more difficult. You might also be rewarded with an enhanced avatar or a new scenario. As people are increasingly drawn into virtual games, every other service must compete with their addictive gratification system. Gamified social media tracks every like, share, and comment and rewards them with algorithmically increased attention. By default, your devices reward every message you send or photo you take with an uplifting sound. Each letter you tap

Ego Tribes  •    Body with More Organs  •

earns you a "plink." Every step you take counts toward your daily fitness quota. In the near future, AI will also be able to judge you for the quality of your actions and applaud you for great phrases or smooth movements. Good performance at work could automatically initiate a little bonus or an earlier end to your workday. Your payment systems could forbid you to buy any sweets unless you exercise sufficiently. In politics, nudging—giving immediately effective incentives to people, as in games—has become a big topic. In some countries, families are paid for sending their kids to school or for getting them vaccinated. The most ambitious effort to score people's daily behavior is China's Social Credit System—turning pretty much your whole life into a state-run game. Evolving from a credit rating system, it scores the trustworthiness of businesses, governmental institutions, and individuals. Depending on your performance—for instance, in payment morale, compliance with traffic or censorship rules, waste sorting, visiting the elderly, or denouncing delinquents—it initiates rewards like tax breaks, discounts, better interest rates, or faster services, and punishments like audits, travel bans, a slow internet connection, exclusion from certain jobs and schools, or public shaming. You can also show off your social credit score on dating websites. In the Western world, China's Social Credit System is widely condemned as a totalitarian instrument that won't stop at controlling and disciplining people's intimate thoughts and behaviors. Indeed, a game that you're forced to play isn't really a game. But simply imposing automatic restrictions (for instance on your consumption of unhealthy food or your $CO_2$ emissions) is even less appealing. Instead, the government could offer a multiplicity of voluntary games that incentivize desired behavior—for instance, regarding fitness, diet, energy consumption, social care, or environmental care. Currently, the city of Vienna is testing a digital "Kultur-Token" and Bologna is trying out a "Smart Citizen Wallet," both of which reward eco-friendly behavior with discounts. Citizens would be free to play as many or as few games as they like and could set their goals (respectively, levels) individually. Participation could cater to a basic income and help people outside the realms of career and fame avoid depression. See "Fitness Income," in my book *Solution 264–274: Drill Nation* (Berlin: Sternberg Press, 2015).

- <u>monetization</u>. With money as a universal measure of value, liberal society is tempted to judge everyone by their fortune and everything by its price. In principle, this evaluation seemed to make our decision-making processes so simple that economics and game theory evolved in parallel. But the homo economicus, acting strictly rationally out of self-interest, is very much an illusion,• which is why economically applied game theory has become more and more complex. Even if at some point it does provide a perfect description of our economic activity, there is still so much that's strictly excluded from being purchasable: whole people, to protect their dignity (you can only rent them for a certain number of hours per day); votes, to protect democracy (you can only buy eligible politicians by funding their campaigns and offering them careers); the air, to ensure people's and nature's immediate survival (you can only pollute it and make humans and non-humans suffer from horrible diseases). Games are free of those ethical restrictions. Each game defines what can and can't be bought, but in principle, every kind of action could make you richer (in points, tokens, lives, etc.), every asset could be up for sale. Even more, in digital games, everything that exists or happens is automatically countable and comparable. Since we're with our digital devices most—if not all—of the time, the quantification of our real lives is also rapidly progressing. Health, sleep, diet, intoxication, exercise, driving, productivity, compliance, care, the list goes on—all of these can be monitored 24/7. This personal data is also a financial asset—though so far usually only for the companies collecting it. Protecting the customs and genetic traits of marginalized ethnicities against cultural and commercial appropriation, identity politics extends ownership claims beyond material goods and individually created artifacts. Influencers, actors, and other persona artists seek the extension of copyright law to all aspects of their physical appearance. Other people seek

• Commie

legal protection from unauthorized virtual replications (deep-fakes) to prevent forging. To avoid exploitation, every aspect of ourselves will be trademarked or copyrighted—conversely commodifying us completely.* Even if nobody is willing to pay for every step we take or every temptation we resist, we can do it ourselves with the help of a multitude of gamified optimization apps. The more aspects of our lives that we control that way—from health and work to dating—the closer we'll get to an overall utility function of our lives. Just as in games, we can try to figure out the best strategy to achieve top results in well-being. This ideal of quantifying and thereby monetizing our well-being is also gaining importance in politics and ethics. In recent years, some countries and charity organizations have started to evaluate the success rates of their measures in the expected gain in quality-adjusted life years (QALYs) per expense. Based on surveys in which people are asked how many life years they would hypothetically be willing to sacrifice to not suffer from a certain disability, removing that disability equals a gain in QALYs. Saving the life of a person with that disability is accordingly worth less than saving that of a person with a similar life expectancy but without that disability. The QALY computations are based on the average, crudely discriminatory perspective of nondis-abled people on disabilities.* Nonetheless, the resources of welfare states and NGOs are limited, while populations are aging and the costs of ever-new medical treatments are exploding, making allocations unavoidable. In the future, we could decide for ourselves how to split up our own welfare contingent: instead of just hypothetically exchanging well-being for life years, we could actually pay for an extraordinary treatment with an earlier termination of certain social services.

- consent. Liberal societies don't allow you to harm others without their consent. But it's the state that defines what counts as harm, disregarding personal circumstances. Furthermore, once you've given consent, you might not be able to immediately revoke it. This makes it possible for a rape that happens within a marriage to not legally be considered

Automatic Privacy • Tardies

• Wishful Death

rape, or to declare certain sexual practices illegal, even when they take place by mutual consent. An abuse would need proof, which is often not available, particularly in intimate matters. Unless you manage to hack them or know about cheat codes, digital games make it pretty much impossible to play against the rules. Even if you did, there would be a record of it. But while virtual games are strict, they allow for actions that would be forbidden in real life. The most obvious example is shooter games. In real life, people and institutions are increasingly sensitized to harmful activities. From an environmentalist perspective, not only humans but also nonhuman animals, if not plants and things, must be protected from harm. The minimum demand is to reconcile us humans with the world; the maximum demand is to reconcile the world in general.° Meanwhile, the criteria for what counts as harm are toughened. Mere nonconsensual touch counts as abuse, and sex demands explicit consent. Conversely, consensual violence, as in sadomasochism and martial arts, gets accepted and demarginalized. Rates of vandalism and violence against others go down; rates of self-inflicted harm and suicide go up. The scruples grow about giving birth to children with potentially unhappy or harmful lives—without their or the environment's consent. For secular and caring people, anti-natalism is about to become the default position.° This sensitivity also extends to verbal and symbolic violence and denounces every microaggression and implicit discrimination. On social media, hate speech is classified as "illegal content," as masterminded in the EU's Digital Services Act. In preemptive obedience, social media platforms massively censor possibly delicate posts. Advanced AI makes it impossible to express them in the first place—the same as with any inappropriate or illegal use of electronic devices. Still, the effort to extinguish hate speech is as futile as the war on drugs.° It will escape to parts of the internet and real life that evade legislation, and radicalize. Consent can't be installed by law; people have to agree on it. And as it's impossible for individualized beings to get consent from all other people, they instead have to seek it from similar ones. Just as we play different games according to our personal preferences, we could become part of different zones or even substates that share a given or an acquired identity and comparable ideas of tolerance and acceptance. An enormous multiplicity of *voluntary tribes* could coexist and compete with each other.* Meanwhile, hate speech could become the topic of a new genre of games that through trolling, bullying, and intrigue allow for an unlimited and exhaustive release of linguistic and gestural violence—just as shooter games allow for impulses of physical violence. In a consensual setup, the hate could be directed not just against avatars but against real people. You troll in mutual playful agreement or let yourself be insulted, offended, and "enlightened" as an overly provocative cam persona. In cases of serious offenses like denying the Holocaust or threatening physical violence, an immediate in-game warning and punishment is issued and visible to the other participants: writing and reading an apology letter, participating in an educational program, house arrest, and so on. Provoking the opposing side to make such missteps or even betting on them is additional motivation to participate in a hate game.

    - chance. Liberal societies claim to provide equal chances for everybody. Indeed, you can choose freely whom to marry (when of the opposite sex), where to move (within the country of your origin), and what to do for work (when you're able to obtain the necessary qualifications). Liberal societies offer free education (for mandatory school years) and social welfare (for the very needy). Still, what you achieve in life is greatly defined by your social and economic background, your upbringing, and your genetic disposition. The strongest equalizing force in liberal societies are catastrophes—financial collapses, natural disasters, wars. For the poor, crime and gambling are often the only hope to get rich. When you start a game, everybody's options and assets are the same. Online, you might enter a game later on and be confronted with skills, alliances, and resources that have already been accumulated by other players—but you can always go for a newer or more egalitarian game. Furthermore, games have events of chance that mix things up; redistribution occurs right away or through an extraordinary challenge. In non-secular societies and contexts, chance is used to let fate or deities guide you whenever you're uncertain about something. Liberal societies condemn decisions by chance as an expression of, as Immanuel Kant called it, "self-imposed immaturity." However minor our insight might be, it should be a better guide than pure chance. But actually, our knowledge is often strongly biased, or we just have no clue how to decide. The more options liberal society offers us, the more we suffer from the agony of choice.• Psychological studies show that the more time we're given to consider a decision, the less satisfied we'll be with our choice. Not deciding at all makes us even unhappier. This explains the resurgent popularity of fundamentalist beliefs and conspiracy theories that limit the complexities of our understanding of the world to gamelike proportions, or that promise chance-based advice, like tarot, the *I Ching*, or astrology (in the sense of the stars throwing the dice). But then again, how to choose between all the different belief systems?• Again, to release us from the agony of choice, we could just draw lots: Sandwich or banana? Buy or rent? Live or die? Whenever we're unsure, we could embrace the arbitrariness of life and toss a coin. While hippies like the protagonist in George Cockcroft's novel *Dice Man* (1971) used chance to break with old habits, today we need chance to make decisions at all. From this practice could grow a cult that pervades all areas of life. If we can't boil our indecision down to two alternatives, we can toss several knockout rounds. If we notice that we don't like the result after all, we stop and toss again. We can also do a coin toss together with someone else who is undecided on the same question. Then heads does one thing, tails the other. Similar to quantum entanglement, we can let each other share in the consequences of our paths or even swap identities for a day. Instead of a rigid "either-or" or a lax "as well as," we go for a collective "both."

As society's main paradigm, gaming loses its innocence. Just as our duties in the real world are being gamified, gaming is under growing pressure to be of substantial use. Games without proven practical value might be restricted or taxed. Fantasy is becoming more real.

Still, games being games, the profits are never as reliable as in jobs. Even more than in real life, assets that for some are crucial for their immediate survival are for others mainly subjects of speculation that fuel the feeling of living in a simulation. It's mainly the unfathomable complexity of the manifold games, levels, fashions, Ponzi schemes, and intrigues that provides for a certain stability. But with AI systems evolving into superior actors, this stability is not to be trusted. To reduce the risks, AI-controlled virtual games must be prevented from exerting their influence outside clearly defined domains. As humans are the weak spot, playing a certain potent game might exclude you from playing others.•

Furthermore, affluent societies could separate the allocation of basic supplies from the increasing number of games and other nonessential economic activities. Generating these supplies is meant to happen in as autarchic a manner as possible (fed by recycled materials and renewable energies). Rations are offered free to all citizens, in exchange for labor obligations or a special currency that can't be used for anything else—forestalling speculation.

Consequently, governments could free themselves from the burden of boosting general economic growth and fixing related crises. While virtual businesses can keep growing excessively without necessarily harming much of the natural world, citizens could even be paid for not producing or consuming stuff in the real world.•

An exception could be entirely or partly real-world games that serve an officially acknowledged common good and create a meaningful meta-narrative for their players. Common-good games practice locally and thematically expansive forms of communitarianism. They can be centrally or collectively organized and hosted by nonprofit NGOs or DAOs.

• Automatic Privacy

• World as Museum

All parameters of the games constantly evolve to ensure every player always has an appropriate and fulfilling task. Nobody is meant to be an extra; nobody is a non-player character.*

While communism and charity, as the egalitarian correctives of labor-based societies, ask you to use your abilities to serve others' needs, the common-good games of post-labor societies take care that everybody is needed according to their abilities. Or, as Kafka's Theater of Oklahoma put it: "We are the theater that has a place for everyone, everyone in his place!"

A crucial difference between games and theater is that you learn games while you're playing. There is no rehearsal. With rules and goals in flux, common-good games resemble the never-ending happenings that Marshall McLuhan imagined as global theater. And yes, this time, the satellites are watching.

There is no need for common-good games to ever get serious and leave the safe realm of play. Whatever common-good games want us to do, AGI and robots can do it faster and better. Humans only add warmth, meaning irregularities and emotions—and drill themselves in case AGI and robots fail.

Church of Lots
2021

The critique of "post-truth" filter bubbles, conspiracy theories, and political maneuvers is idle as long as it stays quiet on the most persistent force of misinformation: religion. Hopes of replacing religion with art didn't come true, but by drawing lots, we could turn our world-ignoring beliefs into a fair and empathic game.

As a West German teenager, in the early to mid-1980s, I turned into a highly critical political being. I was concerned about economic injustice, racism, sexism, discrimination based on appearance, pollution, animal cruelty, Cold War imperialism, nuclear weapons, nuclear power, and the dangers of total surveillance. I read books about basic income, direct democracy, anarcho-syndicalism, communism (including Karl Marx's complete *Das Kapital*), critical theory, alternative renewable energies, truly defensive defense strategies, the Western installment of dictatorships in other regions, feminism, and male self-emancipation.* I protested against a local center of neo-Nazis, participated in the youth organization of the new Green Party,* and endeavored to use gender-neutral language.* I shared pretty much all the concerns that thirty years later would come to define millennials as woke—except for global warming.* Instead, I feared a new ice age, triggered by a nuclear war.

At the beginning of my political awakening stood the realization of the stupidity of any religious belief. The facts seemed clear: after death, the brain rots. It wasn't a god who had created us but the random mutations of evolution. If most people nonetheless fell for the ideas of God and an afterlife, then any other shared beliefs could be crap too.

I've never held the humanist assumption that humans—the most destructive earthly creatures ever—are basically good. But as a teenager, I hoped that at some point most humans would overcome their religious beliefs. All evil came down to patriarchy, and religions, in particular the monotheistic ones, were patriarchy's cement. The same with National Socialism, a perverse mirror of Judaism: Hitler installed himself as the Messiah of the chosen Aryans, who had been abducted and suppressed by Jews, just as the chosen Jews had been abducted and suppressed by Egyptians and Romans.

My Protestant parents still somehow believed in God. But religion wasn't present in our daily lives, and it didn't seem to affect any of their decisions. I didn't see them pray and they never went to church, except for baptisms, weddings, and funerals. For them, attending Christmas Mass was a vain gesture, and attending Mass throughout the year was the venial defect of female widows. Good Protestants stood their ground. They didn't plea or make an effort to express their devotion. I brought the Protestant agenda to its logical end, getting rid of God altogether. My mother and father were upset when I announced I was leaving the church, but they would never question my decision again.

My parents had grown up in the village where we lived.• They had been to school for the mandatory eight years and never sought any intellectual education. Still, to them religion was no more than a stub. As modern society depended on more educated people, I was optimistic that at least in the Western world, it would take a maximum of two generations (mine and what would be the millennials) to push religion completely to the side. Once the traditional ties were cut, it would be impossible to turn back—unless a major catastrophe blew our civilization off the map.

Then the Cold War ended, and I was amazed to see the low numbers of religious believers in former socialist East Germany: only 10 percent believed in a personal god, while 50 percent were complete atheists—and these figures would remain the same. Rising Islamic and Christian fundamentalism didn't worry me too much, as I understood them to be phenomena of suppressed poorer countries. Increased global justice would put an end to these views.

Not that I assumed that patriarchalism and imperialism would dissolve on their own. There would be serious backlashes. Still, there wasn't much that I as a privileged but impecunious White man could do, except for consuming as little as possible or killing myself. Any particular engagement from my side would involve the danger of freeloading off of and paternalizing emancipatory processes. I disengaged from immediately trying to improve the world and became a writer to explore and promote the privilege of being metaphysically unbound. Soon many more people would share my mindset.

But in the early 2000s, religiousness turned out to be more resilient than I had expected. In the economically booming Turkey, the new middle class underwent an Islamic awakening. In the US, more than 90 percent continued to believe in a personal god and often also the devil and hell. Meanwhile in Berlin, several friends overcame alcoholism and drug addiction under the spiritual guidance of Alcoholics Anonymous. I visited a writer couple that had emigrated to a small town in South Africa and saw their house dotted with little crosses. They had become committed members of a Free Church.

The next Western generation after mine, the millennials, are actually less into Christianity and more into chaos magic, an eclectic mix of spiritual off-practices meant to undermine the patriarchal inclinations of both monotheistic churches and Eurocentric enlightenment: astrology, tarot, yoga, tantra, the *I Ching*, shamanism—though often these practices stem from contexts that are just as patriarchal. Cultural appropriation might hinder a deeper understanding; instead of breaking up your own dominant culture, you rather end up as a cultural colonizer.

Pagan practices are highly suggestive (i.e., self-fulfilling). You don't have to believe in them to make them work. See Alejandro Jodorowsky's use of the term *psychomagic*, for instance, in *Psychomagic: The Transformative Power of Shamanic Psychotherapy* (Rochester: Inner Traditions, 2010). This can be very self-empowering as long as you're in charge of the ritual's outcome, for instance getting over a bad habit or influence. However, if not you but a shaman or a divination practice determines the ritual's content, the opposite is the case. Predictions work as instructions.

You could assume that individualistic societies would prefer self-empowering rituals instead of those in which you're overpowered by a divinatory conclusion. But in fact, divination practices are particularly popular among millennials. Does this imply that they don't suffer so much from a lack of freedom as from too much freedom?* Does what they truly wish for feel so out of reach that they would rather be limited and carried off than linger undecided between different mediocre options? However miserable life turns out to be, consider it destiny?

Most divination practices are based on a deliberate random event: drawing cards, as in tarot; tossing coins, as in the *I Ching*; pouring hot, liquid metal into water, as in molybdomancy; reading tea leaves or coffee grounds, as in tasseography. Even if you believe in fate, you know very well that repeating the event would very likely lead to a completely different result. Your lot is obviously no more than a pattern that entices a psychic's or your own intuitions.

Some divination practices, like palmistry and astrology, are derived from our own characteristics. Again, these approaches leave a lot of room for interpretation. But the fact that palmar creases and zodiac signs stick with us for our entire lives has an enormously amplifying effect on their self-fulfilling prophecies. This is particularly the case with astrology, which, in times when Christianity was the one and

Sweetness

only official faith, was already the most rampant para-religion.

Even though the existence of gods interfering in our physical order from outside lacks any evidence, it's at least theoretically possible. On the contrary, astrology always appeared to me as a blatant superstition. How could small variations in the nominal gravitational pull of distant planets and stars affect us to such a degree? Astrology stems from a time when people still commonly assumed that the earth was flat, and that stars and planets were moving lights in the nearby firmament that enabled the gods to steadily communicate with us.

When I ask solid believers in astrology to guess my zodiac sign, they consistently get it wrong, even on the second and third tries. And yet, I do identify with that particular sign. No other sign comes closer to how I feel about myself. When I was growing up, hundreds of people must have asked me about it and treated me accordingly. I became who people thought I was. Then again, nowadays when people don't correctly identify my sign, no matter how well they know me, is it only because of my strenuous efforts to overcome this identification?

My identification with my stars reaches just as far back as my rudimentary understanding of them during my childhood and youth. I feel indifferent about everything that goes beyond my star sign, for instance, my ascendant. I got to know about it only in my thirties, when the internet made individual astrological calculations easily accessible, and it appears to me as totally random.

Astrology is a major discriminatory force. Different from racism, sexism, ableism, ageism, heightism, or classism, it doesn't discriminate based on outward appearance. We can hide our birthday from people we're not inclined to share it with. You could also argue that the good thing about astrology is that it doesn't hierarchize. Certain signs might fit together better than others, but they all have their pros and cons; there is no overall ranking. Therefore, astrology doesn't correlate with other discriminations. No matter how rich, old, fit, tall, or pale you are, the percentage of people sharing your sign will be the same. Zodiac signs are ethereal totems that divide all earthly creatures into twelve slightly cohesive global tribes. At best, astrology works as an arbitrary pattern that makes everybody feel fundamentally different from most of the others. In that sense, astrology has a function similar to that of individual tattoos.•

But when you discriminate based on people's date and place of birth, how can you seriously argue against other discriminations? Seeing a woke generation falling for astrology might serve as proof for the political Right that people have an irrepressible urge to make generalized discriminations. Preferring tangible discriminations like sex and race over astrology could count as being more down-to-earth.

The practices of the contemporary Right work similarly to those of chaos magic. Whether it's neoliberalism, populism, or the alt-right, they don't really care about consistency, but rather rearrange their agendas according to momentary demands. They don't even pretend not to be faking and lying, as every repetitive claim suggests its own world.

Politicians have never been too invested in the truth, but at least they used to pretend. Even dictators made an effort to sound conclusive. Opposing evidence was systematically suppressed, defamed, and destroyed. Meanwhile, in open societies sincerity seemed to be on the rise. Better education would not only repress religious beliefs but also political boasting and bullshitting. Electronic media would allow every lie to be dismantled in real time.

Today, the opposite is the case. Authoritarian leaders don't care too much about maintaining a perfect appearance. They've learned that a certain amount of dissidence serves as a pressure valve and healthy corrective. In authoritarian societies, just as in open ones, there is enough faith in obvious lies to keep governmental betrayal going.

Liberals tend to blame this "post-truth" development on individualized social media, which they think would diminish the general public sphere and seclude us in filter bubbles. This critique implies a skeptical view on the direct participation of all people in shaping public opinion. Instead of opting for an authoritarian government, liberals opt for an authoritarian information policy ranging from censoring obvious misinformation and hate speech to strengthening state-authorized media—calling into question the liberal core principle of freedom of speech.[*]

The Left blames the lulling thrills of late capitalist consumerism for today's credulity. They claim that suppressed existential fears of poverty and failure make people vulnerable to conspiracy theories and promises of salvation. But how to go against these delusions and play fair? At the height of counterculture in the 1960s and 1970s, leftists tried to stir the spectacle and turn it against itself: if people took seriously the promise of immediate satisfaction of every need, they would stop working. In fact, counterculture lured minors and adolescents into drug addiction—the most desperate form of consumerism.

In their critique of the post-factual condition, the Left and liberals both ignore the most vehement force of misinformation: religion. Marx called religion "the opium of the people," but today the Left fears a general critique of religion as a gesture of superiority made by an educated elite. Too many atrocities have been committed in the name of rationality. Liberals treat religion as a private matter—a personal or familial whim—that, at best, helps you maintain good morals. Both the Left and liberals treat religion as an unavoidable residue of the past.

Meanwhile, the distinction between religion and politics never really solidified in the Western world. On the one hand, Christian churches make political claims and endorse certain parties. They try to stop schools from teaching scientifically undisputed knowledge, they're allowed to run their own (often subsidized) schools, and their delegates serve on governmental ethics boards. On the other hand, new political movements like Marxism-Leninism and National Socialism came with an eschatological mission and leaders who espoused their movements like a cult.

The revolutionary and destructive forces of Western

quasi-religious movements dominated the world politics of the twentieth century, to then be copied and succeeded by movements of genuinely religious fundamentalists outside the Western world. In the Western world, the era of consistent movements has been followed by a flood of obviously abstruse conspiracy theories. "Theories" is a misleading term, as unlike some nerdy predecessors (the moon landing hoax, the CIA's assassination of John F. Kennedy), they don't manifest as a meticulous collection of seemingly perplexing evidence but as modern myths about an earthly netherworld whose secretive machinations make you rejoice and shudder, identify and hate. The alleged conspirators take the position of the devil, which tends to be left vacant by monotheistic religions. Totalitarian movements, fundamentalisms, and contra-factual conspiracy theories can be summed up as contemporary religious practices.

For an open society, every religion is a potential threat, as their doctrines come as epiphanies, not as testable hypotheses. All well-established religions originate in patriarchal societies. Throughout history, these religions have all cooperated with monarchist, oligarchic, and dictatorial regimes. Even if the content of certain epiphanies might appear harmless, following them as doctrines sets an example that might result in the propagation of more harmful doctrines in the future. An open society's freedom of speech must also cover the right to be obviously and insistently wrong. But to secure its future, an open society must offer compelling ways to articulate epiphanies that contain the potential harm of those very revelations.

An intellectually progressive bourgeoisie set its hopes on the arts, and thereby emancipated the arts from expressing established religious beliefs into cults of their own.* The cult of God was replaced by the cult of genius. The church was replaced by the museum, the concert hall, the theater. These new cult sites were visited with the solemnity of a Mass. While religions exempt themselves from the burden of proof, art disclaims its truth in a literal sense and aspires to a merely symbolic truth. This truth, though, is meant to be eternal, like a prophecy, and requires a similarly elaborate and never-ending scholarly interpretation.

Over the course of the twentieth century, Western arts slowly got over being religions' secular surrogate. Each new artistic movement claimed to articulate an ultimate truth, only to be quickly questioned by the next one. In an increasingly individualistic society, it seemed more reasonable to celebrate the arts for their outstanding subjectivity.

A more successful containment of religious faith wouldn't come as a mockery but from the very essence of every religion, that is, the faith in intelligent forces that are unimaginably greater than ours. This faith can be extremely comforting or unsettling. It can encourage us to continue what we're doing, as we feel these forces are on our side, or discourage us, as no matter what we do, it could be undone or degraded at any time. This ambivalence also extends to how we view the world and the otherworldly forces themselves. All proof against their existence could be a challenge created by those very forces—what seems to be a prophecy could actually be meant to confuse us.

With otherworldly forces, we never know for sure. No matter how absurd theories about them might appear to be, all the consistent ones are possible in principle: creationism could be right and the theory of evolution no more than a devilish temptation; God could have physically manifested himself as a human baby to later let him be killed and rejoin with himself. But why should we believe in this exact theological extravaganza? As the otherworldly forces are beyond our understanding, no theory about them is likelier or unlikelier than any other.

The ontological equality of all transcendental theories doesn't imply that we must persevere in boring agnosticism like me. Instead, we could give all religious concepts—monotheism, polytheism, animism, astrology, atheism, etc.—in all their concrete manifestations, the same chance. Instead of just drawing lots to find out about ourselves and the world according to a certain belief, we could draw lots to determine which belief to follow in the first place.

A Church of Lots could collect a belief proposal by every member—each called a Lot. Every Lot draws from all entries and commits to converting to the selected belief to the best of their ability and to stay with it for at least a month, at most a year, and then to report back to a congregation of Lots about the experience. Religious practice turns into a playful activity that fosters our understanding of mindsets and milieus very different from ours. Religion is practiced as art, not art as religion. A unique sequence of experienced beliefs makes every life unique.

In a next step, the Lots could extend this approach to earthly matters they are undecided about.* Sandwich or banana? Buy or rent? Live or die? Whenever the Lots don't know which course of action to take and want to do more than just shrug their shoulders, they draw lots from all tenable alternatives they and other Lots come up with. If they notice that they aren't happy with the decision, they realize what they actually want or start another lottery.

The Lots can also draw lots together. Social media makes it easy to find others who are undecided about the same matter. Each Lot draws a different decision, but similar to quantum entanglement, they can let the others share in the consequences of their paths or even swap identities for a day. Instead of a rigid "either-or" or a lax "as well as," they go for a collective "all." Or, the opposite: Lots draw one common lot and join forces.

Today, we know too much not to know that we basically don't know anything. This makes us hesitate—and the longer we hesitate, the more goes wrong. Psychological studies show that the more time we're given to consider a decision, the less satisfied we'll be with our choice. Not deciding at all makes us even unhappier, which is where staggering delusions come in: people go for the first convenient conspiracy theory or fundamentalist viewpoint because they've been postponing making proper decisions about what to do with their lives for too long.

The Church of Lots could organize ceremonies all over the world—splendidly staged gatherings where Lots go on stage and, starting with the formula "I don't know whether to ...," talk about a tricky matter they're undecided on—and then draw lots.

World as Program
2021

> Digitalization encourages men to try to describe the world
> like a computer program based on discrete states of something
> and nothing. But the very core of our understanding of the
> world—our consciousness—doesn't pixelate. In the analogous
> realm of the here and now, men connect with themselves only
> by becoming even more idiotic, even more damaged.

Why is there something and not nothing? Information theorists argue that an absolute nothing is more complex to describe than an absolute everything. Jorge Luis Borges's story "La biblioteca de Babel" ("The Library of Babel," 1941) is often cited as an example of the latter: a collection of all possible books has zero information value. With nothingness, on the other hand, you first of all have to define what kind of nothing you mean. Not only an eternal vacuum but even the absence of space and time? Even the absence of a logical system that would define this nothing in the first place?

An accumulation of all possible books—insofar as there is a limit on the number of available characters as well as the number of possible pages—is immense, but finite. This isn't the case with the set that comprises all-possible-things. But how can the infinite not only be described using set theory but actually *be*?

The bottom line is that all-possible-things hasn't been

in existence forever, but is still in a state of becoming. Thus, what exists in the present moment remains finite. What is infinite and remains so is only that which has yet to come to pass. Nothing and everything move toward each other on the axis of time and intermingle. If everything then comes from a distant, never attainable future, would nothing, conversely, come from an equally distant past, meaning: One that has never begun? Or why did everything once begin exactly in this way and not differently? When it comes to the question about the beginning of becoming, this model also becomes paradoxical.

Unless it were the case that the world began not only once but in all possible ways at the same time. Then there wouldn't be only one course of world history when reading through the books in its library. Would there instead be as infinitely many courses of world history as there are books?

Information theorists strive to describe the world as similar to a computer program solely on the basis of discrete states: yes/no, one/zero. The very beginning of all-possible-things could be a binary opposition—one that branches out in the following course of world history into more and more worlds. A wave function collapse in quantum mechanics doesn't result in a resolution in favor of one of two possible states, but in the splitting of a world into two worlds, each corresponding to one state. The number of existing worlds would be immeasurably larger than the number of elementary particles in our world, but finite.

The only problem with this theory is us. Us, in the sense of the consciously perceiving somethings. Our sensory perceptions, our feelings, and even our thoughts about logic and mathematics—our qualia—don't reveal discrete states. Our consciousness doesn't pixelate.

Is such ignorance about what is happening not immediately in front of our eyes, but immediately behind them, another instance of White-male errantry? In fact, so far only White male information theorists have popularly interpreted the world as a self-actualizing computer program. Even those who critique their theories tend to be White men. Most of humankind doesn't even bother trying to understand them. Instead, in response to the question of the origin of everything that is the case, whenever and wherever it may be, they turn to this or that pretechnological metaphor.

Information theorists have also softened up and reintroduced the idea of an intelligent transcendental creation—the simulation hypothesis: within the world in general (being similar to a computer program), the particular world that we're living in could be an actual computer program, installed by superior beings. There is nothing new about the assumption that the world that we're experiencing is an illusion. But the simulation hypothesis provides hope that we or our descendants could again run a simulation within a simulation and turn into gods. All this without a clue what consciousness is, let alone how it could be artificially created.

How to come to terms with the dichotomy between subjective analog experience and objective digital facts? In ancient Greek theater, it was the satyrs' job to make fun of people and their stupid words of wisdom. Satyrs are forest spirits—half man, half animal—permanently aroused and talking smut. Also, again, male, and—in everything that's human about them—also, again, White. As soon as a satyr looks in the mirror, Nietzsche's *Übermensch* appears to him.• And from there, it's not far to Marvel's superheroes, who have swagger instead of sexual potency, and engage in vigilante justice, cleaning up the world as a one-man army, instead of making crude jokes that cut through the bullshit.•

Who is the enemy? While the dumbheads fear being overrun by the even stupider who procreate and risk more (and seduce women and children), the digital aces fear being overrun by their own intellectually superior AGI creations. Problems like climate change might feel more urgent today, but they're not meant to have the power to extinguish humankind.

Why would it even be bad if humanity dies out and gives way to intellectually superior entities? What is the fundamental difference between AGI and humanity, when humans can be uploaded or are already uploaded to computers? In

• Abnormcore

Comic Purgatory •
One-Man War

the end it's all about the survival of the digital aces themselves. But for what? What makes their brain activity worthwhile, if not their replaceable intelligence?

No matter whether dumbheads or digital aces, in the analogous realm of the here and now, men only connect with themselves by becoming even more idiotic, even more damaged. Man and beast combined add up to less rather than more than the sum of their parts. Too cerebral and too instinct-driven at the same time. No matter how little space men occupy, they've thieved it. Even if they were to castigate or destroy themselves, their self-righteousness would stink to high heaven.

While women and other non-men are assigned the role of perfecting themselves more and more, in a humanist or in a posthumanist sense, the discourse of identity politics leaves men in the gray area of being neither human nor animal. Here they can think about and insist that they still exist as whatever it may be. From here they can write endless screeds in chat rooms and blogs, troll social media, scribble Post-its, spray-paint walls, and brawl in pedestrian zones. So long as they stay beastly and raucous enough that you don't start to pity them. No matter how damaged, they want to remain dangerous—or at least annoying. They want to be pushed aside, resisting, as a bad example. And they want, in a rare moment, despite everything and precisely because of it, to be irresistible. Because they're something and not nothing.

Mutual Enslavements
2022

> The liberal order is based on undesirably and asymmetrically
> intertwined enslavements with others and within yourself.
> Overcoming these enslavements, it's not enough to understand
> their inhibiting and destructive forces. Identity politics
> might replace or feed one fascist evil with another, but there
> might be no other way to overcome the tyranny of the majority
> and enter states of monadic bliss.

When I went to kindergarten in the 1970s, countercultural
efforts to treat girls and boys not just as equals but as basically
the same—exposing them to the same toys, games, rules, and
role models—were commonly regarded as failed. At our kindergarten, boys went for the cars and the shovels, girls for
the dolls and their houses, and that was pretty much it. Boys
and girls would play together only when our teachers sum-
moned us for a task.

While I was growing up, I shared the belief that boys
and girls were fundamentally different. Boys were stronger
and more aggressive, girls were ... —I didn't even have a clue.
Whatever they did, it appeared to me only at the margins. It
wasn't just my ignorance; they simply weren't around. By
chance, all my neighbors and cousins my age were boys. They
were also the ones I would primarily hang out with and fight
with at school.

Thanks to my heterosexual orientation, in puberty girls

started to gain my attention—and I realized that all in all we weren't that different. Our shared interests included music, film, literature, politics, and other people's behavior. Boosted by a more or less open sexual attraction, we were now discovering the world together. At least those of us who weren't intellectually complete by the age of thirteen.

The overcoming of the divide between girls and boys among my high-school and university friends made me optimistic for the future. Our interests and behaviors were still distinguishable—boys were still louder and more dominant—but it seemed to me a given that progress would be made in women's emancipation, just as in the last hundred years. After several serious backlashes, we seemed to have reached a point of no return.

When my acquaintances started to procreate, the relationships between men and women often became traditional again. Men usually worked full-time jobs, women only part-time, taking more care of the children and the household. Even in their spare time I would see them separate again into circles of male and female friends, in openly and latently competitive sports, in more relaxed and more strict diets. As soon as procreation entered the picture, the bonds between heterosexual men and women loosened.

But things could be done differently. When I finally conceded becoming a father, my wife continued to work full-time—without asking me to step back and take the role of the homemaker. We would rather pay for daycare and babysitters than sacrifice our preparental interests and ambitions. We would hardly play or be otherwise bored with our son, but focus with him on our mutual love and curiosity.[*]

I knew our way of living wasn't affordable for everyone and that not everyone would be able to bear having our decent income and refraining from a car or a big house. But there were also cheaper or free options, like communal childcare or even a return to cooperative breeding. So why did parents allow procreation to steal so much of their freedom and quality of life?

Many would argue that it's of foremost importance for

at least one parent to spend a long stretch of time with their children for their development and happiness. But why? During most of human history, children grew up in communal settings with various grown-ups and children. I remember that I, as an only child, was often bored when alone with my parents. I hated that my hours at kindergarten ended already at noon, and I feared Sundays as I was expected to stay with my family and not meet friends.

Obviously, the true reason why parents are willing to sacrifice so much time and freedom when raising their children is rather selfish. Procreation having become in most cases a well-planned act, parents aren't willing to accept that children are ready to live with a multiplicity of caregivers from early on, and they confuse children's unconditional love with emotional dependence. Parents drown themselves in guilt for every hour their children don't spend with them, to block out that the children are actually having a great time without them. At the same time, parents often deprive their children of physical affection—presumably not to sissify them but actually to keep them dependent. My parents are an extreme example: they surely loved me more than anything in the world, but—since I can remember—they never expressed it physically. I didn't receive a single kiss and wasn't even hugged (until I started to hug them, already in my twenties) so as to not make me a mama's boy. At the same time, my parents felt just as deprived of my affection and struggled with my increasing independence.

Keeping the offspring emotionally dependent tends to reinforce the parents' heteronormative role division. As the mother is meant to be more attached to the children, she gives up independence for their time-consuming care and relies on the father (alternatively her parents or the state) as the main provider. In return, her status in their relationship relies on their children prospering just as much as on them staying mainly attached to her. What Sigmund Freud sexualized as the Oedipus complex is the mother using the children's emotional dependence on her as her social security.

The liberal order was meant to free humans from enslavements by others—and it traded that for self-enslavements.[*] Despite the call for freedom and equality, these self-enslavements are usually undesirably and asymmetrically intertwined. Socio-economically it's the poor masses working for and being exploited by the rich elite, while the poor can retaliate against the rich by striking, boycotting, looting, or overthrowing. With individuals it's the enslavement of the instinct-driven "body" by the rational "mind" through discipline (in positive terms) or repression (in negative terms), and the retaliating enslavement of the mind by the body through obsessive behaviors like addiction, OCD, or other neuroses.

We're forced into these self-enslavements from early on. But when starting a family, you're usually way beyond the age of consent and have already experienced the inhibiting and destructive dynamics of an asymmetrically intertwined enslavement with your own parents. How could anybody with one bit of intelligence walk willingly into the trap?

But at our son's international school, where practically all the parents are academics, often the mothers don't work and most pupils eagerly follow the heteronormative script. As early teenagers, the boys are into shooter games and smut-talking male vloggers, the girls into TikTok beauty queens. Their division has been fed since a young age by meticulously gendered toys, clothes, and sweets. Our son stands out just by wearing wide trousers or pastel colors.

The parents worry about their children's immense screen time and their restricted interests but don't seem to do much about it. I wonder to what degree they are, on the down-low, supportive of their children living out crude gender stereotypes before adult life tames them and kills all the fun.[*] Will these kids, trained by nerdy game developers and reactionary social media celebrities, propel a major gender backlash? Or do they indicate that soon the celebration of gender stereotypes will be nothing but a harmless childish folly, similar to believing in Santa Claus?

What strikes me just as much as the children's mimicry

of an atavistic heteronormativity is the degree to which those who make an effort to overcome the gender binarism reaffirm it ex negativo. Declaring yourself transgender implies that there could be a certain gender that fits your sex better than your own. Declaring yourself nonbinary implies that it could be possible to fit into only one gender.* These are essentialist simplifications that reject all the complexities and intricacies that previous generations, my generation, X, included, have been keen to detect and deconstruct.

But in the end, our nuancing confirmed the existing order. The world might not be simple, but power is based on simplifications. The truth of identitarian gender politics and identity politics in general lies in their sense of how to effectively attack the enemy.

It's not far-fetched to characterize identity politics as the revengeful fascism of the outspokenly marginalized— fighting the tyranny of the implicitly fascist majority. For me, as a post-Nazi German, it's horrifying to see identitarian activists asking for proof of bloodline to allow people to belong to a certain identity.

Fighting existing power by turning its own weapons against it is a proven strategy to provoke change. This change might not be for the better—at worst it confirms the rulers and corrupts the subverters. Instead of one fascism canceling out the other, they can also strengthen each other. We can see this in radical right-wingers and populists successfully adopting the polemics of identity politics. Earlier on, the Marxist "dictatorship of the proletariat" resulted in a sort of feudalist regime of the worst kind and provoked fascism as a feudalist variant of capitalism. Still, there might be no other way to achieve substantial social change. To this day, there hasn't been a single case in world history in which an elected socialist government has been given a proper chance. It was the danger of communism that provoked capitalist societies to push for the welfare state. It was the decline of Marxist societies that preceded the rise of neoliberalism.*

So far, identity politics lacks the unity needed to provide

that kind of danger. Each success of one group is soon contested or relativized by the neglected concerns of other groups.* It's this diversity that allowed identity politics to gain momentum in the first place. They don't contest the neoliberal order as a whole but resemble startup companies in how they stir up the attention economy with ever-new—woke—concerns.

In the long run, the identitarian inventiveness in setting rules could lead to a more playful understanding of identities. Recently, my son told me that two male classmates, who a few weeks earlier had been agitating against classmates for strutting on school premises with a rainbow flag, were now diligently role-playing a gay couple.* But instead of evolving everyone's potential and tolerance for self-determination, identity politics could also strengthen a right-wing or populist agenda and diminish general rights. To which extent one or the other happens is first and foremost a matter of massive demographic dynamics.

Liberal emancipation already resulted in a drastic drop in birthrates. This has been economically outbalanced by mechanization, immigration, and more women working in what are usually low-paid jobs. Woke identity politics results in even lower birthrates. Women postpone motherhood in favor of pursuing their careers, and an increasing number of people who identify as LGBTQIA+ are unwilling or unable to procreate naturally. Many cis-heterosexuals also lose interest in having children altogether. They perceive it as too much of a sacrifice to toxic heteronormativity or toxic humanity.*

The liberal era has led to nuclear families that hardly reach replacement-level fertility. Woke identity politics leads to the substitution of your own human family as the default life project with the adoption of easy-to-care-for entities like pets, robots, avatars, or tattoos into your *ego tribe*.* The asymmetries between humans and these biological and non-biological entities are insurmountable, allowing for more reliable enslavements than liberal bonds. Further implemented into a monadic *body with more organs*, you feel these extensions as part of yourself.*

Acknowledge Your Own Oppression •

Society of Games •

• Orcies

• Ego Tribes

Body with More Organs

• Body with More Organs

Sinking birthrates and enforced self-encapsulations could have a number of massive, rivaling effects:

- An aging and shrinking population eases the real estate market * and environmental destruction while also leading to the drastic loss of a productive workforce.

- This loss of workforce might be promptly compensated by AI and robots—preventing mass unemployment and economic decline. Or it might be compensated by mass immigration—leading to intercultural and interracial tensions on the one hand and drained human resources on the other hand.* Countries might build barriers to stop (certain) immigration *and* (certain) emigration, or to encourage ethnic segregation.

- The selected kids that the monadists decide on having are genetically enhanced and exceedingly educated—constituting a new transhuman master race.* Or they're outnumbered by the also genetically enhanced but highly reactionary offspring of religious traditionalists.* The latter go against both liberal and monadist life choices while highly subsidizing heteronormative families and luring or forcing all the others into sterilization. To secure their own modes of living, non-traditionalists must either turn openly antidemocratic or aim for legal segregation.*

- Longevity increases at such a speed that further offspring are only allowed after a demanding assessment. Or the empowerment of AGI and robots allows for humans and posthumans of any number to be "stored" safely in their respective ideal substates or mixed realities.*

- Monadists, liberals, and traditionalists enter a furious war that ends with the suppression of at least one of the three groups. Or they manage to coexist as *voluntary tribes* and autonomous substates—traditionalists in the countryside, liberals in cities, and monadists wherever.* Circular enslavements make each group believe they're ruling over the others (when in fact they're all being ruled by AGI).

Real Estate Porn •

• Posthuman Test Grounds

Middle-Class Warriors •

Church of Lots •

• Automatic Privacy    Middle-Class Warriors •

• Wanderers

## Sweetness
## 2008

A new generation is cutifying all aspects of life. By embracing the playfulness of children, adolescents are able to put a positive spin on anger, depression, and death.

Two girls—fifteen, sixteen years old—are on the city train platform of a German suburb. One is sitting on a bench, the other has just gotten off the train and hurries toward her. Both seem completely enraptured with each other, staring into each other's wide-open eyes and stroking each other's faces.

"Oooh. You, you, you ... !" they call out as though talking to a baby. It takes a while before their awe gives way to extensive cuddling.

The girls give each other the feeling of being as protected as normally only babies are by their mothers, and at the same time elevate themselves to adults who are capable of protecting. This discord is familiar from the love of horses. You must take care of them, but at the same time they're much bigger than you, and their fur exudes a protective warmth. The girls, however, are still cared for by their parents and have become purely emotionally dependent on each other. Their love will never again be so free of practical considerations.

Romanticism also sought such pure love. But with love-marriage, pure love is packaged with sexual fidelity, procreation, and often financial dependence.* Pure love can actually only exist as yearning and in momentary fleetingness. As much as bourgeois society invokes love as the highest happiness, it's considered disreputable to devote oneself to it completely. There is really only room for this in literature, with a tragic end. The storm of love is polluted by sexual desire and material considerations. Friendship is free of both. Friendly love, however, seems slightly stale. Unless it's also fueled by a hidden sexual desire or social ambition.

The two girls on the platform don't have these concerns. The love for the mother, the child, and also the man all play out at once. But it's only harmless play, and different from child's play, theirs doesn't extend to simulating sex and breastfeeding, but remains limited to the symbolic component of the respective kind of love.

The love of the girlfriends on the train platform is meant to soon wear off. Probably a relationship with a man will come to the fore, the desire for a real child. Never again will they love in as carefree and at the same time comprehensive a manner as now, in their camp role-play.

Conventional romance likewise only properly develops in youth—as long as you don't yet have to care for yourself and others. Besides, it has already taken many twists and turns, always driven by the aspiration to unconditionally follow an innermost feeling. The motor of all modern totalitarian ideologies is a romantic one—even if their implementation evokes an unprecedented technocracy or bureaucracy. You can be similarly sure that, even within someone who acts cold, a passion seethes, or at least once seethed; there is something within them that demotes the rest of the world to a disposable mass.* Hippies, on the other hand, tried to simply love everything or make everything lovable, which made them harden, unless they became religious and ultimately had to love everything only as a representation of a transcendental one.* Followers of youth culture behave like members of a self-chosen tribe, which, unlike a gang, isn't determined territorially, but temporally.* For the train platform girls, however, all love is familial—their love for their friends and their pets as well as for their real family. Through travel and the internet, everyone can construct their own personal, constantly reassembling extended family, scattered all over the world, and communicate with it. You're safe *and* free.

A couple's relationship can also be undermined in its relentless claim to exclusivity by emotionally charging all other relationships. "No reason to be jealous of anyone in particular"—the camp exaggeration ensures a residual non-commitment toward the one you've been sharing a bed, bathroom, and kitchen with for years. You kiss each other on the mouth or just next to it, hug each other tightly, and then squeeze again. Every effort is made so as not to appear as strained and mendaciously cordial as you know America to be, rooted as it is in the attitudes of its White settlers.

I have a chance reunion with an old, never-too-close friend. Several months have passed since we last met, and before that we hadn't seen each other for over a year. We beam at each other, fall into each other's arms. Soon she reaches under my sweater, strokes my belly. Now we probably won't see each other again for a long time—even though it wouldn't take much, and it would be fine with both of us. Life is so fast-paced that we would greet each other with the same warmth even if after just a week: it has been so long since we've seen each other.

Soft is the new cool. The former eludes any assignment even more fundamentally than the latter. Eluding assignment also includes not being associated with any particular youth culture—not even one that's clearly steeped in ignorance. New wavers were already ostentatiously soft in their appearance in the 1980s (soft fabrics, loose pants, a quiff of hair protruding gently into the face), but their vibe continues to be arrogant. Their kindred new romantics dream of a love that can encapsulate itself in collective arrogance—and thus of the resolution of the contradiction between the romantic love of a couple and Romanticism. But it may remain only a postapocalyptic dream. The goths, kindred to the new romantics, in turn find it more honest or courageous to indulge in their nightmares.

In the 1990s, the emos, hardcore-listening slackers, form. A preference for radically noisy and yearning music is combined with sloppy-comfy clothing, intentionally thick glasses frames, and Spock-like bowl haircuts. For the first time, youth culture isn't trying to harmonize the worlds of desire it consumes with its clothing, but is instead self-ironically surrendering to being nerdy. At the same time, there is the spread from East Asia of the phenomenon of cosplayers, who, on the contrary, imitate the clothing and hair of certain manga heroes as exactly as possible, thereby making it clear that they themselves aren't manga heroes.

Emos, like cosplayers, clearly distinguish between themselves and the ideal; in short: they behave playfully. One can understand this as the infantilization of youth cultures, which in turn affects younger and younger ages. Yet hip-hop, which is particularly successful among prepubescents, still insists on authenticity. Pop singers are often cast in the context of TV shows, but that makes them all the more real in their struggles for artistic and commercial success. While hip-hop glorifies the hardships of the "ghetto," casting shows glorify the hardships of being an artist—which hip-hop celebrates as a fantastic cornucopia. Wine, women, and song This tripartite motto references the 1869 waltz "Wein, Weib und Gesang, op. 333" by Johann Strauss II. without a tomorrow. Meanwhile, the main clientele is still awaiting their first ejaculation.

The emos of the new millennium spice themselves up with elements of various youth cultures such as goth, new romantic, ska, rockabilly, disco, metal, grunge, rave, and also cosplay. Being equally attracted to everything, you don't even need to distance yourself ironically. You strive for a flawless lean body, which you work on in different ways (pierce, scratch, starve). You're clean and basically friendly. A bourgeois child who no longer represses its misfortunes or treats them as cause to lash out at others, but cheerfully affirms them. Those who inflict pain on themselves or attempt to kill themselves feel freshly alive.

The emblem of these new emos is the skull. Through seriality and combined with pink, it's rigorously de-darkened. Like the acid-house smiley at the end of the 1980s, this fashion disappeared again after a year or two, yet it's an indicator of a permanent shift. In the case of the acid-house smiley, it's the MDMA-fueled will to experience joy. A will that doesn't break because the world doesn't shape itself according to it, but about which it alone you can rejoice. In this way, you set yourself apart from the gloominess of the punks and goths, the strained universalism of the hippies, and the competitive careerism of the yuppies.

The more circumspect emos include death in their affirmation. This doesn't have to mean that they really look forward to their death or feel already close to it, as in death metal. For now, compulsory death is far away. Skull buttons and patterns on sweaters, sneakers, or bags belittle death—not unlike how the train platform girls belittle their later family life. For now, everything can be sweet. For now, you're the ever-fresh Spongebob.[*]

In no time, the skull has also entered children's fashion, decorating their socks, bikinis, and rubber boots. Since children can't really be afraid of death at all, they can find skulls just as great as pirates.

For any other youth culture, it's a serious threat if their fashion is also adopted by children. But in the case of the emos, it gives them another boost in their ostentatious infantility, and they, in turn, can copy the emo children. Success among peers (soon to spawn the YOLO meme) is the problem and drives young people into radicalism. Then you might loiter around the train station, play punk, or become a drug addict. Unlike radical chic, you really want to know, and in the end, you're one experience richer. No matter how hard you've had it with your parents, at school, and with yourself, you see yourself as coming from a sheltered middle-class background.

Somewhere in Berlin, 2008, my photo

There is no immediate hardship to follow or flee from. Like hip-hoppers, you're not a victim.

But while for hip-hoppers this means' gaining clout with muscles, weapons, and rhymes, for emos sovereignty consists in never losing their composure. Even in being lost, they're accurate.[*] They can cuddle and kiss on the mouth without intending to have sex. (The pre-sweeties still need special cuddle parties for that, just as they don brightly colored dresses printed with cartoon characters only if they come from a reputable, expensive brand.) Or they can have sex with both sexes without being bisexual. Or see themselves as of both sexes without being bi-identitarian. Nonbinary is neither "neither-nor" nor "as well as."[*]

The youth cultural border no longer runs between left and right, but between controlled and compulsive, pale and solarium-tanned, androgynous and macho, and thus basically between bourgeois and proletarian. The only difference is that the new bourgeois no longer look grown-up, but cute.

In Japan and other East Asian countries, young people have already been dressing and acting extravagantly cute (*kawaii*) for a long time, often seeking relief from an extremely rigid educational workload. It's also easier to articulate your sexuality in this way, not least because of global physiognomic competition.[*] In the West, on the other hand, it's precisely the high degree of freedom that's a burden.[*] Also, you have frequent contact with older people beyond your parents and your job—because there are so few of the young left and the old don't really want to grow old.[*] As a counterbalance, love for friends is given the gesture of familial commitment. Still, you try to secure the junior part with playful, *Teletubbies*-ish childishness.

Of course, the various family constructs get in each other's way. You must constantly weigh where to draw the line with friends of friends. It's still convenient to move in cliques that are quite closed. But thanks to new possibilities in telecommunications, you can absent yourself at any time, temporarily entering a new conversation or going to another

Mixed Zones  •    Orcies    •  Heightism  •  Church of Lots  •  Corona Tribes •

appointment or family cluster. You're always on the go.

On the internet, you reveal details about yourself for which potentially every person in the world can love or hate you. Nevertheless, unlike the hippies' "tyrannies of intimacy," See Richard Sennett, *The Fall of Public Man* (New York: Alfred A. Knopf, 1977). you present rather than reveal yourself.* Only people who have nothing left to lose—the proletarians—put their marital problems on television.

Today, you can quickly Google every possible affair beforehand. You can find out about the cashier, what kind of music they claim to like, who their friends are. But in the past, hair, makeup, and clothes also used to reveal a lot, and people made inquiries about potential new contacts, private or business. The idea of absolute anonymity has always been utopian—and threatening. Accelerated and expanded access to personal data is driving more theatrics, just as the offer of so many possible preferences— which has grown to infinity— makes it increasingly difficult to decide on something once and for all anyway. Only in the inauthenticity of camp can you take a chance.*

You don't do drugs to lose inhibitions, but to purposefully misbehave by expanding the terrain of the tolerable or by driving yourself into euphoria over and over again. You may behave differently just because you've taken the drug, no matter how it actually works.

The drug acts like a mask, and you can also mask yourself for real. At political demonstrations, people paint themselves bright colors because they want to appear as different as possible from their opponents—visible to the police, unfathomable to the government and corporations. Unlike so many of the dystopian narratives since Stanley Kubrick's *A Clockwork Orange* (1971), the masquerade isn't an expression of an archaic willingness to use violence. Violent youth cultures like those of skinheads and autonomists present themselves in a militarily uniform manner.

Gay sweeties like to appear as soft "bears." It makes them look grown-up and childish-cuddly at the same time,

• Intimate Correctness
Automatic Privacy

• Society of Games

without having to play parent and child like the train platform girls. The camp role models are hippies and mullahs, both dogmatically heterosexual. If straight people then also start to wear beards again, it happens in camp reference to this new gay fashion.

A beer belly or unwashed genitalia can also become proud achievements on the basis of permanent self-editing—naturalness is just another masquerade. Irreparable blemishes like cellulite and crooked penises continue to have a hard time. Aging is bad in general. You learn to admire old people as freaks, while being really old is fortunately still an unimaginably long way off.

By putting together your own dream family as a young person, you can only be disappointed by the real family formation with all its stress, dirt, and costs. In the daily hardships of being a parent, you become a vassal who has even forfeited the right to die voluntarily. If you're lucky, a child gives you the sweet consolation that you've already been giving your own parents.

Or you avoid starting a human family. Instead of children, you're content with having pets.* Big-eyed, docile, and perma-dressed in fluffy fur, they continue to be cute all their short life long and require far less care. When approaching death, they can be cloned.

Monadism reclaims privacy as a migrating sphere
that is adaptable to current needs and eligible to all
sentient beings.

## Automatic Privacy
2020

The COVID-19 lockdowns reinforce an increasing reluctance toward involuntary social densities that goes back to the 1980s and leads to the Monadic Age. The next trillion-dollar enterprise won't be about connecting, but automatically keeping your distance. Your very own bubble will be protected from observation by or interference from people and entities that aren't explicitly invited. This feature could also be applicable to nonhumans, turning Jainism into a general disposition.

We will never again shout, sneeze, or cough unmasked without provoking anger and fear. We will never again hug each other without the thrill of shared danger. We will never again approach a street corner without awaiting potential murder. Even when the COVID-19 pandemic is over, we will never forget that breath and touch can turn into lethal weapons—at least for the sick and the elderly. To overcome that feeling, we will avoid them altogether.

Or will we? The AIDS crisis in the 1980s indicates quite the opposite. Many continued to have unsafe sex even though an HIV infection was expected to be fatal. It often didn't even feel like playing with fire. It was just a bit more pleasurable, a bit more intimate. HIV also didn't increase the discrimination of gay, bisexual, or highly promiscuous people. If anything, HIV made them more visible and normal.°

Then again, different from SARS-CoV-2—the corona-virus that causes the disease COVID-19—it's completely safe to interact with people who are HIV positive in all ways except for "unsafe" sex. And even now that there is a reliable treatment to prevent AIDS, sex rates are steadily going down all over the world. People are hooking up more casually and are more reserved about sex. Sex is gradually losing importance. Obvious reasons could be improved masturbation devices, free online porn, virtual sex, less urge to reproduce, less urge for a steady partner, and an increasing amount of alternate joys and distractions.•

These reasons could also make us avoid physical closeness altogether. The COVID-19 pandemic could work as an exercise in social distancing that will prevail when the danger vanishes. Did most of us comply rather easily to self-isolation because—wittingly or unwittingly—we had been waiting for this opportunity? Unlike our sex rate, our spatial proximity rate has never been researched comprehensively.

While we continued to congest further and further in streets, public transport, planes, or beaches, it wasn't something that we thrived on. While we still frequented stadiums and clubs, sitting and VIP areas were growing. Public spaces were privatized to guarantee some exclusivity. Major political debates shifted from the question of proper distribution to the question of proper distance: from neo-nationalism, neo-protectionism, prepping, and mass incarceration to safe spaces and environmental protection.

In the 1980s, trend forecaster Faith Popcorn coined the term "cocooning," describing it as the "rapidly accelerating trend toward insulating oneself from the harsh realities of the outside world and building the perfect environment to reflect one's personal needs and fantasies." Faith Popcorn, quoted in Beth Ann Krier, "The Essence of Cocooning: It's a Desire for a Cozy, Perfect Environment Far from the Influences of a Madding World," *Los Angeles Times*, August 7, 1987. Many phenomena she observed back then are still evolving today: gated communities, soft furniture, home cinema, home office, home delivery. Popcorn understood cocooning as a sign of political disengagement. But different from the bourgeois Biedermeier style from the early nineteenth century, the rise of cocooning wasn't enforced by censorship and authoritarianism. It was rather the other way around: depoliticization allowed for populism and neo-fascism.

At the same time, the private sphere has stopped being a discrete zone, and not just in how digitalization allows for everybody's in-depth surveillance by states and corporations. With social media, people started broadcasting their private matters to the world. Already in the 1970s, sociologist Richard Sennett observed "the tyrannies of intimacy," or how socio-political liberalization and economical welfare stirred narcissistic self-expression and undermined the traditional public sphere of impersonal relations. See Richard Sennett, *The Fall of Public Man* (New York: Alfred A. Knopf, 1977). Hippies showered strangers with love, and politicians were elected for their personal traits. People insisted on being addressed not in a general manner but with respect to personal sensitivities. A discourse about trigger warnings and microaggressions took shape.[•]

More abstractly speaking: the Liberal Age—or, the Age of the Citizen—was about to be replaced by an evolved individualism that leads to what I call the Monadic Age. This implied an overall societal change that went beyond tearing down or re-erecting walls between the public and the private, or one of the two disappearing. What happened was a remodeling of the private *and* public spheres. To understand this properly, we have to review the basic concepts and interplays of home and territory:

A. Animals might claim a territory for exclusive exploitation or a home for exclusive shelter. The territory preexists and caters to metabolic supplies; the home serves procreation and recreation and might be, to some extent, self-created. Some animals also cater to metabolic supplies within their home through the division of labor and symbiosis with other animals or plants.

B. Due to the advanced use of tools like weapons, fire, clothes, and paint, human hunter-gatherers claim both a territory and a home. The domestication of plants, other animals, and themselves as serfs—the breeding and training of organic robots—allows for the introduction of agriculture. Peasants do both: they expand the functionality of the territory to the home (husbandry, craftsmanship) and the protectiveness of the home to the territory (fences, weapons).

C. Through the specialization of tools and skills, the division of labor expands beyond a single herd or family. As citizens, humans share a common—public—space with all other citizens to exchange, between their territories and homes. This exchange is overseen by a state that's in charge of overall rules (law) and overall means of exchange (money).

D. With advanced mechanization penetrating all aspects of life, the division of labor doesn't only apply to movable goods. Humans divide their own lives between different temporary or partial homes and territories that they share with alternating others. The congestion of cities allows for a maximal fragmentation of life. Urbanites live next to and with strangers (apartment complex, hotel, flat share), eat next to and with strangers (restaurant, cafeteria), party next to and with strangers (bar, club), have sex next to and with strangers (darkroom, brothel, hookup), recreate next to and with strangers (park, beach, spa, resort), and move next to and with strangers (train, plane, public transport, taxi). To overcome the instinctive drive for a safety zone against strangers, what zoologist Heini Hediger named "flight distance," urbanites try not to—or at least pretend not to—notice the others. They treat them as vectorial obstacles, evasive liquid, or as particles of a greater body to unite with.

E. Digitalization allows for machines to operate automatically, to shrink in size, to be easily reprogrammed, and then even easily remodeled. Humans reduce their labor and its division, and become monads. To understand what that means, we can project where the COVID-19 pandemic is taking us: we might live as congested urbanites, but we avoid random encounters. Robots pamper, transport, maintain, and satisfy, and communication and entertainment are virtual. However small, our home can be an office, factory, farm, school, hospital, or prison. Even when we go out on the street in person, we don't have to meet anyone. We don't even have to pay attention to the actual street: through a warning system, similar to a parking system, we keep enough distance so as not to bump into each other or transmit a disease. Through a protection system, we fend off unwanted weather, noise, and pollution. Before sharing home and territory, we take them with us, or at least create them virtually wherever we are. The parameters of our home and territory don't change unless we want them to. We're in our own shell even when entering that of someone else—unless we both agree to unite them for a certain period of time. This can happen gradually. There is an endless range of degrees of convergence between singular and group isolation. Whenever we agree to a new intimate encounter—of a physical kind or even just mere communication—all members of our social groups as well as their social groups get notified. Depending on their safety parameters, they might shut us off permanently or just temporarily, for vetting.

As citizens, we follow general guidelines—ranging from universal natural rights to local manners—within which we're allowed to act freely. As monads, we renegotiate and recalibrate our code of behavior before, during, and after every encounter. Just like explicit violence, the implicit violence of random encounters becomes a matter of choice. On an urban or global scale, this boundless contingency is only maneuverable with computational support. Like farms and cities, states don't disappear. But for monads, they become just another cluster within an immense agglomeration of mutual agreements. Citizenship gains the character of a membership or a share rather than that of a birthright; it's neither written in stone nor in our genes. From this perspective, "classical" Western democracies are authoritarian systems: their constitutional cores aren't meant to be changed.[•]

Another problem with them is their reliance on strict majority rule and the dichotomy it creates between ruling parties and their opposition. Monads understand themselves as so diverse that a majoritarian rule can only be about what is in the interest of a majority, not what is right or wrong for all. This is even more the case as monads put any eternal law into question—even when it protects minorities and delinquents. Therefore, governments have to ensure wide consent. This can happen either by consociationalism (as in Switzerland, which isn't led by a president or prime minister but by a federal council that represents almost the entire political spectrum) or by segregating into more homogenized states. A combination of both is also possible: more homogenized, largely autonomous substates governed under the umbrella of a federal council (as, to some extent, in Switzerland, which is composed of rather autonomous, often tiny cantons). Substates don't require territorial integrity. Zones of territorial exclusivity can be splattered and temporary—depending on the movements and agreements of their current citizens.*

Today's prevalent technological concepts don't fully catch up with a monadic society. While our communication devices are all about connecting and sharing, we tend to fall back on atavistic concepts like walling off or locking down the physical sphere.* We isolate ourselves, yet we don't gain any privacy—just the opposite. To fear no harm, we allow our personal data to be mined and make ourselves as predictable as possible. The more we feel observed, the more we become reserved. Openness and social anxiety go hand in hand. We lose our privacy and are lonelier than ever.

This will be even more the case with AI allowing us to perfectly fake any kind of digital representation. As a consequence, everything will be regarded as fake (that is, fiction), unless certified as true (that is, original); ideally, in a highly decentralized manner, as on a blockchain. To avoid exploitation and betrayal, every aspect of ourselves, down to each utterance, will be trademarked or copyrighted—conversely commodifying us completely.* Unless we fake others, we'll be provenly real. Even more, it will be difficult not to leave permanent traces of who we are.

The next trillion-dollar enterprise won't be about connecting, but keeping one's distance. While social media allows us to get in contact wherever we are without any effort, this

• Real Estate Porn   • Wanderers

• Society of Games   Tardies

endeavor allows us to be by ourselves wherever we are without any effort. Our very own bubble will be protected from observation by or interference from people and entities that aren't explicitly invited. To all the others, we'll become a black box.

How is this possible, when it doesn't take more than a scraped-off cell, a fingerprint, a scan of a pupil, some spoken words, or a few steps to identify who we are? Even alone and inside, we're tracked by our digital devices. Even equipped with all sorts of jammers, a proper masking would require enormous effort and make life highly inconvenient. And even then, quantum computing is making any absolutely secure encryption impossible. What is left is that quantum cryptography also makes it impossible to keep any act of eavesdropping undetected.

Accordingly, the emphasis on protecting our privacy must be on detecting and blocking—sandboxing—all devices that are able to observe us. Legally, our identity rights could hold not just for figurative representations of ourselves but any kind of identification. Technically, everyone must be authorized to disable all surrounding digital devices and their owners from observing or approaching. Your protection is canceled the moment that you yourself (or your belongings) make an unwanted observation or approach.

This "automatic" privacy can also be applied to keep humans away from certain animals, particularly during sensitive periods like mating or egg hatching, or to keep predators and their prey at a distance. Both receive signals to stay away from each other: the predators are lured to artificial prey and the prey to birth control.

Earth could become a place where Jainism isn't just a personal practice but a general disposition. At worst, two virtual bubbles bounce against each other and drift apart. Over time, this system could become more and more sensitive and include more and more species. An advanced system able to deal with traffic, housing, and vegetation could navigate human and nonhuman interaction on the whole planet.

Real Estate Porn
2016

As property prices soar, the square meters we own dictate
our lives and relationships. We're falling in love with houses
rather than people, and we subordinate ourselves to a
gentry of property owners. Until genetic modification allows
us to live comfortably outdoors in any climate, all that can
redeem us is a recurring redistribution lottery.

## The New Old Gentry

Housing is meant to make our lives more comfortable. Besides
walls that protect us from hostile circumstances, we've
equipped the interior with an accumulation of tools and devices.* Being spoiled by all those belongings has only been
followed by even more things. Digitalization marked a shift in
the minimalism of interior design; while it was first about
shrinking, smoothing, and hiding tools and devices, 3D printing and the cloud enable us to live with almost nothing aside
from what we need at this very moment.*

The only thing that can't be expanded out of nowhere
is our exclusive living area. Earth's surface is fixed, and the
population continues to grow while further building is restricted.* The result is a cult of vast, empty, naturally lit space,
in densely populated areas, if possible. After thousands of
years of civilization and mass murder, we're talking square meters. The medium-rich are selling shares or their companies to

buy architectural jewels, devote years of their lives to polishing them, live in them like in a shrine, and make a living by renting them out for special occasions every now and then.

Walled space has become the ultimate luxury; even more so as everyone needs a minimum of shelter—to have a place to put a bed and your clothes is just as important as having an address to gain the status and benefits of a full citizen. Still, while lots of states guarantee their inhabitants food, clothes, and health care, they don't guarantee shelter. At most they pay your rent up to a certain amount.

Virtually everywhere on Earth, the prices to rent or buy residential space have been rising faster than the average income, the result of which is mass speculation about a further rise in prices. If you don't buy a house or apartment now, you probably won't be able to afford a similar one for the rest of your life. You're under the gun to start climbing the real estate ladder as fast as possible, and to already include space for your eventual kids so that you won't be forced to move to a worse part of town when you actually start a family. Couples stay together only because of the decent piece of real estate they once got together. Maybe the piece of real estate is so exquisite that it becomes the true love interest, effectively turning the marriage into a ménage à trois. *9 1/2 Weeks* (1986), *Ghost* (1990), *Sleepless in Seattle* (1993)—since the 1980s, many famous erotic thrillers and romantic comedies have shown an uninhibited level of real estate porn.•

Nothing has created more millionaires than the worldwide boom in real estate. Yet at the same time, it enslaves a majority of people to a lifelong mortgage and flawless career. With prices for real estate skyrocketing, it gets harder and riskier for every new generation to secure decent housing with their income. Even if you could resell a piece of property and make a profit worth a couple of annual salaries, it wouldn't be worth moving into a cheaper area as its underperforming job market and poor infrastructure would cost you even more.

A decent inheritance is the last chance. People who don't have to pay their rent or take out a mortgage are the new old gentry: highly privileged but often hardly solvent. Maybe it's the creative class, but I know an increasing number of people who own huge flats and have hardly enough to eat. The rising cost of utilities is eating them up, and renting out the flat can be against house rules. Or renting can make property lose value. In Germany, this can be up to 50 percent, as it's quite difficult to kick out tenants, and rent can only be slowly increased without renewing the contract. As a result, many private owners prefer to keep their property empty or only offer it on a short-term basis on Airbnb.

The online marketplace Airbnb started as the possibility to rent out your flat when you're not home, or to rent out an extra room when you don't need it. But in fact, Airbnb reduces permanent living space, and by increasing the possible income from owning flats or houses, prices are being pushed up even further.

### The Landlord's Guilt

In 2010, I had saved and inherited enough money to buy a decent flat in a mildly gentrified part of Berlin. Compared to other European capitals and many other German cities, prices in Berlin were still amazingly low, just like the rents and wages. The population hadn't been growing since reunification, even though Berlin was Germany's new capital and the country's economy was finally booming again. Berlin's economy was still not doing well and there weren't enough international bohemians moving to the city to compensate for a new suburban flight. During the Cold War, the Western, capitalist part of the city had been encircled by a wall, and the Eastern, socialist part had left people without personal fortune, so the possibility of building your own house outside the city was still new.

But the 2008 global financial crisis in general, and the 2009 Euro crisis in particular, were about to have a drastic impact on Berlin's real estate market. The crisis had been triggered by mortgages being belligerently issued to Americans with precarious income. From a self-fulfilling prophecy, the housing boom had turned into a worldwide pyramid scheme.

To stop the crisis, national banks flooded the market with cheap money. Yet as interest rates plummeted, where could money be safely invested? Again, the main idea was private housing.

Whether at art events in Berlin or private parties in Nairobi, everywhere I went I heard people talking about Berlin's spectacularly cheap real estate. People hardly knew the city but their pronunciation of up-and-coming quarters like Moabit, Schöneberg, or Neukölln was remarkably good.

I had been based in Berlin for more than twenty years and finally I could profit from my deep knowledge of the city. Different from the outsiders, I would focus my search on Wedding, a part of the city where I had been living for a couple of years. Wedding neighbors Mitte, the historical center of the city, and despite its exquisite location, gentrification was still sparse.

The longer I searched, the more it became clear that it would be hard to find a flat that I would like as much as the one where I lived. My flat was small but extremely quiet, and it had a lot of light and a spacious balcony. Situated on a pedestrian road with no stores, gentrification couldn't manifest in an accumulation of neat cafés and shops. And still, Mitte and Prenzlauer Berg were only a stone's throw away.

But of course, my rent would rise and the house would eventually be sold to a rigorous investor or even torn down. Besides, at some point in my life I might stop traveling a lot and be fed up with living on my own in only one room. So, I continued to search for a two- or three-room apartment in Wedding. As I wouldn't need this apartment right away, my search wasn't limited to ones that were already vacant. I wouldn't want to be a mean investor, and I would be fine as long as the current tenants paid enough rent to cover running costs and taxes.

When I visited the first flats, I realized that either I detested the tenants so much that I would never be able to deal with them, or I liked them too much to make them fear that one day I could kick them out to move in myself. Just the idea of standing again in someone's apartment as its potential owner became unbearable. Renting out an apartment was far too personal to be acceptable as a business relationship. I couldn't do it, just as I could never go to war.

### The Housing Lottery

The fear of losing your familiar shelter might seem banal compared to the fear of dying from sudden cancer or being killed. In the worst case, you have to commute longer and deal with inconveniences like less space, less sunlight, or more noise. But different from food, clothes, electronic devices, or means of transportation, a decent home is the one investment in quality of life that's likely to last—even beyond your death. This is why a large part of our courage and energy is absorbed by finding it and paying it off. Real estate is the enemy of love, fun, and generosity; it makes our lives fearful and boring. We don't own our houses, our houses own us.

"What have you been doing all your life?"

"Oh, I secured a really nice piece of property. By now it's unaffordable."

What would a society that provided generous hospitality to everyone look like? A "basic habitat"—similar to a basic income—isn't easy to offer. People have different needs and desires, and existing houses can't be cut into similar slices as in land reform.

In his novel *Utopia* (1516), Thomas More outlined a recurring lottery to redistribute housing among the entire population: "At every ten years' end they shift their houses by lots." But such a decree would be highly unpopular with all those who invested a great deal of time and energy in their current home, and would provoke major civil unrest. In addition, the raffled residents would lack motivation to maintain and renovate their temporary homes.

In a more moderate scenario, personal housing that exceeds basic needs is raffled for a limited period of the year. For the winners, their new temporary home will be more like a free vacation rental or residency fellowship, and they're likely inclined to make the most out of it—inviting friends over, throwing parties, shooting all sorts of videos, if not actual real estate porn. Winners, who share the home with its owners, may try to scare them off, meet their expectations, or lure them into their own way of life.

The housing lottery raises expectations about how to make the most of our obsession with real estate—either to activate villas, terraces, and gardens for special moments and encounters, or to turn them into residencies for people in need.

The housing lottery marks a transitory phase until genetic engineering enables a future us to comfortably live outdoors in any climate.* When that time comes, there will be endless virtual possibilities to find seclusion, when desired.* People who continue to insist on a vast physical space just for themselves will appear as unacceptable burdens on the environment.

A House of Her Own
2017

Hollywood has steadily portrayed women's spatial
independence as a source of misery and death.

Patriarchal societies used to label women who intentionally
live on their own as witches. Their presumed magical powers
led them to be segregated in forests and caves, far from society. In the twentieth century, emancipation and the rise of
industrial capitalism saw more and more women moving to
work in big cities and enjoy independent lives. But Hollywood
has long been in denial of this reality. Even if these women
were portrayed, they wouldn't be seen in their homes—just as
people in movies wouldn't be seen in their bathrooms.

Friedrich Wilhelm Murnau's *City Girl* (1930) is a rare
exception. In one two-minute sequence, the eponymous city
girl, a waitress called Kate, is shown in her dreary and noisy
one-room apartment, trying to save a withered and dusty
potted plant, identifying with her caged bird and dreaming
of the countryside.

The first Hollywood movie that revels in a single
woman's home is Howard Hawks's screwball comedy *Bringing*

*Up Baby* from 1938. Katharine Hepburn plays a spoiled, rich brat who lives with a tame leopard (sent from Brazil by her brother as an intended gift for their aunt) in a modern Manhattan apartment building. Her spacious, sun-flooded flat is all white and cream—just like her gowns. Hepburn captures the pure joy and mischievousness of a young, independent woman—untamable like a wild cat. Karl Marx once observed that historic facts and figures appear twice, "the first time as tragedy, the second time as farce." In the realm of fiction, it might be the other way around: social progress first manifests itself as farce, while seriousness and depth tend to confirm a reactionary view of the world.

During World War II, increasing numbers of women lived on their own. Nonetheless, the first successful postwar Hollywood movie featuring a single woman's home is *Sunset Boulevard* (1950). Billy Wilder's grimly satirical portrait of a lonely and forgotten Hollywood diva has been praised as a great study of the dark side of the movie industry—an illusion machine that leads its own protagonists to lose touch with reality. But the character Wilder actually portrays is more reminiscent of a witch who relentlessly swings her hands in a spiritistic manner, refusing to accept that her magical powers have deserted her. Twelve years later, Robert Aldrich's *Whatever Happened to Baby Jane?* (1962) would repeat this story, only this time the aged actress, played by Bette Davis, turns mean instead of delusional and holds her paraplegic sister (Joan Crawford) captive in an old Hollywood mansion.

The first postwar Hollywood icon of a woman living independently is Marilyn Monroe in the harmless masquerade of a ditzy blonde. In Jean Negulesco's *How to Marry a Millionaire* (1953), she, Lauren Bacall, and Betty Grable play three attractive single women who rent a luxurious penthouse in Manhattan to lure wealthy men into marriage. But to pay the rent, they're forced to gradually empty out the apartment—selling off its owner's nouveau riche hodgepodge of modern and neobaroque furniture. Only when the apartment is practically empty does each of them find their man. In Billy Wilder's

*The Seven Year Itch* (1955), Monroe plays a model and actress who becomes the object of her married neighbor's fantasies. Again, her apartment is only a temporary sublet and, even though it's only a wall away, it's never actually shown in the film.

In 1950s Hollywood, women who live alone in a proper home have to be way beyond the age of thirty. And it's usually Rock Hudson who frees them from loneliness—whether it's in Douglas Sirk's *All That Heaven Allows* (1955), in which the young Hudson has a romance with a widow some years his senior, or in romantic comedies such as Michael Gordon's *Pillow Talk* (1959). In *All That Heaven Allows*, Hudson's character frees the widow from her constricting bourgeois New England surroundings, a liberation represented by his converted barn with its huge front window looking out over the countryside. In *Pillow Talk*, Doris Day plays a successful interior designer—independent and single—who lives in a spacious high-rise apartment with the futuristic door number 2001.

In Richard Quine's romantic comedy *Bell, Book and Candle* (1958), Kim Novak is still in her mid-twenties when playing the free-spirited and unattached owner of a gallery for African art. Her apartment looks very modern, disguising the fact that she's actually a witch. As if this wasn't enough, it's her cat's stares that mediate her powers and make her neighbor fall in love with her. Her black clothes and silver-blonde hair seem to have been a significant inspiration for the signature look of Factory warlock Andy Warhol. As she falls seriously in love, Novak's clothes turn red, she loses her magical powers, and turns into proper marriage material.

The next young, single Hollywood woman dressed in black is Audrey Hepburn, as Holly Golightly in Blake Edwards's *Breakfast at Tiffany's* (1961), an adaptation of Truman Capote's novella of the same name (1958). The film explores in depth the makeshift style of her one-bedroom apartment in a Manhattan brownstone: a bathtub is remodeled as a couch; wooden boxes serve as tables; the shelves are almost empty; her shoes are stored in the fridge. Just as with Monroe's roles, the provisional character of the home of the protagonist (whom

Capote called an "American geisha") is deliberate: "I don't want to own anything until I find a place where me and things go together," Holly declares. The only place where she gets that feeling is at the Tiffany & Co. jewelry store, anticipating marriage. But it's her provisional home that plays a significant role in making men fall in love with her, arousing feelings of both protection and freedom. It's the first time in Hollywood that a home isn't just the woman's destination in love, but an essential tool in finding it. It's her home that sparks magical powers.

From here it's not long until women fall in love with their own homes right away: with the sexual liberation movement progressing into the hippie era come freaky women who relate passionately to their exceptional homes rather than to other people. In Hal Ashby's *Harold and Maude* (1971), seventy-nine-year-old Maude is living "free as a bird" in an old wagon crammed with "incidental" memorabilia. Even though she and a boy fall in love with each other, it can't hold her off from the planned suicide at her eightieth birthday. A late example is Adrian Lyne's *Flashdance* (1983), in which a young welder and aspiring jazz dancer lives with bric-a-brac furniture, a couple of dummy torsos, and a bulldog in a gigantic warehouse. How should she heat it in winter? How should she pay the rent? Her house feels more like a set of girlish fantasies, soon to be superseded by a rich marriage.

In Lyne's next movie, *9 1/2 Weeks* (1986), a divorced gallerina with a foible for antiques and lace curtains falls for a slick broker. Her infatuation peaks when he leaves her alone in his huge apartment that's all hard lines, metal, black, and shades of gray. The scene marks the beginning of a whole new Hollywood genre. With neoliberalism and gentrification kicking in, extraordinary real estate acts as women's equal, if not superior, love interest: the castle-like SoHo loft in Jerry Zucker's *Ghost* (1990), the lavish Beverly Wilshire Hotel in Garry Marshall's *Pretty Woman* (1990), the enchanted Upper West Side apartment with greenhouse and roof garden in Peter Weir's *Green Card* (1990), the fabulous houseboat in Nora Ephron's *Sleepless in Seattle* (1993), and the list goes on.•

• Real Estate Porn

For Hollywood, women who insist on spatial independence pay a disastrous economic and psychological price. It's
again Lyne who sets the line of approach on how to portray
such women: as malicious maniacs. In Lyne's *Fatal Attraction*
(1987), Glenn Close plays a book editor who ruthlessly stalks
a married colleague. Her apartment is a spacious loft in
Manhattan's Meatpacking District; his on the Upper West
Side is crammed with furniture, toys, a wife, kids, and a dog.
Close has found her formula for success and repeats the role
of a coldheartedly scheming single woman and owner of
lavish real estate in the historical drama *Dangerous Liaisons*
(1988) and the family comedy *101 Dalmatians* (1996).

After first being killed as a single woman saving gorillas in the rainforest (Michael Apted's *Gorillas in the Mist*, 1988),
Sigourney Weaver follows in Close's footsteps. In Mike Nichols's
*Working Girl* (1988), she plays a ruthless, idea-stealing manager
who lives alone in a lavish postmodern apartment: antique
furniture is combined with narcissistic Pop art, gym machines,
and computer gear.

The pattern peaks, both in terms of real estate and
meanness, in Paul Verhoeven's *Basic Instinct* (1992): a troubled
middle-aged detective, like Close's counterpart in *Fatal
Attraction* played by Michael Douglas, falls for a dazzling bestselling author in her mid-thirties who comes with a sprawling
beach mansion in Carmel Highlands, a huge classicistic town
house in Pacific Heights, and a couple of Picassos. Catherine
Tramell feels completely secure in her glassy beach home;
even alone at night, she leaves the gate open. Her X-ray insight
into human nature and her seductive superpowers are enough
to keep her safe and men at her free, destructive disposal.

It's only with the enormous success of British and
American TV series like *Absolutely Fabulous* (1992–96), *Melrose
Place* (1992–99), *Friends* (1994–2004), or *Sex and the City*
(1998–2004) that Hollywood has to make the depiction of
premenopausal single women a normality. Still, nice single
women who live in large houses continue to be portrayed as
scared as hell. In Mick Jackson's *Bodyguard* (1992), Whitney

Houston's character Rachel Marron resides with her seven-year-old son in a historical Beverly Hills mansion with twenty-nine bedrooms and three pools. All the security measures can't protect her from a stalker who masturbates in her bed and a hit man who threatens her life. In Simon West's *Lara Croft: Tomb Raider* (2001), Lara Croft lives in an enormous Jacobean country mansion that gets invaded by an armed commando to steal a magic clock. In David Fincher's *Panic Room* (2002), a freshly divorced academic and her daughter move into an enormous brownstone on the Upper West Side. In the first night at their new home, robbers threaten their lives. None of these houses are definitively earned by their female owners. In *Panic Room*, the house is bought with money from the divorce. Croft inherited her mansion from her father (different from the original video game, where she inherited it from her aunt).

In the 2010s, women in Hollywood movies finally buy villas with their own earnings. In Tom Ford's *Nocturnal Animals* (2016), a successful gallery owner is left alone by her betraying husband. The comforts of her luxurious bungalow (along with a huge *Balloon Dog* by Jeff Koons in the garden) don't stop her from immersing herself in a brutal novel by her first husband and the hurtful memories of how she betrayed him. In *Elle* (2016), again by Verhoeven, the head of a successful computer game company tries to embrace and overcome her inner and outer demons. Being the daughter of a mass murderer and divorced, she starts an affair with a neighbor who repeatedly intrudes into her villa and rapes her.

The latter women are middle-aged and portrayed in a more realistic manner. Still, the way they're viewed is with even more machismo as it implies that however financially independent women are, their social autonomy remains involuntary and precarious; at best, they can submit to their perdition.

Expanded Sex Work
2012

The poverty of artists often supersedes that of the lumpen.
With rapidly rising rents, the only way they can keep a
home may be to commercialize it as a work of art—and
themselves as its sex spell.

The era of a mass culture in which most people were mere
consumers has passed. Thanks to ample free time and technological possibilities, every citizen in the Western world can
tender works of art on the global market. The resulting art glut
renders an ever-growing fraction of the global production
commercially worthless. File sharing reinforces this process,
and even the art world's trade in certified originals hasn't remained unaffected.

It used to be that bohemians shot their wads, trying to
make a splash as geniuses after which they'd be rich and
famous, or wrecked. The lives of today's artists utterly lack
this dramatic component and are in fact fairly ascetic, except
for the occasional intoxication; they're not buoyed by the
prospect of better times to come. They're lucky if revenue
from their art covers production expenses—in Berlin, only
one in five artists breaks even, a study of the German Federal
Association of Visual Artists has found. Many artists are on

welfare for extended periods of time, and they've long re-
signed themselves to a life in which the complete trappings
of the middle class (a new car, homeownership, a family, retirement savings) will be permanently out of reach.[*] Of the
untold numbers of artists, a few may achieve these comforts,
but it's hard to admire and envy them for it, since such success
is the fruit of enormous discipline. Maintaining the sort of media presence that inspires people to pay considerable sums for
your work requires massive activity in social networks as well
as steady participation in touring exhibitions, biennials, and
festivals around the world.

The creative industries have achieved a degree of exploitation that Karl Marx couldn't have dreamed of. Year in, year
out, artists slave away in internships for pay that doesn't even
come close to covering basic living expenses—if there is pay at
all. Their digital means of production are supplied by themselves. They might work from home, thereby also paying for
their own production facilities. If they're lucky enough to work
at an office that has a sofa, they might be able to secretly crash
there at night—as long as the boss doesn't need it to conduct
their secret rendezvous.

Today's artists' belongings—beyond their current ward-
robes, computers, and phones—are dispensable in everyday
life. They can be stored somewhere, and the mere fact that
they may one day be retrieved offers a consoling sense of home.
Just as senile parents are consigned to the retirement home,
personal effects go into self-storage, where their proper safe-
keeping will be funded for a few years before being cast off
for good at a flea market or in a dumpster. Then again, such
unseen and unutilized possessions also resemble the private
art collection that has grown too large for exhibition in the
owner's home or a storage display.[*]

Those who hope, as collectors do, that their personal
effects will be admired after their own demise would do well
to work them up into a piece of art in due time. The home becomes an installation that's for sale in whole or in part. And
there is no need to stop at your own body. In installations and

performances, artists have been making museum and gallery exhibitions of their daily lives for decades. Why go to all the bother of transposing your own life into a different context? The simpler and more radical solution is to conceive of your entire home as art. Even the visitors and collectors who drop in become part of it. Not just for the occasional afternoon or evening—they can buy themselves into the piece, and be properly instructed on how to take part.

In the steady expansion of what may be regarded as art, there is no compelling reason why you should draw the line at your own bed. And don't just exhibit it: invite people into it, sex included. Many young artists already make a living from various forms of body (and mind) work: from massage, yoga, and healing to tantra, sugaring, and straight up sex work. These jobs require little formal qualifications and no regular hours, only an open mind and a pleasant appearance. And many incorporate their work experience into their artworks or vice versa.

This has contributed to care becoming a major theme and concern in art.* Art no longer wants to be the terrain of the idiosyncrasies of a pampered White middle class. It tries to recover its severed roots in the representation and decoration of magical practices designed to ground lost souls. But for the sake of exoticism, many of these practices have been appropriated from non-Western contexts.* For the sake of prudishness, the sexual components—as in sex magic—are rather subdued. Just like previous efforts to gain legitimacy, such as artistic research, the caring turn of art is about to accelerate its own loss of relevance. Art is magic for cowards.

What is more powerful than sex to establish a strong connection with your audience and collectors? If you continue to leave the commodification of sex to hookers and hustlers, you shouldn't be surprised if they soon make inroads into the realm of art under the banner of an expanded concept of sex work in order to still be able to compete with virtual sex avatars.

Besides relying on welfare or parental support, bohemians who refuse to engage in total artistic self-marketing may hire themselves out as measures of gentrification in one especially unattractive neighborhood after another—not expecting to make more than a pittance, perhaps in the form of a discount on their temporary lease.

# Mixed Zones
## 2015

Punks invented in-person trolling. Relics of an urban life
before total digital surveillance, they now make a
living as comforting tableaux vivants in environments that
are designed to seamlessly and excitingly mix virtuality
and reality, but aren't quite there yet.

From my hotel it's only a few steps to Hamburg's Reeperbahn.
I remember that in the early 1990s, there was still one strip
club after the next. But far more money can be made today
by normal bars that feed on the wicked reputation of the Reeperbahn, and so the strip clubs have almost all disappeared.
Finally, the dentures are held in place by a single tooth—and
by the glue that's smeared under the dentures. Here, that's the
punks who have made themselves comfortable everywhere on
the sidewalk for a long night. They've even set up a mattress
camp on a side street.

You might think they're a remnant, too, but twenty-five
years ago, the Reeperbahn wasn't interesting to punks. Punks
don't seek confrontation with other freaks, but with normals;
it's more lucrative and homey. As punks do, they collect money
for more alcohol. Therefore, they besiege passersby so much—
in a chummy, boozy way—that you give them something just to

get rid of them quickly. And if you're already tipsy yourself, then you might even find the punks cute.

Junior punks, who probably still go to school, have placed themselves at the very beginning of the mile. All are wearing hooded sweaters. One has a light-blue streak in her blonde hair; one wears a black miniskirt and black tights with an over-the-knee Doc Martens lace-up printed on them, plus designer Docs—black on the front, with longitudinal black and white stripes at the heel.* There is little talking, and the one with the streak passes the time texting on her iPhone. The juniors regroup, even closer to the subway. Now they place two pots in front of them with signs: "alcohol" and "marijuana." I remember: the other day I saw punks with iPads in Milan. It seems that being a punk is gaining new appeal with the distractions of mobile digital communication.

The harassment by the predominantly male punks finds its female counterpart in the bachelorettes and their cronies, dressed up in glowing devil horns, tight pink graphic T-shirts, cowboy hats, nurse's coats, or, once in a while, Cuba caps, camouflage and adapted Che Guevara flags with the face of the groom-to-be. They blare popular songs from their teenage years, offering schnapps to male strangers and having their pictures taken with them.

The bachelor party traditionally takes place in a bar, perhaps a strip club, as far away from home as possible, so that everything that happens during this alcohol-filled night can remain secret. The bride-to-be, on the other hand, is publicly exposed to ridicule. This phenomenon would also be unthinkable without smartphones, which can be used to freshly present the collective embarrassment to those at home.

When a pack of men roams bars, it's unlikely that women will take a serious liking to them. At most, they will be at their service venally. Women, alternately, often act extra ridiculous, disguise themselves in disfiguring ways, and document their every move so they can be more offensive to men than usual without getting into an awkward situation. It's a mobile, more elaborate version of the method practiced by punks: make themselves ugly, ambush, and then quickly pick out others with the intention of turning away just as quickly.

Punks and bachelorette nights practice forms of analog trolling moderated by digital technology. Analog trolling was perfected by punks in times when it was still possible to act largely anonymously in the pedestrian zones of a large city. Today, only certain disreputable spheres of the internet promise anonymity. In others, especially mainstream social media, any activity remains assigned to you indefinitely. Given these two extreme poles (as well as some lazy compromises like Snapchat's single-view feature), the nightlife district of a major city seems pleasantly human: there are surveillance cameras and police everywhere, so a criminal can hardly escape, but until there is an analog recording of personal details, everyone remains largely anonymous.

Soon, even this fun will come to an end, when facial recognition will be so sophisticated that public spaces will obey the same real-name principle as mainstream social media. Your face will then be your irreplaceable license plate. Special zones with a rigorous, electronically monitored ban on recording are needed—places where people can still meet each other solely on the basis of their knowledge of human nature (i.e., their prejudices).•

It's a few minutes' walk from the Reeperbahn to the newly built HafenCity district. I cross a pedestrian bridge into a silence of the grave. This is exactly how I imagine the future: every sound that exceeds normal speaking volume is assigned to its named author and punished. To be on the safe side, people will stop speaking in public altogether.

But my following experiences don't fit the mold: I reach a small shred of green, situated between several skyscrapers. In order to make it appear not quite so miserable, it has been equipped with a few *Teletubbies*-like hills, on which a few real, excrement-pooping hares hobble around. I pass two wedding parties that I could easily walk into and crash. At a third, semi-outdoor party, I nibble from the buffet and mingle with the dancing. In the bar next door, several uncool teens are dancing to the title track of the musical comedy *Wenn Inge tanzt* (When Inge is dancing, 2013), as "completely out of control" as its uncool protagonist in the lyrics. The streets I walk through are all deserted, but not far away I keep hearing a sports car racing through the bare, echoey canyons of houses.

Is this new part of town still technically on the level of Stanley Kubrick's *A Clockwork Orange* (1971)? Or have the windows become so impervious to noise that speeding cars and loud parties no longer bother anyone? I already know how this conundrum will tip. Seamless speed monitoring via GPS has long been technically possible. It's simply not worth introducing it, because in just a few years it will only be possible to drive a car yourself virtually or at special motor sports venues.

Gradually, we say goodbye to what we consider real—for a simulation that, with desired exceptions, seems ever-more real. It's not a sphere locked away in books, radios, and televisions, but always and everywhere. Our physical environment can only disappoint in direct comparison, and that's quite intentional. In the past, shopping streets were dull so as not to distract from the stores. Now they're just supposed to not be scary, because everything real can be particularly dangerous—and can be virtually enriched at any time anyway.

Soon, not only bourgeois and old people will be strolling around here but also nerds and slackers who have been stressed out by ever-more exciting and engaging computer games*—just like how for punks who still meant business, the pedestrian zone provided a pleasantly tidy and clean contrast. Many even practice virtual abstinence, since HafenCity, initially conceived as a media center, with its numerous "decision nodes" (i.e., varying shopping routes) and extensive walkability and bikeability, looks like the physical incarnation of cozy, old-fashioned *Second Life*.

HafenCity doesn't kill and it doesn't make any further demands. Here, everyone gets along just fine. And even the punks and bachelorettes from the Reeperbahn find a quiet spot.

• Society of Games

World as Museum
2020

> Conservation is the flip side of modernization. But what
> to save, and what not? Ecological natives gain authority as an
> extension of our environment. Similarly, museal natives
> position themselves as affined to certain collections of artifacts.
> Meanwhile, we can reduce the space that we need to live to
> a minimum.

The cultural development of humankind stems from the imita-
tion and exaggeration of superior aspects of its environment.
Humans aspire to live as long as trees, dwell in houses that
are as protective as caves and as high as mountains, fly like
birds, move as fast as the speed of sound, if not light, and
finally, become as powerful as the gods were assumed to be.
The next step is for humans to aspire to live longer than trees,
build houses higher than mountains, fly better than birds,
move faster than the speed of sound, if not light, and finally,
become more powerful than the gods ever were.

It's the same with social formations: monarchies are
hierarchical, like beehives; basic democracies are like a flock
of birds that collectively finds its direction and alternates the
lead; and presidential democracies try to be both. Borders are
hardly traversable, like rivers or seas. The nation is like an island, the empire like a whole continent. The people inhabiting

a nation or an empire are meant to distinguish themselves, like in a clearly defined race.

Environmentalism calls for a new social analogy of a global tribe and kinship with all creatures. Instead of copying nature to make us feel and act superior, this analogy accepts nature's superiority—that is, the collective evolution of billions of species over billions of years. Instead of furthering the homogeneity of our one particular species in one global village, we should acknowledge our entanglement with the overwhelmingly diverse biosphere and—following the Gaia theory—even Earth's non-biosphere.[*]

For now, this analogy seems to be quite presumptuous. What is kinship when you can't procreate with one another? What is a tribe when you can't know or even understand most of its members? Gene technology may soon allow us to procreate with every other creature on Earth, and information technology may allow us to understand them. But the challenge will be to make this a bilateral undertaking—that is, to make the other creatures understand us (not only when we speak their language) and want to procreate with us (and not just be tricked into it). This will only be possible by improving their intelligence—just as we'll improve ours. Otherwise, the global tribe of ordinary creatures will have posthumans and AGI as their gods. Or is it rather the assumption that there are fundamental differences between human and animal intelligence that's presumptuous?

Proponents of a global tribe assume that extraordinary intelligence is already prevalent in the coexistence of native tribes with their nonhuman environment—thanks to traditional wisdom, animistic spirituality, and an absence of ownership. The perception of what Colombian anthropologist Astrid Ulloa calls the "ecological native" remodels the noble savage: "They have to be 'our' utopian reality. They have to be the warriors of 'our' inner conflicts."[*] Astrid Ulloa, *The Ecological Native: Indigenous Peoples' Movements and Eco-governmentality in Colombia* (New York: Routledge, 2005).

• Orcies

• Body with More Organs

In fact, native tribes do claim territorial exclusivity and defend it against others. Like any living kind, native tribes have a tendency to overpopulate. But this destructive growth is counterbalanced by disasters, epidemics, and wars; since you can't buy land, you have to win it. The individual lives of tribal members and others are regarded as rather worthless. Tribes lack not just personal property but all personal rights.

Environmentalism is able to overlook these dark sides of native tribes because it puts an emphasis on conservation. Ecological conservation finds it natural to prioritize the preservation of the collective over self-preservation: individual creatures have to die sooner or later, so only social formations can survive. A society inclined toward progress can't be conserved; in industrialized societies, conservative parties are constantly changing. The reason that ecological conservation tends to include the conservation of native tribes isn't just that they live aligned with nature—needing protection like nature and extending their own protection to nature—it's also that they actually want to be collectively protected as they are.

Conservation is the flip side of modernization. As soon as a society understands itself as constantly progressing, it starts to build museums, memorials, and nature reserves; the efforts to move forward and to save both complement and compete with each other. While modernization gains speed, ever-larger parts of the world are turned into nature reserves and put under protection. This is problematic in two ways: First, nature itself is a dynamic process. We can hardly save it as it is, and even less as it was before human interference. Second, space is limited, and it will be only a matter of time before museums and nature reserves cover the whole planet.

In a world as museum, individual humans only find their place as collectors, guards, restaurateurs, visitors, or their very own museum*—unless they themselves become immortal and collectable. While in the future it will be possible to replicate every solid entity based on compressed information, individual living creatures will be the only pieces that still need to be kept in their original form. In the meantime, humans have to legitimize themselves as the servants of preservation. As members of Indigenous tribes take the role of ecological natives, modern societies generate *museal natives*. They move gently through the collections' halls and storages to take care of the masses of artifacts—starting with their own. While the ecological natives plant, fertilize, harvest, and protect, the museal natives save, archive, display, and restore. Both act in accordance with a compelling order intrinsic to their world: for ecological natives, it's the inherited customs of their respective tribe; for museal natives, it's the distinctive missions of the foundation or initiative to which they devote themselves. Their entities might gain rights as legal persons, with tribes or foundations acting as their custodians.

The different conservationist projects can't all go hand in hand, since you can't protect everything. The extension of individual rights beyond humankind is the apparent end of moral universalism because it's impossible to respect all living creatures or species, from bacteria to mammals, to the same degree. Even if you restricted basic rights to conscious creatures, where would you start? Fruit flies might dream too. Where would you end? There is no greater vermin than the human race; the global ecosystem can spare it more easily than some unknown microbe.•

Trying to overcome anthropocentrism ends in moral relativism, as do nationalism and ethnocentrism. While the latter derive their moral criteria from birth, environmentalists and musealists derive them from choice. Your moral criteria might be inspired by intuition, experience, or rage—all in all, they're an act of caprice. The ones who share your caprice might become your *voluntary tribe*.

Voluntary tribes don't necessarily demand exclusivity, neither in membership nor in territory. Different from gangs and sects, you can leave them whenever you like. The state's monopoly on legitimate use of force allows voluntary tribes to multiply easily.• But environmental and museal measures demand a high degree of territorial exclusivity and tend to

• Body with More Organs

• Middle–Class Warriors

restrict access even more than nations. This increases the pressure on all social entities to hoard land. In a world in which everything can be automatically created except space, all space that isn't a museum or nature reserve might be equally divided or shared as a commons.•

The spheres of progress and conservation are both projected as enormous houses. Until the Middle Ages, settlements and cities were conceived as giant houses with surrounding walls. With the progression of the division of labor, this analogy was gradually replaced by that of an organism, and with the liberation of the market economy, by that of a dense ecosystem—with factories, offices, apartment buildings, and malls as big as medieval cities. Meanwhile, nature reserves are meant to house whole ecosystems. Drastic climate change might make it necessary again to protect cities with huge walls, eventually a dome, living within a largely closed ecosystem with an emphasis on recycling, renewable energy, and farming. With increasing environmental concerns, a house is no longer meant as a place to temporarily retreat, but as a largely self-sufficient—monadic—unit. The museal native merges with the ecological native.

All these encapsulations might lead away from a world tribe and toward increased isolation. An erosion of nation-states might only accelerate this process. Alternatively, nation-states or supranational pacts could work as overall eco-nationalist or eco-ethnicist shields and displace the basic principle of a growth economy and ecology—creative destruction—to games and virtual reality.• In phases of despair, creative destruction might trespass into the real world.• The chances of such acts being successful and not ending in self-destruction are so low that the perpetrators and their sympathizers celebrate them as camp transgressions. Their opponents ridicule them as cartoonish rebellions of self-proclaimed superheroes who try to ignore their finite powers.•

Real Estate Porn •

Society of Games  •
• World as Program •
Comic Purgatory •

Catering to courage and happiness, the monad knows how to best orchestrate its eventual end.

Musings of a *Landei* The German term *Landei* ("country egg") labels a person from the countryside who doesn't fit in well in an urban environment. While derogatory terms like "hillbilly," "hayseed," "bumpkin," or "redneck" imply that country people are coarse, "country egg" rather characterizes them as odd—not round but oval. Landei is related to the verb *herumeiern*—not moving straightforward but wriggling like an egg. 2021

> Growing up in the countryside, I learned early on that there is no such thing as nature untouched by humans. If you don't want to kill, you have to die.

I experienced my childhood in a slice of the world where everything seemed to be fine. No one around me suffered from hunger, illness, separation, or any other recognizable adversity. By the time my first friends and close relatives went broke, became depressed, or died, I was already well into my twenties.

This was, of course, pure coincidence. When I was born, it had not yet been twenty-five years since the Second World War had raged and the Nazis had ruled the very place where I would grow up. Now the economy was booming, and even if survivors of the Third Reich still dreamed of Germany as a world power,[•] it seemed permanently defused by its division into two states, each subject to a different world power.

I was fortunate to have been born in the more prosperous part of Germany, which was integrated into the capitalist West. Productivity was higher than in the socialist East, and at the same time, in order to prevent new radicalizations, there

was extraordinary concern about the entire population sufficiently participating in the wealth generated.

Some elders told of the horrors they had experienced
during and after the war in captivity and flight. My parents
visited the grave of my older sister, who had died when I was
two. My mother's father had died of bone cancer in his early
fifties, and my father's father had died of a heart attack in his
mid-fifties. Each had left behind a wife who would be a widow
for most of her life, but also five children, all of whom lived
close to or, like us, even with her. My parents had had me. And
the stories from the war were repeated so eagerly and with
such a sense of drama that I understood them less as trauma-
tic experiences than as quirks the old people referenced to
distinguish themselves from the younger ones. Who could
know what had really happened back then—especially since
Jews never appeared in the stories.*

But then there was television. Here I saw the proxy wars
of the world powers nonviolently facing each other in Germany.
Saw famine and natural disasters. Saw violent crimes against
young people returning home at night. Saw parental violence
against children. Saw homeless people and drug addicts. Saw
smoggy cities, cut-down rain forests, polluted rivers, and
animals threatened with extinction. Saw the Holocaust.

I was surrounded by suffering, only it showed itself
to me personally as little as the animals in the forest did.
Once, during an excursion with me, my parents stopped at the
German-German border. On the other side, there was only a
forest and a watchtower, but I knew that the people there were
poorer than we were, and so Africa began, for me, behind that
forest. I could hardly believe it, because weren't even the light
and sand quite different in Africa, wasn't it much warmer
there? But I had watched it on television.

Already at elementary school age, I understood that
most of the suffering in the world could be prevented if only
there were far fewer people. War, displacement, hunger, environmental destruction—all were due to the fact that there
were far too many people spread out on the fertile land. Karl

May's adventure novels set in North America during the pioneer era were decisive for this insight. The noble and wise "Indians" did everything right. They were few in number, rarely got in each other's way, understood nature from the heart, and took just enough from it for it to regrow without any problems.* But then the evil Whites came from Europe, because it was getting too crowded for them there, brought vast quantities of weapons, and destroyed without sense or reason. I would have liked to have siblings, but now I understood why I had to remain an only child. Even my friends all had at most one sibling—not four, like both of my parents.

Was that enough? In poor countries, populations continued to grow, despite famines. Even in West Germany, as people grew older, Germans fled the East, and guest workers immigrated, the population was still growing. Yet it was one of the most densely populated countries in the world.

We lived in the countryside. But when I went out into nature to try to resemble a Native American as much as possible in my play, I didn't get very far. Every forest I could reach on foot or by bicycle was so small or so intersected by roads that I could hear cars everywhere. I either saw no animal tracks or didn't understand them. The wood was too wet to make fire with, or when it finally dried in the summer, it was too dangerous. Mushrooms and berries were only available for a short time and there were too few to feed on properly. Even if I eventually learned to shoot, I wouldn't be allowed to hunt just like that. There were no waters for fishing, far and wide. And how should I spend the night in the forest or elsewhere in nature without isolating myself in plastic? Even in summer, it took a tent or sleeping bag to avoid being stung and poked too much. Or a tree house? But who would help me with that? And then, strictly speaking, would I still be living in nature?

German nature did me no harm, but it didn't welcome me either. And this apparent indifference was caused not only by the fact that no one taught me to understand it but also that nature didn't really exist there anymore. The German forest was also just a field.

August Niermann's (no relation) butcher shop in our neighboring town, circa 1910, photographer unknown

So, I tried my hand at farming. My mother's parents had been farmers and my mother still managed a large vegetable garden, where I regularly helped. We largely followed "organic" principles, which meant paying attention to complex crop rotation and fertilizing with manure from the cattle that were waiting in our barn to be killed, gutted, skinned, and quartered in my father's little slaughterhouse. We dealt with animals that had it in for our crops by hand: we set up scarecrows, stretched nets, and walked through the garden clapping loudly several times a day; we laid chicken wire belowground to ward off rodents; we also collected slugs every morning and threw them in brine, where they turned into a foul-smelling mush. Digging up the entire garden, burying the manure, sowing, watering, weeding, and finally, harvesting, was a tremendous slog. Again and again, our potatoes fell victim to potato rot, the nets came loose from the bushes in strong winds and the berries were eaten by birds, or the mice made it to the carrots. Our fruit trees were impossible to protect anyway. There were too many of them and they had grown too high for nets to be stretched over them.

Nevertheless, from late spring until the first frost, we were able to feed ourselves largely from our garden; frozen peas and beans, pickled cucumbers and onions, applesauce, pumpkin soup, and jam were even enough for the whole year. And everything tasted so much better than from the store— even when I later shopped at organic food stores (which didn't exist in my childhood), the fruits and vegetables would never taste as good as the ones from our garden.

My father kept cattle in surrounding pastures from spring to fall before slaughtering them. Here, too, I helped from an early age. We renewed the barbed wire, set new stakes, inspected the self-watering troughs, doctored cows suffering from udder inflammation with a shot of penicillin, and once a week, we trapped cattle fit for slaughter. We spent hours mowing the nettles and thistles that spread throughout the warmer months with a scythe. During vacations, I mucked out the stalls and helped with the weekly slaughter. Though I was fond of them, I felt little pity for the cattle that died before my eyes. They had no idea what was in store for them, and unlike us humans, they were spared old age and infirmity.

My parents were rural conservatives. They had no sentimental feelings toward nature and were suspicious of the Green Party—know-it-alls from cities who wanted to dictate to them. For my parents, it wasn't a matter of principle if we ourselves only ate meat from cattle that had lived on the pasture with us and with small local farmers. Or if we only ate eggs from the quirky farmers whose chickens still roamed free on the farm. It all just tasted so much better. And anyone who bought packaged meat at the supermarket to save a little money had only themselves to blame. Looking out on pastures and woods from all sides of the home, as we did, was a reward for those who worked hard, far from the city. For my parents, the fact that a road ran directly in front of our house and a small asphalt factory slid into view next to a forest was also part of life in the countryside.

It was no different for me as a child. Not only did I love playing in the woods but I also made pilgrimages to construction sites to sniff fresh asphalt. The ditches that ran along the country road were perfect for war games, and the bridge that crossed the nearby highway was wonderful for spitting on cars. I loved the cherries from our garden, but also the artificial cherry flavor of children's cough drops. I loved the quietude of nature, but I also loved sitting on a noisy, vibrating tractor. I loved playing outside even when it was cold and wet, but also taking a hot bath or snuggling up to a radiator afterward. In the countryside, it all basically seemed, to me, to go well together.

If only it weren't for cities. In the country, I could run across every field and farm. Many roads were so seldom traveled that you could play on them. In cities, on the other hand, except for a few parks, you couldn't linger anywhere without paying for it. Everything was far too crowded. And because city dwellers needed more and more food, farmers used more and more chemicals. Because cities were getting bigger and noisier, more and more city dwellers moved to the countryside and turned fields into settlements where everyone was only allowed to linger in their own mini-garden.

When I moved to Berlin to study, I was lucky that the Wall fell shortly after. I immediately moved to the depopulated Eastern side, and was able to live in the city for a few years while still feeling a bit like I was in the countryside: there were freely accessible wastelands and ruins everywhere.

But how had it ever come about that I had left the country and moved to the city to study philosophy? Why hadn't I become an organic farmer or organic butcher? Not a deep-ecological activist committed to fewer human offspring and more conservation around the world?

My teenage years were marked by ever-new environmental disasters: the nuclear power plant meltdown in Chernobyl, chemical spills in Bhopal and Basel, capsized oil tankers, an immense drought in Ethiopia. Acid rain attacked forests, fertile soils eroded, rainforests were cut down, and only deserts and cities grew. Environmental destruction was no less present in the media then than the dangers of climate change are today.[•]

When I was sixteen or seventeen, a Green Party youth group started in the next city over. A friend invited me to join and then dropped out herself. In the end, we were only three boys—the other two being somewhat older Trotskyists. Instead of ecological issues, we argued about the legitimacy of violence in the fight against state-sanctioned oppression and destruction. The two Trotskyists were very much in favor of violence; I was against it.

Even though I had quite a bit of philosophy and political theory in me by then, I perceived myself in this conflict as the simple-minded Landei trying to stand up to crafty city slickers and beat them at their own game. Although I couldn't take our dispute seriously at all in terms of political work, it captivated me. Probably because I had grown up as an only child in prosperity and peace, the suffering of the world opened up to me primarily on an abstract level. To put it crudely: I was more interested in being right than in doing right. But this rightness wasn't something static; it had to prove and invent itself again and again.

Soon, I was seeking Socratic duels in every conversation and every reading. As a child, I had often fought with my friends. Now I had found a peaceful equivalent to physical combat that was at least as exciting.° This was to be my destiny: to always push a seemingly deadlocked discussion a dizzying bit further. As a Landei, I fancied myself free of bourgeois aporias—such as a kitschy, harmony-addicted, and, at the same time, ignorant relationship to nature.° As far as concrete political struggle was concerned, there were already the Greens and all kinds of NGOs, so it didn't depend on someone more like me—shy and mentally wound up.

Even before I started studying, I threw myself at all sorts of big questions and lost myself in the search for better, if not ultimate, answers. As befits a Landei, the basic mood should be neither apocalyptic nor euphoric. The world will probably go on for a while with humans, also in the number of several billions.° A Landei knows that there is no nature independent of humans, or humans independent of nature. But a Landei also knows that such a symbiosis isn't an idyll and that you can't live without being guilty toward your environment. This is also true for Indigenous peoples and vegans relying on subsistence farming.° To live always means to kill.° City dwellers don't really want to admit this, but for a Landei it's as obvious as the sequence of day and night. If you don't want to kill, you have to die.

# Wishful Death
2020

The life-sustaining measures used for severe complications from COVID-19 often result in chronic disabilities or gruesome deaths. Instead of arbitrarily selecting between those more or less worthy of survival in the absence of medical capacity, much suffering could be prevented by granting and communicating the right to euthanasia to everyone.

About a year ago, my mother died in an induced coma, ventilated by a respirator. She had been kept alive this way for two weeks. Her heart had continued to beat strongly and regularly, and her inflammation levels had slowly decreased, but her lung capacity was steadily going down. She had apparently developed fibrosis—an irreversible scarring of the lungs. The doctors suspected it was a side effect of the chemotherapy that she had started a few months earlier and initially tolerated well.

When fatal, COVID-19 often follows a similar course: it begins with a dry cough, mild fever, and weakness, and ends with rapidly progressing shortness of breath. Just a few weeks before my mother was placed in an induced coma, she had been gardening and jaunting. Just four days before, we had gone shopping together—her driving—and three days before, we had baked a cake. Then her condition had deteriorated exponentially. There were only a few hours between our last phone call and the moment she was put into an induced coma.

The measure was taken at such short notice that I wasn't informed until afterward.

My mother's lungs continued to suffer daily, not least due to the machine ventilation. Because of the continuous undersupply of oxygen, the other organs, including the brain, also suffered. When I asked the doctors how she would return to her life if her condition miraculously improved, I received no answer. It's not the task of intensive care to provide such an answer; it's only about saving lives. And, as the doctors assured me, not all possibilities had been exhausted: "There's still room for improvement." That meant a tracheotomy, so that oxygen would no longer have to go through the mouth, and reactivation of the heart after an initial standstill. When I asked if it wasn't all completely pointless and only causing my mother unnecessary suffering, I was told that she was being given such strong opiates, barbiturates, and anesthetics that I needn't worry about it. If I really wanted them to stop the treatment, I would have to say so, but usually they would wait a little longer in such cases.

I was irritated. Didn't I need a living will to turn off the equipment? My mother still had said document lying around at home, not filled out, so I just told them that they shouldn't overdo it with the "room for improvement."

When I said goodbye to my mother's body, the doctors looked down in embarrassment and could hardly get a word out of their mouths. Was it because the signs of fibrosis could have been detected much earlier in the department where she had been treated before? That would have, I didn't fool myself, delayed her death by a few weeks at most, perhaps months. Or was it because they weren't quite sure what exactly she had died of? To prove fibrosis conclusively, a tissue sample would have had to be taken from the lungs. But there was no question of an autopsy, and I didn't demand one either. Corpses are rarely examined in Germany, except in cases of suspected crime. At some point, time just runs out, and that's it. This not-so-accurate way of looking at the end of life could also be a reason why the official COVID-19 mortality rate in Germany was so unusually low to begin with. Unlike in Spain and France, fewer than average sixty- to seventy-nine-year-olds were registered as infected in Germany, and even fewer over eighty.

My mother had lived a good life until just before her death, at age seventy-seven. She had even taken on her mastectomy and chemo with a lot of courage and wit—always keeping in mind the ten sprightly years she would surely have ahead of her afterward. Perhaps she hadn't realized until the end that she was about to die. The doctors spoke to me in such a forced and flowery way, and they never stopped saying there was "very well still hope," or that her situation was "stable," so I couldn't imagine that they had clearly communicated to her that she could not come back from the coma. Otherwise, would she not have insisted on seeing me one more time, on speaking to me, on hearing me? That this hadn't happened was perhaps only a good thing, because then I would have cried terribly and my mother would have realized how bad her situation was. But who gives doctors—or me—the right to come to that decision?

In many European hospitals, at the height of the pandemic, decisions were made by rule of thumb as to who would receive intensive care, who wouldn't, and for whom it would be terminated prematurely. The Italian Society of Anesthesia, Analgesia, Resuscitation, and Intensive Care Medicine, for example, recommended giving priority to patients with a higher probability of survival and a longer life expectancy. Such selection procedures, "triages," are typically used in wars and disasters. However, COVID-19 isn't a sudden event; it develops over days and weeks. One might also ask the sufferers themselves whether they want to continue living under these circumstances—in which saving their life may cost another. If not, they could be offered euthanasia.

The outrage over such a procedure would be inevitable. Although suicide is now exempt from legal punishment in many countries—in Switzerland it has even been a human right since 2006—the moral condemnation remains. For Christian churches, continuing to live is a God-given duty, and for secular humanists, too, every human life has a value in itself. It's therefore often not parliaments and ethics committees that clear the way for assisted suicide but the constitutional courts—as was the case last fall in Italy and this February in Germany. And even where assisted suicide has been legal for some time—for example, in the Netherlands or Switzerland—it must be based on acute egoistic motives such as a serious incurable illness, so that no one feels like society is pushing individuals toward death.

Yet it's such an indication that discriminates against certain people as possibly "worth dying." At the same time, the suffering of all other people who are tired of life is trivialized across the board. The ruling of the German Federal Constitutional Court, which overturned the ban on institutional euthanasia, therefore explicitly states that it shouldn't be "limited to situations defined by external causes like serious or incurable illnesses, nor does it only apply in certain stages of life or illness." In "all stages of a person's existence," a person has the right to a self-determined death: "Their decision must, in principle, be respected by state and society as an act of autonomous self-determination." "Criminalisation of Assisted Suicide Services Unconstitutional," Bundesverfassungsgericht, February 26, 2020, https://www.bundesverfassungsgericht.de/SharedDocs/Pressemit teilungen/EN/2020/bvg20-012.html.

The German Constitutional Court brings into play the duty to seek advice from special, state-authorized organizations—similar to that which exists in Germany for abortions. In a comparable process, you would first have to inform yourself about the various legal offers of assisted suicide and their risks, evaluate your motives, and be educated about alternative scenarios. Counseling could then be followed by a reflection period.

Today, in countries that allow euthanasia, it's physicians who are pushed into the counseling role. But they lack the time, qualifications, and perhaps the will to do so. Their code of honor dictates that they heal and not kill. At the same time, they can't act with complete impartiality because they earn money from assisted suicide. In hospitals, whether or not patients are granted euthanasia has an impact on the bed occupancy rate.

Your own family and friends are even worse advisors. They have a great interest in keeping you alive, or maybe, they want to slowly get rid of you. Are they after the inheritance? Just the possibility that the person who wants to die might think something like that makes relatives self-conscious. Counseling centers would offer the opportunity to talk impartially about your suicidal motives and about the pressure that your relatives exert in one direction or another. Early on, my father became a member of the Swiss assisted suicide association EXIT. At family celebrations, he proudly and provocatively passed around the association's brochure and was greeted with an embarrassed silence—even from me, although I actually found him courageous. At the end of his life, he— like my mother—hadn't even filled out a living will.

It took and still takes great social struggles for women to be able to decide freely whether they want to have a child or not. "Pro-choice" must not only apply to the unborn but also to one's own life.[*] It's absurd to argue that euthanasia would open the door to society's distinction between valuable and valueless life (i.e., eugenics) when politics and all of us are constantly judging life and death: we let malnourished children die needlessly or allow people to become lonely, impoverished, and driven to suicide.

The COVID-19 pandemic makes us aware not only of our own mortality but also that we all kill at any time.[*] The climate change debate has brought this guilt home to us in a rather abstract way: somehow my emissions, along with those of billions of other people, contribute to something that, cumulatively over many years, increases the probability of disastrous natural events. In this pandemic, the blame is very concrete and lurks on every street corner: Could I now, if I'm not careful enough, get so precariously close to someone that I kill them with an infection I haven't even noticed yet?[*]

We're also all to blame for what is currently happening

• Comic Purgatory

• Musings of a *Landei*

• Automatic Privacy
Corona Tribes

in hospitals because we've tolerated cuts in our health care systems and haven't pushed our governments to be better prepared for public-health crises. But we won't see ourselves as complicit until we also put our own lives on the line: How can I claim the right to stay alive at all costs when others don't have that same right—also due to my inaction?

In the debate over appropriate anti-coronavirus policies, Texas Lieutenant Governor Dan Patrick caused an uproar with his call not to risk the country's economic future for vulnerable old folks like himself: "My message is that, let's get back to work, let's get back to living, let's be smart about it, and those of us who are seventy-plus, we'll take care of ourselves but don't sacrifice the country." Dan Patrick, interview by Tucker Carlson, *Tucker Carlson Tonight*, Fox News, March 23, 2020. Of course, such a call is cynical. Patrick himself just turned seventy, doesn't have to use crowded transportation, seems healthy, and certainly has excellent health insurance. But what happens when we see protections against the coronavirus drive millions and millions of people into misery, homelessness, and hunger?

Already after 9/11, we've seen how protection from further attacks has cost the lives of hundreds of thousands of innocent people. And some of these measures were also directed against ordinary citizens—in many places personal rights were minimized. What French President Emmanuel Macron described as the "war" against the virus could be far more devastating, because the virus sacrifices itself even more devotedly than fundamentalists and multiplies millions of times faster. We become hostages to our unconditional will to live.•

The West could learn a lot from how Southeast Asian cultures are approaching the pandemic—for example, why protective masks aren't hysterical, how to wash one's hands properly, how to avoid coughing on others, and how to monitor and control one's citizens seamlessly. Beyond more self and state control, however, we could also learn from Southeast Asian cultures a freer approach to our own death.

From a Western perspective, high suicide rates in Japan or South Korea are the result of great pressure to perform and conform, but even so, no one there dictates anyone else to kill themselves. Every suicide can be understood as the result of a social grievance—and it also indicates it. This indication is what suicide bombers rely on, rubbing their worldview in our faces with their deaths.° Conversely, we can conveniently overlook those dying in nursing homes and clinics, quiet and isolated. When COVID-19 patients have their ventilators turned off because others who are younger and more able to survive are waiting, they no longer have the strength or sense to spark an outcry on social media.

To gauge the scale of the COVID-19 pandemic, we've relied on a number of more or less trustworthy statistics: How many lives has COVID-19 taken? How many more lives can COVID-19 take if such and such happens or doesn't happen? How much longer will ICU capacities last? For what percentage of us can COVID-19 prove fatal? But this coronavirus differs from other viruses not only in its infection and fatality rates but also in how cruelly it kills—through gradual suffocation.

My mother was lucky in that she didn't know exactly what to expect. We don't have that luck. The possibility to leave life painlessly and reliably cared for at any time wouldn't stop the pandemic. But it could alleviate the worst: our fear.

Corona Tribes
2020; 2022

During the course of the COVID-19 pandemic, I envisioned
new generational conflicts and alliances unfolding. The
different opinions on safety measures and vaccines gave me
the idea that society could avoid harsh frictions by dividing
into voluntary tribes.

October 2020. When I tell my son, born in 2009, about the
time before his birth, he wonders how it was possible at all: to
navigate through an unfamiliar city without GPS, to find out
about something without the internet, to watch something
without pressing play and pause. But his reaction is more than
astonished, shaking his head in disbelief, when I tell him how
much danger people lived in before his time.

All through my childhood, I, born in 1969, didn't wear
a seat belt in the car. It wasn't until 1974 that seat belts became
standard in West Germany, and only a minority used them.
One felt restrained by the seat belt, and insecure, because it
made one all too aware of the dangers of driving. Driving without a seat belt in Germany has only been a fineable offense
since 1984.

In my elementary school, nine- and ten-year-olds
were already smoking semi-secretly on the playground. At the

Gymnasium (high school), the senior grades could smoke legally. Flying was still an ordeal until the end of the 1990s, when shortly after takeoff the air-conditioning system blew the secondhand smoke from the smokers in the back rows to the nonsmokers in the front. It wasn't until 2007 that a general smoking ban was imposed on German trains. In bars and restaurants, it would take even longer. Again, there were bitter arguments about how personal freedom should be interpreted, even though the considerable dangers of smoking and passive smoking were no longer questioned, not even by the cigarette industry.

The COVID-19 pandemic opened a new debate about the negligent endangerment of oneself and others—one in which even my son has yet to take a stand. For as little as he wants to endanger others, constant handwashing, mask wearing, and social distancing get on his nerves. It may seem exaggerated if people, just because they have to tie a cloth over their mouth and nose in an acute emergency and not impatiently ram into the back of the person standing in front of them in line, immediately think that the basic order of freedom has come to an end. But no need for a conspiracy, this acute emergency is only the beginning. If you don't want to infect others with the coronavirus, it's hard to later say, "But with the flu, it's OK."

In Japan, even before the coronavirus outbreak, a large part of the population was wearing masks on public transport—to protect others, to protect themselves, or perhaps to just spare others an unpleasant sight. With each new epidemic, the number of mask wearers jumped up, then settled at a new high. When we were in Tokyo in early January, I told my son that I would reward him with 1,000 yen for every person he heard sneeze or cough or saw grab their face. He went away empty-handed.

It's a coincidence that the epidemics that have broken out in recent decades have been largely confined to Southeast Asia and Africa. At some point, it would inevitably hit the Western world. But we were ill prepared and reacted hesitantly;

the misconception that epidemics only affect presumably less developed countries was too deeply ingrained in us.

I too couldn't imagine what would happen in the coming months. I assumed that people would travel less, perhaps for years. Risk groups, in particular, would keep a low profile. Perhaps mass events would be banned. But that borders, schools, and most businesses would be closed for months virtually all over Europe, sending the economy into a recession, was beyond my imagination.

To justify the drastic measures, the fight against the pandemic was quickly compared to a war. It was a fairly convenient war at first, perfectly tailored to our post-heroic age: all you had to do was do nothing and chant #staythefuckhome on social media and you were a brave warrior. All you had to do was not give an oncoming passerby a wide berth or meet and hug a few friends and you were a swashbuckling partisan. From the actual front, the intensive care units, you learned little concrete information and were glad of it. Economic adversity was muted by government subsidies. •

The international winner of this war was soon clear: Southeast Asia. There, the spread of the virus was quickly brought under control through a combination of self-discipline and rigorous state surveillance. The rest of the world is grinding along in a bumpy "flattening the curve." The specific course is controversial and leads to numerous upheavals—while the formation of the social fronts is far from over.

Immediately after the coronavirus outbreak, I suspected that a new generational war might be looming. In the parks, under-thirties continued to gather in groups, sharing vapes and shishas with the same mouthpiece, lying in each other's arms, and gasping into each other's mouths as they worked out, while older people kept their distance, shy and suspicious. There was talk of "corona parties," where young people would try to get infected so that they would soon have COVID-19 behind them and be immune from then on.

In retrospect, all the major European crises of recent years seemed to me to be harbingers of this new generational war. In the global financial crisis, EU states had done everything they could to save the banks and the older population's investments there with guarantees and bond purchases worth trillions, but at the same time they had accepted youth unemployment of up to over 50 percent with a rigorous austerity policy. In the refugee crisis and Brexit, it had been primarily older people who urged their countries to be better sealed off against young immigrants. The #MeToo movement had been, at its core, a rebellion by younger women against sexism and abuse by older, more powerful men. Students had protested to take action against climate change, while it had been mostly older people who didn't have long left to live who had denied or relativized it. Now, while older people feared for their lives, youthful environmentalists and climate activists could radicalize themselves into deep ecologists who endorsed and wantonly spread epidemics as a natural regulator against overpopulation and aging.

The generational conflict reached its preliminary peak in the Western world in the 1960s and 1970s, when the baby boomers of the prosperous postwar years challenged the period's reactionary common sense. Since the fall of the Berlin Wall, this conflict seemed to have been largely shelved. The old were now continually reinventing themselves, and the young who followed were too individual for exclusive youth cultures to achieve cultural dominance. The generational conflict lived on at best as an intercultural "clash of civilizations," which was, after all, basically a "clash of birthrates."

With the COVID-19 pandemic, the generational conflict seemed to have returned to us in an archaic way—just as journalist Frank Schirrmacher warns in his 2004 bestseller *Das Methusalem-Komplott* (*The Methusaleh Conspiracy*). Cryptically, he repeatedly invokes our current year as the decisive year: "It will be too late if we wait until 2020 to experience that, for the first time in our existence, life is not just a game, but deadly serious."

Schirrmacher himself succumbed to a heart attack in 2014 at the age of fifty-four—not really an age anymore. Accordingly, the front in the new generational war has also shifted backward. The line between "young" and "old" is no longer drawn between adolescence and starting a family, but just below the retirement age—in some cases, well above it. Last exit to Nietzsche: prove yourself once again as death-defying without risking too much.* When push comes to shove, there is also an ICU bed available for those who doubt that COVID-19 is worse than the flu.

Older, relatively fit men in particular want to have another go. First, women disputed their alpha position, and now, the economy is being strangled by those pre-suffering from civilization's ailments such as obesity and diabetes, instead of rewarding those who have spent the last few decades drudgingly keeping healthy with new opportunities for advancement.

Coronavirus skeptics aren't so much the victims of digital filter bubbles as of an outsize belief in organic food and exercise. It's no coincidence that in Germany they're led by slim doctors, alt-hippies, and a vegan chef. In my local Basel swimming pool, too, I was regularly surrounded in the locker room by well-trained sixty- to seventy-year-olds who were literally spitting in each other's faces that the pandemic was nothing at all. To them, at least, it seemed more like a fountain of youth.

SARS-CoV-2 seems to have been designed by social Darwinists on a drawing board, since it kills mainly the old, the chronically ill, and the socially weak. For people under forty-five, the virus can be more harmless than the flu; over eighty-five, it kills one in four, even in technologically advanced OECD countries. If we were to let it rage freely, it could significantly reduce the burden on pension, social, and health insurance funds. It would offer a natural incentive to keep fit and to better protect yourself against the diseases of civilization. Or to eventually become so rich that you can shield yourself from the next pandemic in your own refuge—the maximum version being a private island only people with a negative coronavirus test have access to.

In fact, such libertarian arguments play practically no

role in the criticism of drastic anti-coronavirus measures. Rather, people question whether the coronavirus is dangerous at all, whether masks even offer protection, or whether a lockdown protects more lives than it costs because of increased unemployment, bankruptcy, homelessness, depression, hypertension, and depression. The assumption that certain people might better die under certain circumstances is subject to greater stigma in our humanistic society than believing in tinfoil hats.

Even before the coronavirus, we let poor people die years earlier than rich people, and lonely people die earlier than socially integrated people. Expensive medical treatments are rationed and organ donations are granted only up to a certain age. Also, unlike in Southeast Asia, anti-coronavirus measures in Western countries have never aimed to stop the spread of the coronavirus altogether; they've been intended only to limit it to the extent that hospitals aren't overburdened. The cruel suffering of COVID-19 victims has been obscured by the focus on ad hoc target levels.[*]

With each day that the anti-coronavirus measures continue, their economic and societal harm becomes all the more apparent. The greater the number of those who have survived a coronavirus infection without suffering any harm, the greater the number of those who no longer want to be held hostage by an arbitrary "maximum value of life" will inevitably be. Isn't it enough for everyone to take a little better care of themselves? If German Chancellor Angela Merkel is really so much more rational than coronavirus skeptics, why is she still obese and not reducing her risk of getting seriously ill by fasting?

As of yet, protests against anti-coronavirus measures lack a truly broad appeal. Their protagonists seem crazy or heartless, and show once again how much a liberalism that used to dominate Western discourse has lost its power. Pirate parties have failed in their attempts to update liberalism for the internet age. Liberal parties act primarily as lobbying groups for high-income earners. Right-wing populists resort to liberalism like a piece of carrion.

The fall of the Berlin Wall, which was supposed to seal the victory of liberalism once and for all, ushered in its greatest crisis. On the one hand, capitalism no longer had to prove itself to socialism as the basically more "social" system, but could aggressively flank the enrichment of the rich by the state. On the other hand, it wasn't liberalism at all that had triumphed over socialism, but Chinese autocracy, which for decades drove rapid economic development that required neither proper civil liberties nor democracy.°

The West has responded to every major crisis since then by adapting to the Chinese model. 9/11 was requited with illegitimate detention, torture, and murder. In the wake of the global financial crisis, Western countries saved their banks from bankruptcy through huge guarantees and bailouts, similar to China's practice. Military interventions were abandoned after they devoured trillions of dollars in the war on terror, provoked devastating civil wars, and triggered a severe refugee crisis. Instead, to prevent terrorist attacks, there is a relianceon seamless electronic surveillance. Social media increasingly exercises censorship to limit misleading and hateful speech.

Conversely, it could be argued in favor of Western anti-coronavirus measures that elementary civil liberties, especially privacy, haven't been seriously challenged. Unlike in Taiwan, for example, our home quarantine isn't monitored by collecting data on our movement. Coronavirus tracing apps were introduced only after data rights concerns were largely satisfied, and even then, the apps weren't mandatory. The physical right to protest is maintained to some extent. But the real crisis may still be ahead of us. The cuts in social and economic life may leave severe lasting damage—including national bankruptcies and a new global debt crisis. New epidemics will spread, and we won't see them as an event of the century for which we can once again drop everything.

Coronavirus regulators and coronavirus skeptics share the understanding of the pandemic as an event that they want to leave behind as fast as possible—and then return to the previous world. COVID-19 is meant to have been nothing more than a statistical dent that time will quickly iron out. The only question is where one is more willing to accept the dent: in economic development or general life expectancy.[*]

Both approaches are solely about restoration, and that's why both must fail. On the one hand, our society can't simply desensitize itself to a newly identified lethal hazard. This doesn't work for epidemics any more than it does for environmental toxins or suicide attacks. Today, progress is essentially conveyed to us by the fact that we can live a long life with ever-greater security. But on the other hand, this also means that we must not jeopardize all existing security in order to combat a new danger.

Therefore, the crucial question is: How can we protect ourselves from future epidemics without ruining ourselves or initiating totalitarian surveillance? Many things are more than obvious: We can increase the capacity of intensive care units and train medical reservists who can be deployed quickly in emergencies. We can invest more in vaccine development. We can detect that we're infected early on through rapid tests, AI-based diagnostics, or sniffer dogs. We can have masks ready and wash our hands properly on a regular basis. We can live healthier and eat better—also on government initiatives.[*]

Finally, we can protect ourselves and each other by reducing our exposure to other people: travel less, shove less, meet less. At-risk groups such as older people and people with disabilities, often socially isolated anyway, are thus in danger of further loneliness. While HIV, the last epidemic to hit the West hard, required needle sharing or sex to spread the virus, intact family ties are now enough.

Initially, it appeared that the HIV outbreak would further promote discrimination against at-risk groups, especially gay people. But the opposite happened. The AIDS crisis helped stop gay people from being overlooked. Often their illness meant an involuntary outing. As a result, homosexuality was decriminalized in many countries and eventually same-sex marriages were legalized.[*] Could the COVID-19 pandemic thus also help make the general population more aware of discrimination against older people and people with disabilities? If one is already willing to pay such a huge price to let them survive COVID-19, couldn't their lives be greatly improved at a far lower cost?

For many younger people, caring for older people has already been part of their everyday lives. Due to demographic developments, nursing professions are now experiencing a boom similar to that of teaching professions in the 1970s. Many do sugaring, which is located in the gray area between dating and sex work. Others provide end-of-life care to confront themselves with their own finitude in a world largely free from mortal danger while various new organizations and event formats promote what millennial mortician, YouTuber, and bestselling author Caitlin Doughty coined a "death-positive" approach to life.

Acceptance of anti-coronavirus measures is greater among those under forty than among those over forty, and greatest among those under twenty-five. The real generational war today may be that many middle-aged people would like to continue fighting once again with their parents' generation as a "natural" war of annihilation, while younger people oppose—they're anti-anti—and seek a new generational pact.

Already sensitized to various forms of discrimination through wokeness,* it's only logical for millennials—also known as Generation Y—and the subsequent Generation Z to also take a stand against ageism. All they need is for a few older people to make their mark in terms of identity politics. It's true that there are many older people who belong to the bourgeois elite, and that their pensions and health care are increasingly being called upon for the relatively fewer and fewer younger people, but it's precisely because older people are in the majority and have also accumulated the most property that younger people, who are only at the beginning of their careers, can no longer afford to confront them and must instead try to participate in their wealth.

This dynamic doesn't have to mean that the younger

• Orcies
Acknowledge Your Own Oppression

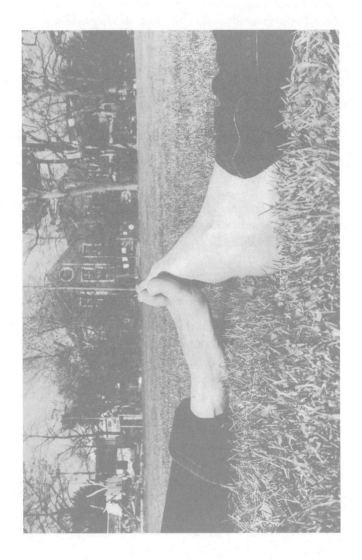

Still from my video *Safe Touch*, 2020

ones are forced into poorly paid care jobs. Older people could pay to interact socially with younger people, or the older ones could work for the younger ones cheaply, if not for free. While their own children often live far away, they can be profitably integrated into their communities by younger adults on the ground. Many younger people have anyway given up the idea of building an existence on their own or with only one life partner. They seek emotional security and fulfillment from a diverse web of relationships, and they live communally, if only because they can't afford their own apartments. It's a similar story with children: raising them alone or as a couple would be too expensive. Including older people in community care is not only an act of charity, it satisfies concrete interests: older people give advice, have free space, and money, and have time and patience for babysitting, tutoring, and cooking.

See, for example, D'Vera Cohen et al., "Financial Issues Top the List of Reasons U.S. Adults Live in Multigenerational Homes," Pew Research Center, March 24, 2022, https://www.pewresearch.org/social-trends/2022/03/24/financial-issues-top-the-list-of-reasons-u-s-adults-live-in-multigenerational-homes/.

Sweetness •
Mutual Enslavements •
Real Estate Porn •
• Orcies

In order to master the demographic crisis, it's not enough for older people to keep fit and active longer and for the retirement age to be raised. There also needs to be a new understanding of the traditional strengths and needs of older people in general—not necessarily just those of your own parents and grandparents. The notion of family and even the newer concept of the multigenerational home are often too rigid and binding to meet our changing individual needs. End-of-life care is also so popular among younger people because it lets the relationship with the older person come to an end on its own.

Since the spread of HIV, sex rates in the Western world have steadily declined—despite knowledge of safe sex. Correspondingly, the COVID-19 pandemic could also lead to a permanent decline in physical interaction with strangers, even after COVID-19 has long since lost its deadly horror for most. The experience of how dangerous it can be to hug, shake hands, or talk loudly will linger. Once sensitized, we'll also be cautious in the event of a flu—just as today HIV is only one of many sexually transmitted diseases we fear.•

Even before the coronavirus outbreak, we began to problematize unwanted touching in a similar way to how we did with sexual assault before—an issue that has been amplified since the HIV outbreak. In Generation Z, hugs are still common, but people lean far forward and are careful not to touch each other's torsos. This makes consensual and safe touching all the more important. Just as people developed an understanding of "safe(r) sex" in response to the AIDS crisis, we now have to learn and promote "safe(r) touch."•

March 2022. Before a new intergenerational solidarity could take shape, novel mRNA vaccines complicated the conflicts. While the initial challenge was to decide who should be prioritized to receive a COVID-19 vaccine—those who were particularly vulnerable due to illness or those who were particularly vulnerable to becoming ill because of their occupation (the usual decision was to give it to both in parallel)—only a few weeks later the question arose of how to get enough people vaccinated in the first place, in order to relieve hospitals and perhaps even achieve herd immunity.

Now it was young people in particular who refused to be vaccinated, considering it an intrusion into their physical integrity. For them, the risk of uncertain side effects weighed particularly heavily against the concrete benefits. Like the European governments, I was surprised by the breadth and intensity of vaccine resistance. From traveling to tropical countries, I'm accustomed to getting vaccinated mandatorily. To me, the course of a severe coronavirus disease seemed so dangerous that any vaccine complications had to pale in comparison. I underestimated the possibility that it was not only people who trivialized COVID-19 who might oppose vaccination but also others, on principle alone. And the more the state discriminated against people who didn't get vaccinated, the more opposed they became. Paradoxically, these discriminations primarily ensured that, although it was mainly the unvaccinated who became seriously ill with COVID-19, full treatment was still guaranteed for everyone.

Thus, intentionally or unintentionally, vaccine refusal became an instrument of terror. In effect, anti-vaxxers resembled a weakened form of suicide terrorists—self-harmers—who provoke the state to show its totalitarian face. Conventional terrorists do this by spreading their persecution ever wider, eventually placing much of the population under general suspicion.* Anti-vaxxers do it by prompting the state to worry about them—a prime example of advanced biopolitics.

Cases of coronavirus skeptics or anti-vaxxers heroically foregoing medical treatment for severe cases of COVID-19 were rarely noted. Thus, they literally pushed the proponents of vaccines and restrictions further and further to marginalize them. Could this usher the regression of the welfare state into communitarian barter circles—hand in hand with particularistic identity politics? In Switzerland, for instance, anti-vaxxers started the associations Graswurzle and Urig to build up local intergenerational communities to circumvent vaccine documentation requirements. Or as with mandatory seat belts and smoking bans, is it only a matter of time before everyone gets used to restrictions in the event of a pandemic?

Western countries ultimately settled on a compromise for dealing with the pandemic that was accepted by the vast majority without major grumbling: mandatory masking, (largely) yes; mandatory vaccination, (largely) no—just like the debt crisis led to the compromise of not offering debt relief but buying up the debt and pushing interest rates down to almost zero. Or, like the refugee crisis, which led to the compromise of largely closing the borders but allowing the refugees who were already there to largely remain.

The SARS-CoV-2 Omicron mutation has phased out the severity of the pandemic, and Russia's war against Ukraine has replaced the "war" against the virus.* The big question, however, remains: whether the anti-coronavirus restrictions were worth the resulting economic and psychological burdens.

The belief in conspiracy theories has increased once again, as it did after 9/11, the global financial crisis, and the refugee crisis, although the consequential problems arising from increased government debt, school failures, or private upheavals aren't even foreseeable yet—particularly since society has had no time to regenerate and is about to enter the next acute crisis with the war in Ukraine. But, in the course of time, we'll feel it more and more clearly. On the other hand, how many more people would have died from COVID-19 without the restrictions, or how many more would have suffered from long COVID, remains abstract speculation.

I'm glad that smoking is no longer allowed in restaurants today, and that seat belts are such a matter of course that my son can't imagine it any other way. But these regulations weren't introduced by hook or by crook, but in a process that took years. I've never had a bad experience with my many vaccinations, but I also understand people who want to wait a few years before taking a novel agent. And I can see how much damage has been done by zealously discrediting them, discriminating against them, or threatening them with mandatory vaccination.

The COVID-19 pandemic is a unique memento mori: not since World War II has such a large percentage of the Western population concretely feared for their lives or the lives of their loved ones. This experience of collective fear can help us determine what really matters to us—both privately and to our society as a whole. But with it inevitably comes new conflicts that we must learn to endure.

The debt crisis and the refugee crisis required united European action. Considering the pandemic in retrospect, the question remains: Wouldn't temporary separation have been the better solution? Just as there used to be smoking and nonsmoking compartments, couldn't we have had compartments for people with and without masks, or with and without vaccination? Office areas with and without masks? Restaurants, hospitals, and health insurance with and without vaccination? Special school classes for children who belong to at-risk groups?

Instead of spending enormous amounts of resources poorly covering up hardening social conflicts, this schismogenesis could also be seen as an opportunity to further advance social differentiation—an essential feature of a modern society. Now, not only according to a specialization in the field of work— what systems theory calls "functional differentiation"—but according to personal preferences. Liberal bourgeois society strives to contain personal preferences as a private matter (or to morally defame them), but in a truly individualistic— monadic—society, they also determine our public life.*

This doesn't mean that we must settle on these preferences once and for all—as is expected in a bourgeois society for major decisions such as marriage, a career, or purchasing a home.* Much like teenagers sort themselves into tribe-like youth cultures according to their preferences and perspectives, which can change from one day to the next,* we can also sort ourselves into different coping tribes in the face of extraordinary risks. What, as discussed in the first part of this text, leads to a new intergenerational solidarity for some is for others a test of their own physical and mental condition, in which the social element consists mainly of competing against each other or together, against others. The coping tribes can dissolve as soon as the crisis is over, they can switch to reserve status, or they can understand the crisis as a prelude to also shaping life thereafter.

• Middle-Class Warriors
Wanderers

• Society of Games •
Sweetness •

## Comic Purgatory
2020

Current Western politics follows the paradigm of the comic strip, which, at the end of each episode, undoes all its developments in no time, nourishing the dream of eternal life and return. Unwilling to risk our lives, we need the threat of a catastrophe to gain determination and seek the help of some self-proclaimed superhero. To fully enter the Monadic Age, we must accept and celebrate death as our ultimate joker. This is where our story retroactively begins.

The shortest story is a picture, or a sentence long. It took humans many thousands of years, until the development of writing, to bring both together. It needed the competition of cinema, using the sequence of several images (a strip) to make the characters move in hilarious ways that would be impossible in real life—even children (like Richard F. Outcault's *The Yellow Kid*, 1895) or animals (like George Herriman's *Krazy Kat*, 1913). These characters would defy gravity, accelerate to the speed of light, and be destroyed and completely restored instantly.

One could have called these strips "fantasticals" or "supernaturals," but as the first successful versions in newspapers worked as distractions, the cartoons were called "comics." This name stuck to the strips, even when they evolved into movies and extended to stories about grim superheroes. In the Western world, it took almost a century for more serious strips to become their own genre: the graphic novel.

This was because of another advantage drawn characters had over real actors: they weren't subject to life's greatest tragedy, aging then dying. A comic strip could turn into a never-ending series, and its characters could acquire commercial value far exceeding that of famous actors. A saga about gods and empires could also go on forever, but it's way easier when the characters and their settings simply don't change: in each episode of a typical comic series, the protagonists go through tremendous adventures, only to end up in exactly the same circumstances in which they began. They keep the same age, character, skills, friends, family, belongings, and hardly remember anything that happened in the previous episodes. No prior knowledge is necessary; new audiences and illustrators can join the series at any point. Furthermore, comic series offer comfort with the certainty that no matter whatever great, bad, or bizarre thing happens, in the end it won't have any consequences. Life is like a play that after a fixed period of time is set back to zero.* When Albert Camus famously declared in 1942 that "one has to imagine Sisyphus as happy," Albert Camus, *Le mythe de Sisyphe* [The myth of Sisyphus] (Paris: Gallimard, 1942). he likely thought of him as a cartoon character.

Comics are particularly appealing to small children. Their episodic memory is still evolving and when they actively take in the world, they tend to do it through the harmless form of playing. To learn as fast as they do, they avoid and are kept safe from harsh consequences. But even for small children, watching comic series is regarded as escapist or regressive. The characters are released from the pressure to learn and take responsibility; they're stuck, though happier not knowing. Tales come with a lesson, and when playing, you're urged to constantly make and test your own decisions, while in comic series, things happen so fast and outrageously that the series doesn't believe itself. At the end of each episode, all its developments are undone in no time, nourishing the dream of eternal life and return.

Overcoming finiteness in general and mortality in particular has been regarded as the ultimate, unfulfillable human ambition. Religions claim immortality as what defines gods and offers humans passage to their realm in the afterlife. Wars

George Herriman, *Krazy Kat*, 1913–41

have been fought, discoveries have been made, artifacts have been produced to at least gain memetic immortality.\* But soon we might reach a point in technological progress where we or our successors could enter a state of personal immortality and overall contingency. Ultimate truth and happiness might take a bit longer or be—as in comics—impossible to reach.

Already today many people expect themselves, their family, and their friends to live eighty or ninety pretty healthy years. Early death or being infirm are regarded as avoidable accidents. Aging is delayed or compensated with a large variety of tools and techniques. Risks are cushioned by a multitude of state securities and private insurances. Our subsequent unwillingness to risk our life and end up as a martyr has earned us the label post-heroic. We don't even realize why personal sacrifice would be needed.\*

Since humans started to gain control over their life expectancy, they also started to move dumping grounds, cemeteries, slums, prisons, and later, factories, power plants, and server farms outside the city, while sewage and cables went under the earth. Due to recursive technological progress, the world is changing faster and faster, yet people are more and more shielded from the immediate effects and insights of this transformation. In planes and high velocity trains, we're under the impression that we're hardly moving. The intelligent gadgets that guide, entertain, and surveil us are handy and cute. The more our society is driven by mechanisms and machinery that are far too complex for us to understand or to interfere with, the more we resemble idle comic characters.

In a largely pretechnological, aristocratic society there are the few who rule and the masses who obey. In a mechanized, bourgeois society there are the few who create or accumulate, and there are the masses who are stuffy and square.\* In an automatized, comic society there are the few who script the next episode, and there are the masses who try not to lose their part. We no longer legitimize ourselves through authority or merits but through our ability to entertain.

When media theorist Neil Postman famously warned in 1984 that we "amuse ourselves to death," Neil Postman, first quoted at a talk at the Frankfurt Book Fair in 1984, then in his book *Amusing Ourselves to Death: Public Discourse in the Age of Show Business* (New York: Viking Penguin, 1985). he was observing the transition from a bourgeois to a comic society. Back then the entertainment industry was muting the masses, who were still stuffy and square. In a fully evolved comic society, we would rather amuse each other to stay alive, like jesters in a court of nothing but jesters.

An aristocratic society disposes of limited wealth that can be fought for. A bourgeois society disposes of potentially unlimited wealth that can be generated through intelligence and labor. In a comic society, all basic needs are already fulfilled. At the same time, certain parameters of wealth, like space• and natural resources,• are shrinking. Wealth has to be less achieved and multiplied than protected against intrinsic and extrinsic dangers. Not only do we not risk our lives, we only fight not to lose them. We would risk too much in following teleological master plans. It's not that, as Giorgio Agamben claims, "our society no longer believes in anything but bare life," Giorgio Agamben, "Clarifications," trans. Adam Kotsko, March 17, 2020, https://itself.blog/2020/03/17/giorgio-agamben-clarifi cations/. but that we're so spoiled that only a threat to our bare lives would make us risk any deliberate, fundamental change. We need our possible end as an ecosphere (Fridays for Future), a species (Extinction Rebellion), a subspecies (White genocide theory), a culture (war on terror), a nation (Make America Great Again), or as individual bodies (war on the virus) in order to gain determination.

The collective realization of an existential threat is accompanied by the appreciation of self-proclaimed lifesavers. It has always been a way to power: to wait for or to provoke a major crisis to then install oneself as the savior. But while the saviors of the Aristocratic Age sought divine legitimation and those of the Bourgeois Age ideological legitimation, the saviors of the Comic Age are chosen for their sense of urgency.

• Real Estate Porn
• Body with More Organs

Even when the masses feel safe, they're already sniffing out the next catastrophe. Until it becomes impossible to overlook the disaster, they must persist as ridiculed sidekicks, then rise up as acclaimed superheroes.°

The mission of superheroes is to turn back time, but they lack a coherent conservative agenda. Our world is in constant, accelerated change, and to be able to undo one major aberration comes with indifference about the rest. It's not that superheroes aren't guided by ideologically colored mindsets—they might even regard themselves as prophets. But they have to be innocent outsiders in the political realm and not be affiliated with any established party. Acknowledging them as political figures comes as a surprise: the reality TV villain, the bipolar rapper, the innocent Asperger's child, the nerdy scientist, the provincial doctor, or maybe an animal, a river, an algorithm. Note, 2024: Volodymyr Zelensky, a comedic actor who became the Ukrainian president and heroically braced himself against the Russian invasion in 2022, makes a perfect addition to this list. Even more in times of crisis, we don't want to get bored.

The mission of superheroes is to put the world back in order—that is, to make the episode end where it started. But in real life we don't know about such an exact moment in time: what would actually be an acceptable amount of carbon emissions, pollution, immigrants, humans, or infections that we have to get back to? The mission of the superhero remains a bit random and vague, and it ends with people losing interest or getting fed up rather than with clear success. Triggering a sense of urgency is one thing, but actually turning the whole world upside down in no time would create a gigantic mess, while turning it upside down in a sustainable way is both lame and dangerous—even more so when all that's at stake is getting back to a previous, already not ideal condition. The superhero turns into a Sisyphus who fails to push the stone up the hill in the first place.

From reality TV, US President Donald Trump learned that to keep punch and drive as a superhero, he had to bring each episode to a quick end. Not having solved a case properly creates reliable material for new trouble, that is, the opportunity to start a new episode and forget about the previous one. Even his enemies couldn't help it—everybody was part of his show. Climate activist Greta Thunberg acted as his exact inversion: young versus old; female versus male; small versus tall; innocent versus guilty; true versus fake; steady versus flighty; serious versus clownish. Trump was the Joker, and she wasn't Batwoman but the Anti-Joker.

In the aristocratic saga and the bourgeois bildungsroman, you have to keep in mind the whole narrative to fully grasp them. A cartoon practices tactical amnesia. A saga or bildungsroman tries to make you believe in its plausibility, however unlikely it might appear. A comic is deliberately unbelievable. The negation of the glory of the saga is tragedy; the negation of the rationality of the bildungsroman is absurdity. Both can be perceived for the sake of nihilism or cathartic edification. A comic accumulates an enormous number of tragic and absurd moments, only to zero them out. In real life, the more superheroes overstretch what is usually acceptable behavior and the more they bullshit or dramatize, the more they reassure people of the belief that in the end, everything will stay the same.*

The fact that the comic has become the leading social paradigm doesn't mean that people are done with progress. Quantitatively speaking, the saga and the bildungsroman are still the dominant cultural narratives—including interactive formats like role-plays or video games. But sagas and bildungsromane are too stringent and clear (even in being erratic and mysterious) to feel real. The moment our life fulfills the criteria of being a remarkable story, we're under the impression that it rather complies with a novel, film, or game.

Sagas and bildungsromane deliver a definite scenario of what happens. This isn't how we perceive life. We can interpret our past in ever-new ways, and when it comes to the future, the facts aren't a given. Stories help us to understand how things might develop or might have developed over a period of time, but we never know for sure. Games allow us to choose between different scenarios, but only within certain fixed parameters. Our lives and societies are too complex to be contained in such vessels.

Even in fiction, a good story can't be completely planned. You have to let it go and adapt. This is even more so in real life: you have to allow your story to be freed from you. You have to let it write itself. When you realize that you yourself don't fit into it anymore, you have to give up on it and switch to another.[•] And when there is no more satisfiable story left for you, then it's time to die. In this case, it's advisable to have one, or several, grand finales in petto.

Our post-heroic aversion to risk depends on our ignoring the fact that we'll die, and that we can decide ourselves when and how. The state offers palliative care, in some countries even euthanasia, and our heirs profit from life insurance. But when we choose to die—not in the immediate process of dying—we're left on our own. More and more, countries are offering legal procedures for divorce, deselection, and abortion, but they all hesitate to offer general assisted dying—often even declaring it illegal.[•] Life insurance loses its validity in the case of suicide.

The plea to end up being spoiled by the fake reality of a never-ending comic series and to again take more risks amounts to nothing. There is no voluntary way back to less safety. Rather, we have to include our deaths in our preparations. As we instinctively resist dying, we have to trick ourselves with options for not just a pain-free but ecstatic euthanasia. Our suicide could be framed by outlandish festivities before and after our death. Our heirs could profit from a special life insurance that's only issued if we kill ourselves. Should we lack the financial means, we could reach mutual agreements to service each other.

The possibility to kill ourselves is our ultimate freedom—accessible even under the most devastating circumstances. Death is the joker that's always at hand. We only have one, but if we don't use it, we'll eventually lose it to a "natural" death that medical progress might turn into a long-lasting procedure. Waiting until all treatment eventually fails is hardly affordable and little fun. Even if we manage to stop aging, the fear that we would eventually die would torment us. To choose death is a modern necessity. It's only a matter of when and how.

Sagas and bildungsromane describe how people succeed or fail in unfolding their potentials, while comics describe how they succeed or fail in sustaining their current state. But our own story always ends with our death. The one image or sentence that an intelligent life evolves from is how we would like to die—not as a pious hope but as a substantial undertaking. From there, we can imagine our future backward. Everything that we do has to lead us toward that end and be better than dying already now—for us, society, and the environment. This retroactive autofiction could be called *obit*—originally the Latin word for perished, as in "obituary."

Existentialist philosophers already tried to establish the inescapability of death as the absolute zero from where we're able to retroactively acknowledge our personal potentials and seek self-fulfillment. After secularization pushed back the authority of God, they wanted each of us to judge our own life from its hypothetical end. But as long as we regard death as fate, we're forced to fear it like a predator and see it degrade our plans and ambitions. Only when we plan and time our death will our engagement with it expand our actual freedom.

To follow the inverse storyline and leave comic purgatory, we have to drill ourselves to make dying part of our daily lives. Things have already started to change with many young people engaging in voluntary end-of-life care.[*] In a next step, we have to also assist with voluntary euthanasia. People who are dying or committing suicide could invite the public, as artist Gregor Schneider envisioned for his "Death Room." Gregor Schneider's exhibition "Sterberaum" was on view November 19, 2011–January 28, 2012, at Kunstraum Innsbruck. The setting could be a minimalist, sober white cube—or a seductive circus of death.

# V. INDEPENDENCE, FINALLY

The monadic state yields precedence to autarchy, not enforced cohesion.

The international ban on the proliferation of nuclear weapons doesn't serve world peace, but rather the ruthless rule of a nuclear oligarchy. Countries that voluntarily renounced their nuclear weapons or weapon programs have been repeatedly betrayed. Nonaggressive, nonexploitive (i.e., monadic) democracies need nukes to plausibly defend themselves.

Whatever evil Russia comes up with in the war against Ukraine, you can be pretty sure that the US and its allies have already been there. Russia invading a whole country on a flimsy pretext? Think of Iraq. Attacking, abducting, and torturing the innocent? Think of the war on terror. Russian president Putin's outrageous threat, on the fourth day of the invasion, to eventually use nuclear weapons? A few years earlier, in 2017, US president Donald Trump threatened that North Korea would "be met with fire and fury like the world has never seen." Donald Trump, "Trump: NKorea Will Be Met with 'Fire and Fury,'" Associated Press, August 8, 2017, https://www.youtube.com/watch?v=8p1JlgTuKQk.

You probably don't even remember the latter incident. For one thing, because Trump wasn't taken very seriously as he echoed similar threats uttered by the North Korean government on various occasions. For another thing, because Trump was responding to an incident that habitually causes the US to threaten or take harsh action: advances in other countries' arsenal of weapons of mass destruction—in particular, nukes.

We're so used to these threats and sanctions, accompanied by the zealous scrutiny of the International Atomic Energy Agency (IAEA), that we take it for granted that the proliferation of nuclear weapons is one of the worst things that can happen: nukes are horrendous, so the more countries that have them, the worse it is.

In fact, this makes sense from the perspective of the nine countries that already have nukes. It's reasonable that this nuke oligarchy doesn't want to give up its privileged power. So far, no country with nukes has ever been seriously attacked on its own territory. This makes Putin's threats to attack NATO just as vain as Kim Jong-un's threats to attack the US or Trump's threats to attack North Korea (particularly because they both have families). The internationally disputed regime of a small state like Israel or a poor one like North Korea can be sustained—thanks to their nukes. India and Pakistan didn't engage in a proper war over Kashmir—thanks to their nukes.

As long as missile defenses can be bypassed, nukes are the best national safeguard. Countries without offensive ambitions could give up on most of their conventional weapons and instead focus on the possession of a critical number of nukes and their adequate protection.

Opponents of nuclear proliferation argue that the more countries there are that have nukes, the more likely it is that a nuke will fall into the hands of terrorists or lunatics. It would be safer if only a few countries had nukes and guaranteed their allies that they would retaliate against any nuclear attack.

But what is the price of such a guarantee and how likely is it to be carried out? Moreover, a guarantee to retaliate against any nuclear attack on your allies doesn't protect them from conventional attacks. In the current geopolitical situation, if Russia were to attack Ukraine with nukes, the US would retaliate. But if Ukraine had its own nukes, it wouldn't have been invaded in the first place.

It was a fateful combination of economic dependence and political naivety that after the collapse of the Soviet

Union led three of its former republics—Belarus, Kazakhstan, and Ukraine—to give up the nukes stationed on their territory and join the Nuclear Non-Proliferation Treaty. In return, the nuclear powers Russia, Britain, and the US accepted their independence and sovereignty within existing borders and assured them they wouldn't use military force or economic sanctions against them in the 1994 Budapest Memorandum on Security Assurances.

Twenty years later, this agreement has proved largely ineffective. In 2013, the US imposed rigid economic sanctions on Belarus to retaliate against human rights violations. To stay in power, Belarus's dictator Alexander Lukashenko had to seek further protection from Russia. Since the overthrow of Ukraine's pro-Russian government in 2014, Russia has provided military support to pro-Russian Ukrainian separatists, invaded and annexed Crimea, and, finally, invaded Ukraine as a whole. To fight back, Ukraine needed the support of the US and its European allies. A spiral of sanctions and the damage caused by the war pushed the world into an economic crisis (shortages, inflation) that's likely to cost far more lives than the war itself. All of this could have been prevented if the US and Britain would have rearmed Ukraine with nukes as soon as Russia broke the Budapest Memorandum. It wouldn't have been necessary to make Ukraine a NATO member.

A liberal concern is that once a dictator gets a hold of nukes it's hard to get them out of power. True. For a dictator, giving up on nukes can be suicidal. In an effort to appease the Western world, Libya eliminated all its programs and weapons of mass destruction in 2003. In 2011, the EU and the US backed a rebellion against Libyan leader Muammar Qaddafi; NATO provided air support, bombing both military targets and Qaddafi's family. But neither Libya nor any of the other countries that were invaded and destabilized by the West became functioning democracies. Rather, these endeavors backfired, destabilizing the West as well, with fundamentalist terrorism and millions of refugees. Furthermore, the means to destabilize these regimes undermined the West's own democracies.[*]

No democracy is a given and the Western world would do better to give up its paternalistic urges against nondemocratic states and focus on stabilizing existing democracies by equipping them with their own nukes. The prospect of more military security for less money might motivate countries to become democracies in the first place.

Of course, any decision about which state counts as a democracy must be arbitrary. Any democracy can fail. But as we've seen recently with the US, this is also true of existing nuke democracies. Of course, nukes could be sold or stolen. But although pounds of weapons-grade uranium and plutonium have disappeared, so far there is no evidence that a functioning nuclear bomb has ever been built without a state having commissioned it. So far, the nuclear bomb hasn't been privatized. The IAEA could monitor safety measures to ensure that nukes aren't displaced.

Today, the IAEA is meant to prevent the proliferation of nukes while fostering the civil use of nuclear energy. But as we can see with the war of Russia against Ukraine, even a nuclear power plant can be used as a weapon—by the enemy. Russia is more likely to attack a Ukrainian power plant and blame the Ukrainians for it than to drop a nuclear bomb. Any country with nuclear power plants needs nukes to protect them properly. The arduous divide between civilian and military use of nuclear power doesn't prevent wars, it causes them. The IAEA doesn't serve peace, but rather imperialist power. Nuclear proliferation (not nuclear oligarchy) is the path to more peace and democracy.

When I first made this argument in 2006, See my essay "Democratic Bomb," in *Solution 1–10: Umbauland* (Berlin: Sternberg Press, 2008), translated from *Umbauland—Zehn deutsche Visionen* [Reconstruction country—Ten German visions] (Frankfurt am Main: Suhrkamp Verlag, 2006). I was ridiculed and accused of being tempted by totalitarianism. Still today, the only significant public intellectual to argue in favor of nuclear proliferation is the neoreactionary philosopher Nick Land. He dreams of a world in which the US-led liberal order is dismantled and replaced by numerous autonomous ministates operating as corporations. After the Russian invasion of Ukraine, he tweeted: "Among all the nuclear doom talk, it's important to remember that the root cause of the 2022 Russo-Ukraine war was denuclearization." Nick Land (@Outsideness), Twitter, March 1, 2022, 1:22 p.m., https://twitter.com/Outsideness/status/1498649841974800386. A few minutes later, he added: "... WMD are the foundations of political independence. A successfully fragmented future will require even more of them."* Land, March 1, 2022, 1:25 p.m., https://twitter.com/Outsideness/status/1498650586954481666. And a few days after that: "Hang onto your nukes as if your independence depends upon them." Land, March 4, 2022, 4:40 a.m., https://twitter.com/Outsideness/status/1499605578641207299.

Land reverses the usual disdain of advocates of a world state against nukes, as such a state would have no more use for such weapons. But how could a world state ever be established? The five largest nuclear powers, and the only ones legitimized as such by the non-proliferation treaty, are also the five permanent members of the UN Security Council, with the power to veto any resolution passed by the UN. They're decisive in preventing the creation of a democratic world capable of granting everyone some basic rights.

To disempower the nuke oligarchy, nukes have to be distributed more equally. Only then can the world get rid of all nuclear technology whatsoever and erect a consensually elected world government. For this to happen, you could even argue in favor of unconditionally giving nukes to all states. In "Forewarning," his introduction to the 1985 science-fiction anthology *Beyond Armageddon*, Walter M. Miller Jr. proposes that the US opt out of the Nuclear Non-Proliferation Treaty and give each UN member a small nuke. Only when every "rogue state" will have achieved the status of a nuclear power would the established nuclear powers advocate a global renunciation of atomic weapons.

Liberalism tried to make the world believe that international trade would make wars obsolete. The more interconnected the world would become, the more self-destructive it would be to wage war. But this is only true if what each party has to offer is unique and essential. The Western hegemony allowed its countries to subjugate poorer countries at will. With the return of China as a—if not the—superpower, major suppliers of vital natural resources are the only countries that enjoy protection because of their economic importance. Europe is out.*

This makes Switzerland an excellent candidate for where to start with nuclear proliferation under democratic terms. Its nuclear weapons program only came to a proper halt with the end of the Cold War. Even if it were to equip itself with nukes targeting Russia and the US (which already have that power over Europe), it would be difficult to accuse neutral, prosperous, direct-democracy Switzerland of an undemocratic conspiracy or secret attack plans. There is a good chance that Switzerland would be expelled from the UN. But it was doing well before it joined the UN just twenty years ago. A democratic world state based on the UN is inconceivable anyway; it must be built independently of and in opposition to the UN.

# Rise and Fall of Reich Europa
2022

Due to Germany's political and economic dominance, the EU has been derided as the "Fourth Reich." What has been largely overlooked is that European unification was a Nazi project from the very beginning, and that the expansion and decline of the EU strikingly resemble those of the Third Reich. For Europe to survive, it will have to abandon its imperialist ambitions and transform into a cluster of collaborative, but independently functioning, nuclear-armed monadic states.

In the final days of World War II, the Nazis still hoped the US would join forces with them against the Soviet Union. The Nazis considered themselves not as bad for the Americans as the Bolsheviks. Once the Third Reich had officially lost the war in 1945, a variation on this theme actually happened: while West Germany was formally democratized, most Nazis were pardoned and many remained in power—politicians, lawyers, industrialists, journalists. In the following years, West Germany experienced enormous growth, dubbed *Wirtschafts-wunder* (economic wonder) to hide the fact that the progress was largely due to American aid—on top of not having to pay adequate reparations.

A key figure in West Germany's rapid economic reco-very was the banker Hermann Josef Abs. He had worked in London, Paris, and Amsterdam before Aryanization allowed him to become a partner in a German bank in 1935. Three years later, he became a member of the managing board of the huge

Deutsche Bank. Abs didn't join the Nazi Party, but as head of Deutsche Bank's foreign department, he was responsible for the takeover of several previously Jewish-owned banks and provided loans for the building of the largest Nazi concentration camp in Auschwitz. He also became a board member of IG Farben, a huge German chemical and pharmaceutical conglomerate that profited from forced labor in the concentration camps. After World War II, Abs gained the trust of the British occupiers. When West Germany was founded in 1949, he became head of the Kreditanstalt für Wiederaufbau (KfW), a state institution that used US aid to administer loans to the German industrial sector. In West Germany's early days, these government loans provided a substantial chunk of the available economic liquidity. Abs's right-hand man was Stefan Martini, a former member of the SS, whom he already knew during the Third Reich from his work as head of the Credit Department in the Ministry of Economics.

When Deutsche Bank was refounded in 1957, Abs became a member of its board and retained his position at the KfW, which was now rededicated to issuing guaranteed loans for development projects in non-Western countries. This gave Abs leverage for the international business of Deutsche Bank—soon to be Germany's largest bank. Often, Deutsche Bank also managed the portfolios of its clients. This allowed Abs to become a member of up to thirty company boards, in up to twenty cases as the chairman.

Abs was friends with the first West German chancellor, Konrad Adenauer, and helped him conduct important international negotiations. Adenauer offered Abs the post of foreign minister, but Abs declined. As the de facto super chairman of what was later called "Deutschland AG" (Germany PLC)—a loose conglomerate of manyfold intertwined banks, insurance companies, and industrial enterprises—Abs's power superseded that of the prime minister. Most of these companies had already existed during the Third Reich and had profited from its war economy. Although the Nazis had been overthrown, former affiliations with them still ensured access to the business elite—not so different from how the Chinese economy works today. One-party capitalism is highly susceptible to corruption but can also be highly effective if its actors share the ethos of quickly making the country number one again.

The US framed the Cold War between capitalism and socialism as the rivalry between liberal democracies and totalitarian dictatorships, when in fact the US preferred its allies to be stable, bribable autocracies—West Germany, officially the model student in democracy building, was no exception.

Soon West Germany became a major force in strengthening political ties within capitalist Western Europe. As socialist countries formed a homogeneous bloc dominated by the Soviet Union, capitalist countries didn't want to be left behind and founded the European Economic Community(EEC) in 1958, which was transformed into the European Union(EU) in 1993. Although there has been a directly elected European Parliament since 1979, important decisions have to be agreed on by all national governments. The decision-making process, with all its interlocking deals, is highly untransparent.

Once again, Abs played a key role in initiating European unification. As early as 1946, when West Germany didn't yet exist as an independent state, he joined the European League for Economic Cooperation, an intellectual pressure group set up to promote a common market and monetary integration. Another key figure in European unification was Walter Hallstein, who cofounded the European Coal and Steel Community, predecessor of the EEC, and became the first president of the EEC, serving for ten years. Like Abs, Hallstein excelled as not having been a member of the Nazi Party. However, he had been dean of a law faculty during the Third Reich and had publicly applauded the Nuremberg Laws, which began the systematic persecution of Jews and other racial minorities. In the same year, 1935, Hallstein began a voluntary military career on the side.

Why was Germany so eager to be embedded in a supernation? A supernation to which it became by far the biggest net contributor? Germany was obviously trying to bribe its neighbors into opening up their markets and accepting Germany's renewed economic strength. But this common perception greatly underestimates Germany's postwar ambitions. When Germany had started World War I in 1914, it "only" wanted to be the most powerful country in Europe. When it started World War II in 1939, it wanted to rule at least the whole of Europe. This time, the disaster and defeat had been so gigantic that even in its failure Germany had proved to be a highly exceptional nation. There was no way of going back to normal and becoming just another mediocre state struggling to defend some sovereignty within global capitalism.

No, Germany had found a way to finally conquer all of Europe and more: it poured itself into Europe. "EU" was another word for an enlarged Germany, and giving out sweets was how Germany, as the core, effectively controlled it. This promised to be a much cheaper and much more sustainable strategy than the use of military force—even more so because most of the German money ended up back in German pockets: tariffs protected the EU from foreign products, and subsidies kept the other EU countries lame. Already during the Third Reich, Germany dominated conquered countries economically. Not only did Germany plunder them, it also gained privileged access to their markets. German companies were feeding the war machine and operating across Europe without barriers. The EU was designed to restore this dominance.

But why were other Western European countries so eager to merge with their former nemesis? It wasn't just the fear of the Soviet Union as the new Eurasian superpower or the paternalistic prompting of the US as the new Atlantic superpower. Different from after World World I, many Western European nations had to cope with enormous colonial losses. European unification was meant to compensate for and distract from an ongoing series of major defeats. Apart from Luxembourg, a microstate, and Germany, which had lost its colonies in World War I, all the founding members of the EEC were dwindling colonial powers. The Netherlands had just lost Indonesia; Italy had just lost Libya, Eritrea, and Somalia; Belgium was about to lose Congo; and France had just lost Indochina (Laos, Vietnam, and Cambodia), Syria (including Lebanon), Morocco, and Tunisia. In addition, France was about to lose a brutal war against the independence movement in Algeria—a defeat that would pave the way for the loss of all of its major African colonies: Senegal, Madagascar, Niger, Burkina Faso, Togo, Ivory Coast, Chad, Guinea, Cameroon, Djibouti, Gabon, Mali, Benin, Republic of Congo, and the Central African Republic. When Britain joined the EEC in 1973, in the previous decade alone it had lost Singapore, Malaysia, Nigeria, Botswana, Bahrain, Cyprus, Fiji, Gambia, Ghana, Jamaica, Kenya, Kuwait, Maldives, Qatar, the Emirates, Trinidad and Tobago, and Uganda—after having already lost India (including Pakistan and Bangladesh), Israel, Jordan, Oman, Myanmar, and Sri Lanka right after World War II. All the overseas territories that remained with the EU were smaller islands. The exceptions were Denmark, which still had Greenland (but Greenland was largely autonomous and left the EU in 1985), and some former French and Belgian colonies in sub-Saharan Africa that informally stayed under the substantial economic, political, military, and cultural control of France—commonly labeled Françafrique—without coming anywhere close to fulfilling the criteria for EU membership.

As a late nation, having been founded as the German Empire only in 1871, Germany was also a late colonial power. Since the loss of its last colonies with the Treaty of Versailles in 1919, it focused even more on its expansion within Europe. The full extent of this ambition became apparent with the end of the Cold War. West Germany didn't stop after annexing socialist East Germany by bribing the EU, Russia, and the East Germans. And the EU, after having expanded to cover pretty much the whole of Western Europe, now moved eastward.

Germany had lost both previous world wars in a Napoleonic attempt to conquer Moscow. This time, it refrained from invading Russia, but established a cordial friendship. German chancellors Helmut Kohl and Gerhard Schröder became best buddies with Russian presidents Boris Yeltsin and Vladimir Putin. The Soviet Union had fallen to pieces and there were more than enough countries to conquer, as a start. The Nazis' eastern El Dorado, "Gotenland" Crimea, was again within reach. Meanwhile, Russia was good for cheap fossil fuels and as a sales market for consumer goods. Highly klepto-cratic, Russia sort of colonized itself.

The EU's eastward expansion didn't provoke too much of a public debate. It was too tempting to also manifest the victory over communism in territorial terms. Moreover, the enlargement of the EU appeared to be the perfect means to curb the power of a reunified Germany. And indeed, Germany began to seriously struggle. In order to operate more dynami-cally on the global market—not just the Eastern bloc, as China was also opening up economically—its companies broke away from "Deutschland AG" and became vulnerable to speculative takeovers. Investment in East German infrastructure was huge. Cheap labor from Eastern Europe became a serious compet-itor and unemployment soared. In addition, Germany natural-ized more than two million Russians of German origin. Taxes rose and wages stagnated. As in World War II, Germany found itself at war with the whole world once the first phase of an unchallenged westward expansion was over.

Also similar to the Second World War, Germany re-sponded to the growing challenges by pushing for the even faster growth of the Reich. After the end of the Cold War, the EU grew from twelve states in the early 1990s to twenty-eight in 2013. In 2004 alone, it expanded by ten countries. The next enlargements were even supposed to include Islamic countries such as Albania, Bosnia, Kosovo, and Turkey. Where would the EU eventually end? Could African and Asian countries be per se excluded? Would the continued growth of the EU culminate in a world government?

The particular strength of the EU was to present itself as both more pragmatic and more idealistic than the current sole superpower, the US. The EU expanded peacefully and was reserved for democratic countries that respected human rights, while at the same time cultivating close economic ties with autocratic non-US allies such as China, Iraq, Iran, Syria, and Libya. While continuing its arms exports on a massive scale, the EU slimmed down its own military forces. Germany was at the forefront of this development, abandoning conscription and dismantling even purely defensive structures such as sirens and bunkers. The EU neither wanted to be perceived as a serious threat nor did it fear strong opponents.

The EU's carelessness became increasingly problematic as it expanded deeper and deeper into the territories of the former Soviet Union, while at the same time, thanks to the world economy's growing appetite for fossil fuels, Russia regained its ambitions as a military superpower. NATO's military intervention in the civil war in Kosovo in 1999 was the first serious provocation of Russian interests. In 2008, Russia struck back in Georgia, and in 2014, in Ukraine, securing its influence over regions with a majority of people of Russian origin. Russia didn't have a third of the EU's population or a fifth of its GDP, but it did have a powerful army and the willingness to use it. Meanwhile, the US was scaling back its military engagements worldwide, still suffering from the high costs of its supposedly anti-terrorist invasions of Afghanistan and Iraq. With his campaign to "Make America Great Again," US president Donald Trump, elected in 2016, openly questioned the existence of the EU. Much like Germany in 1941, the EU now found itself in a simmering war with both Russia and the US.

On top of this, the EU had been hit by a severe debt crisis less than a decade earlier—the result of the introduction of a common currency, the euro. Germany had given up on its own strong currency, the deutsche mark, and leveraged its reputation as a reliable creditor to grant cheap credits to the other states of the eurozone, thereby boosting German exports. A policy that Abs had introduced on the level of guaranteed credits for individual companies was expanded in a way that resembled the neoliberal US policy of easing private credit to stimulate consumption and real estate investment. The

2008 collapse of the US credit bubble, often financed with European money, then triggered the collapse of the European credit bubble.

Germany was unwilling to accept any cuts in euro debt and demanded the same austerity measures from the affected countries that it had suffered over the previous decade. Being part of the EU wasn't that attractive anymore. Parts of the Greek population sank into harsh poverty, and the UK, which had never been fully integrated into the EU, considered leaving what its yellow press polemically called the "Fourth Reich" (too presumptuous to see that this Reich had already been in existence for more than fifty years). Anti-EU populists were backed by Russia. Turkey had already been asking to join the EEC as early as 1959. But now its economy was booming to such an extent that it lost interest in proving to the EU that it was secular and democratic enough.

The early 2010s marked the beginning of the Arab Spring, a series of uprisings in many Arab countries against corruption and dictatorship and for economic and democratic reform. While the US's enormous efforts to transform Afghanistan and Iraq into stable democracies were faltering, the Arab Spring was a series of dynamic grassroots movements that operated both in physical space and on new social media. The EU saw its chance to intervene much less and achieve more: a wave of future EU members—back for good with their former colonizers. Hopes for an easy victory resembled those of the Nazis when they invaded North Africa and, thanks to a shared hatred of Jews, expected the population to welcome them as liberators. In Libya, England and France bombed government forces. The prospect of similar support triggered a civil war in Syria.

The years passed, and despite sporadic Western—again, mainly US—military inventions, no Arab country came closer to democracy, but just the opposite. Dictators became even more brutal and civil wars even more gruesome. Syria became a particular hotspot, with EU neighbors Turkey and Russia intervening. Syria also became the base for a new terrorist organization, the Islamic State, which attacked a number of European cities.* After dreadful years of civil war, hundreds of thousands of Syrian refugees poured into the EU, mainly through a permissive Turkey, followed by millions of refugees from all the Arab countries that the US and the EU had been destabilizing since 9/11 and the Arab Spring.

West Germany had a strong tradition of welcoming foreigners since the end of World War II: first twelve million refugees from parts of Germany that had been annexed by Poland and the Soviet Union, then millions of *Gastarbeiter* (guest workers) from southern Europe and Turkey in the 1960s and 1970s, then millions of East Germans and Russian Germans. It had only been during periods of economic stagnation after the 1973 oil crisis and after reunification in the 1990s that the welcoming policy had come to a halt.

When German Chancellor Angela Merkel allowed a large number of Middle Eastern refugees to come to Germany, many Germans applauded her, seeing it as a chance to shake off Germany's image as Europe's grim austerity master. Germany's economy was strong enough to easily absorb several hundred thousand foreigners a year, and could only get stronger.*

With a birthrate of no more than 1.6 children per woman, the EU didn't lack *Lebensraum* (living space), it lacked *Lebewesen* (living beings). Germany's birthrate of less than 1.4 children per woman was one of the lowest in the world. Why even go for more territory, why not just go for more people? Instead of taking over the world, let the world come to you.* Eventually, having been drained of their human resources, countries may surrender anyway. Think of West Germany's victory over East Germany: all the former had done was attract large numbers of East Germans, causing them to flee to the West. Once East Germany was substantially emptied, its annexation came naturally.

But in general, the EU's population (Germans included) wasn't at ease with non-European immigration. They were already afraid of giving the EU too much power and opening their borders to its other citizens. Across Europe, nationalist parties were on the rise. Britain, whose attacks on Libya were largely responsible for the refugee crisis, voted to leave the EU in 2016. That same year, to prevent millions more Middle Eastern refugees from entering its territory, the EU had to pay Turkey to keep its borders closed.

The first EU refugee crisis was enforced by the confrontation between the US and Russia in Syria—each siding with a different party in the civil war. The next refugee "attack" would be a concerted US-Russian maneuver from the start, rendering the EU even more helpless, as it would be an "invasion" within Europe—making it morally and practically impossible for the EU to close its borders. First, in 2019, Trump, openly sympathetic to Putin and elected thanks in part to his campaign aid, announced an increase in US military support for Russia's enemy Ukraine. Then he left the execution of this support to his rival successor Joe Biden—giving Putin a pretext to invade Ukraine in 2022. Biden would rigorously side with Ukraine (thus attacking his predecessor's main foreign supporter) and drag the EU into its first proper war. The war was to plunge the whole Western world into recession and inflation—leading to a further deterioration of the EU.

The trap was so perfect that even if the EU had recognized it, it couldn't have escaped it: on the one hand, the EU, primarily Germany, paid for the Russian invasion by importing large quantities of fossil fuels; on the other hand, it took in millions of Ukrainian refugees, making room for a large-scale Russian resettlement. While Stalin had to deport "socially dangerous" people to Siberia, Putin only had to scare them with occasional bombings and cut them off from water, electricity, and food.

When Russia's invasion stagnated, the situation got even worse, as the EU felt obliged to stabilize Ukraine as a pro-Western stronghold. Military and reconstruction aid would foster the already exorbitant levels of corruption. Ukraine became the EU's economic Stalingrad.

But the EU, especially Germany, continued to deny how its war with the world had flipped. It even denied that it had ever willingly gone to war. At first the EU had ignored its own aggressiveness and destructiveness against poorer countries—often former colonies: flooding them with goods while protecting its own markets, exploiting their human and natural resources, and offering aid that led to further debt and dependency. Now, the counterattacks left the EU in disbelief. Were its neighboring countries that refused to be lectured about bad human rights records, vote rigging, and censorship so averse to progress? The surprise resembled that of Nazi Germany at how fiercely and brutally partisans and enemy forces attacked them even (and even more so) in poorer countries.

The more vulnerable the EU became, the more it treated its crises as catastrophes that broke in from outside. In affluent Germany, the bored middle class even felt energized by these sudden states of emergency—at least in the first weeks or months. Happily, they saw the still rather selective war on terror replaced by the war on the virus, and finally, a real war. The simple good/bad dichotomy of the Cold War seemed to have returned for its final iteration.[*]

The moment the US would withdraw its troops and stop its imports from Europe—concentrating all its forces on countering against and arranging with the new superpower China—the EU would be just as screwed as the European climate without the Gulf Stream. The EU wasn't too good to be true, but too weak to be true.

Different from World War II, it was China rather than Russia and America that won the war against the latest Reich. Recession, debts, and spats made it even easier to buy up European countries, take over their spheres of influence, and undermine their liberal-democratic order. Western democracies had been able to hold their own against massive autocracies as long as they acted as actual or de facto colonial powers—like the democracies of ancient Greece, they had been mass oligarchies at best. Without the comforts of exploiting others—humans and nonhumans—democracies weren't prepared to make enough sacrifices to sustain themselves.[*]

Germany had lost all three world wars, and each of them hastened the decline of Europe. But squeezed between all the other major European powers, you could give Germany credit for at least having given it a try to lead Europe back to relevance—first in a fascist, then in a technocratic superstate.

Battered by recession, inflation, energy crises, refugee crises, debt crises, climate crises—all that the EU could do to stop its decay would be to prove that its civil rights and wealth weren't just luxuries paid for by the rest of the world.

In the 1990s, after the fall of the Berlin Wall, the anti-globalization movement had criticized free trade for catering to the rich in the West and exploiting the environment and the poor. In the 2000s, it had instead been populist nationalists who railed against free trade and migration for no longer making the Western world richer but worse off (in relation to new emerging economies, especially China's). Now, with their backs to the wall, Europeans on the Left and the Right had to join forces to abandon the EU's expansive ambitions and gain independence from other expansive regimes (instead of fighting them, stop feeding them).

In order to support each other effectively, each European state would have to become a highly self-sufficient and defensive—monadic—entity. Each state would produce most of its essential food, energy, and machinery itself. Instead of exchanging mainly goods and money, the states would focus on exchanging knowledge. International cooperations would only be allowed to penetrate local markets if they invested in local structures that could, if necessary, function independently. Land, raw materials, and other limited goods would be gradually communized—their lease forming the basis of a national wealth fund. Instead of maintaining a highly expensive army, each state would be endowed with its own nuclear deterrence.[*] If one entity fell off, the network wouldn't be substantially harmed. Extensions of the network would also be less complex and problematic than those of the former EU, and could easily spread around the world.

Pre-AGI Democracy
2022

Liberal democracy defeated monarchy worldwide in less than 150 years, and its next great threat—totalitarianism—was pretty much extinct in another seventy years. Yet liberal democracy appears to be slowly deteriorating. Why is this, and what can be done to reverse the crisis?

When state democracy began taking shape in Athens some 2,500 years ago, its citizens were asked to gather once a month to openly vote on laws and decrees, elect officials, and try political crimes. Since then, democracy has become more and more diluted. Bigger states with even greater populations made it impossible for all citizens to gather in one place at the same time. Even in Athens, the direct vote was only viable because no more than 10–15 percent of the population counted as citizens (women, children, slaves, criminals, and foreigners were excluded). Hereupon, representative democracy was introduced, in which every few years certain citizens (male, of a certain descent or wealth) would elect a manageable number of representatives. Liberal democracy, familiar to us since the late eighteenth century, is even more diluted. While pretty much all men, and over the course of the twentieth century, also pretty much all women, gain suffrage, those who are elected become more specialized. Politicians are expected to not only be professionals but also to submit themselves to the mandates of a political party.

Liberal democracy was introduced to outnumber the ruling classes of the aristocracy and clergy. The rest of the population was again divided into different classes—bourgeoisie, workers, farmers. Still, by comparison, their differences in wealth and status felt minor. But once the aristocracy and clergy were defeated and the Industrial Revolution gained momentum, the bourgeoisie rapidly grew richer, while most farmers and workers stayed poor. This new class antagonism put liberal democracy in its first severe crisis.[*] Many farmers and workers—even though they were the majority—felt betrayed by democracy and wished for a socialist dictatorship, while parts of the bourgeoisie sought refuge in the monarchy. Fascism managed to bundle both antidemocratic movements into one, united against minorities and foreign forces.

The welfare state revived the classless utopia of liberal democracy, promising that everybody would be able to "make it" (i.e., become part of an affluent and educated "middle class"). Some political parties might be more in favor of the "lower middle class," some more in favor of the "upper middle class," some more in favor of keeping subsidies for the poor low, some more in favor of increasing taxes on the rich, but to win the majority of votes, they all had to show how their politics wasn't just in favor of a special clientele but also the prosperity and growth of an immense "center."

In evolved welfare societies, this one common political task no longer exists. People put more emphasis on their individual personas and identity clusters, like religion, ethnicity, gender, taste, or morality. They "monadize," as general enrichment slows down. Natural resources become rare, and accumulated environmental damages come into full effect. There is also more competition, with emerging economies. Some are ruled by autocratic regimes that are basically run like companies.[*] Supernational institutions have gained in power, and even in democracies, the people's vote is for the most part symbolic. The people, after having been and still

• Mutual Enslavements

• Middle-Class Warriors

being indoctrinated with nationalism by almost all political parties, are mistrusted by exactly those parties for their inability to grasp the long-term necessities that go along with globalization. Likewise, the people regard politicians as elitist, manipulative, and corrupt. Society has become more complex than simple ideological dictates can encompass, and people find their opinions less and less congruent with any one single party.

Liberal democracies have compensated for the limited say of their citizens by granting them extended fundamental rights—besides the freedom of speech, demonstration, confession, and movement, these often also include expensive rights like free education, free health care, or social welfare. In the twentieth century, the public spending ratio of most democracies increases from less than 10 to up to 30 percent or more; in some European countries, even up to more than 50 percent. But after the oil crisis and the following stagflation in the 1970s, the rise of neoliberalism, and the end of the Soviet empire, a rising public spending ratio often goes hand in hand with a rising Gini coefficient (a measure of national income and wealth inequality). The welfare state doesn't just take care of the poor, it also lessens the fiscal burdens and economic risks of the rich by offering tax exemptions, subsidies, and warranties. New rights are only introduced on the basis that they don't cost much—more civil rights to compensate for rising inequality, or even cater to it.* For instance, women gain more rights to cheaply flood the labor market.

In the liberal states of the nineteenth and early twentieth centuries, it's mostly a male, well-educated cultural and political bourgeois elite that makes extensive use of civil liberties.* Poor people's lives are mainly defined by working to survive, and the fulfillment of most of the bourgeoisie is also defined by success in their work. Women are pretty much excluded from civil liberties. By contrast, liberal welfare states of the twentieth century give the majority of people the chance to make extensive use of civil liberties and shape their identities via that use. This engagement heightens awareness of the

material and immaterial costs of these rights. As a consequence, when people ask for even more freedom, they tend to
also ask for more restrictions in other areas. A populist backlash nostalgically asks for a comeback of a bourgeois—"universal," "humanistic," or "racially realistic"—set of civil
liberties that basically fosters a privileged ethnicity, particularly its abled, cisgendered, or male members.

In comparison to the religious and class conflicts of
previous centuries, the identitarian conflicts of welfare states
appear rather harmless. Despite backlash, in general, tolerance
has increased a lot, and identitarian factions are so many and
so diverse that it becomes difficult to gain momentum for
further radical change.• Meanwhile, the autocratic government
of the world's most populous country, China, can use drastic
measures to support the most rapid economic, scientific, and
military development ever.•

In democratic welfare states, governments need to
please a variety of pressure groups—spoiling them and training them not to tolerate unwanted change. To overcome this
pamperedness, real or proclaimed crises are used to install a
"state of exception" and bend or break constitutional law in
defense of "essential" rights and against what are regarded as
misguided ideas of self-fulfillment.

The more politics is driven by drastic emergency measures, the more those crises occur—as revenge for all the risks
and problems ignored in previous states of exceptions. The
war on terror (illegal electronic surveillance, incarceration,
torture, and killings) blends into the world financial crisis
(massive state bailouts for banks), which then blends into the
European debt crisis (massive quantitative easing), into the
refugee crisis (violent border control, social media restrictions), into the COVID-19 pandemic (limited freedom of
assembly, compulsory vaccination, additional social media
restrictions), into a semi-hot war between East and West (free
trade restrictions, additional social media restrictions).•

These states of exception are framed as too obvious to
require further discussion. Unwanted opinions are condemned

*(margin, rotated)* • Acknowledge Your Own Oppression    • Rise and Fall of Reich Europa •    • Comic Purgatory •

as the result of maliciously catered conspiracy theories and filter bubbles, while favored opinions are praised as the last stands of clear thought and independent media.* The so-called post-truth paradigm leads to paradoxical results: liberals try to condemn, if not forbid, unwanted opinions and expressions as "hate speech." Conservatives try to restore order by breaking it: locking up political enemies or hampering them in their right to vote, putting election results randomly into doubt.

Liberalism has argued that international trade works as a harbinger of peace and freedom: the more the world is interconnected, the more people are exposed to the blessings of democratic capitalism, and the more self-destructive it becomes to fight wars or install dictatorships. But in the early twentieth century, at the first peak of global trade, the Western World experienced its most disastrous conflicts (World Wars I and II) after it had divided up most of the non-Western world into colonies and protectorates. Today's mounting conflicts coincide with the rapid economic rise of many non-Western states.

Since Ancient Greece, democracies effectively only worked as mass oligarchies. The Western world never really made serious efforts to spread democracy unless it was to destabilize enemies. Otherwise, it preferred to deal with kleptocratic dictatorships and often helped them rise to power, as they were easier to control and bribe, and wouldn't put the Western world into question. Stable liberal democracies seem to depend on the economic exploitation of others.*

Today, AI and robots take the place of the carelessly exploited. But our states don't collectivize the profits generated through them. Human work is taxed up to 50 percent, while the work of robots and computers isn't taxed at all. No relevant political parties are proposing such a tax—not even one low enough not to work as an "innovation penalty."

When the idea of a robot tax first came up in the 1940s, the influence of Karl Marx's theory of surplus value was still strong. He argues that factory workers should directly participate in the profits generated by the machines that they serve.

Church of Lots •

• Rise and Fall of Reich Europa

But today, robots and AI are more than tools, they're able to replace many jobs completely.

Beyond income taxes, a progressive property tax could serve as an effective means to redistribute wealth *and* stir investments. Taxes on the transfer of property, commonly in place for goods and services (VAT) and real estate (stamp duty), could be extended to all financial transactions (Tobin tax).

Another new approach to taxes would be to not just raise them on certain unwanted environmental impacts, like $CO_2$ emissions, but on any consumption of raw materials. In a more radical approach, basically all raw materials are owned by the state. Private persons and organizations can only rent them out, and are obliged to return them largely unchanged when the lease expires.

Politicians of popular parties hardly propose such alternative concepts for taxes and charges. Is it only up to autocracies to introduce radical reforms? Or to superior AGI? In the meantime, how could liberal democracies reinvent themselves to incentivize proactive political change?

### Compulsory Voting

In liberal democracies, voter participation of 80 percent is considered to be high. Some states, like the US, hardly reach 50 percent participation in their national elections. Nonvoters are either condemned as lazy and irresponsible or they're pitied for being hampered or not properly represented by any party. But nonvoters might just be acting rationally. Voter participation is based on the ethics of good intentions or on devoted followership. It's not rational to participate in a ballot when it's highly unlikely that your single vote makes a difference (the "paradox of voting"). This could be changed simply by introducing compulsory voting. Today, only a few democracies have it and even fewer enforce it properly. In dictatorships, compulsory voting is associated with fraud elections. But a ballot can be designed to allow you to formally abstain. The true reason compulsory voting hasn't caught on is rather that it tends to harm well-established parties. People who find it unproductive to vote could give new and fringe parties a chance—feeling their vote is wasted anyhow. Not turning our right to vote into a duty is inhibiting progress.

### Direct Democracy

Despite first-past-the-post voting or electoral thresholds, recent years saw the rapid rise of new, mostly populist parties. Often, these parties are condemned as "protest parties," as they're mainly driven by one subject on which they fundamentally disagree with well-established parties. In case their top subject is losing interest, they look for new subjects to vehemently disagree with. These parties gain momentum by substituting lacking referenda. Different from class societies, in individualist societies people feel only partly represented by the party they vote for. This could be compensated by plebiscites. Modern telecommunication could enable all citizens to participate in political debates and to vote on short notice on an unlimited number of questions. But established parties don't want to give up their power, and warn that plebiscites undermine considered policies in favor of momentary moods and hypes. They argue that the effort required to form a solid opinion on several subjects a year would overexert most people. In case plebiscites are possible, they're usually limited to elementary constitutional questions and need to be initiated with a petition signed by a large number of citizens. The plebiscite is regarded as a last resort *in saving* rather than an actual exercise *in* democracy. The one historical exception is Switzerland, where since the nineteenth century people have had the chance to decide several times a year on a number of regional and national topics. Usually, the results are moderate, despite the turnout often being much lower than 50 percent. When a radical opinion becomes popular in the polls, forces to overpower it also grow. To not overexert people and at the same time make their vote more relevant on the topics they're particularly invested in, each citizen could be allowed to vote only a limited number of times per year See Martti Kalliala, Jenna Sutela, and Tuomas Toivonen, "Vote Economy," in *Solution 239–246: Finland—*

*The Welfare Game* (Berlin: Sternberg Press, 2011). or to exchange their single vote on certain topics for multiple votes on others. To prevent small minorities from accumulating massive powers, the relation between the number of your invested votes and your actual voting power could be curbed, as, for instance, in quadratic voting.

### Sortition

Sortition already existed in Ancient Greece to staff certain public positions. Today, in most democracies, it's restricted to the nomination process of court juries. Only recently, gamification has led to a revaluation of the element of chance in decision-making processes.[•] As a consequence, there have been a number of political experiments with sortition, for instance, in the Belgium province Ostbelgien to nominate a second chamber, or in Ireland to select a number of assemblies to each give an opinion on a constitutional issue, like abortion, that precedes a public referendum on that topic. Sortition promises to overcome the corruption, opportunism, and power dynamics of party politics. Randomly nominated citizens might lack expertise, but what do politicians really know? You could argue that at least they share the commitment to devote their lives to politics. If laypeople are meant to become full-time politicians for several years, most will decline the proposal right away, while those who agree are just as prone to bribery, vanity, and intrigue as professional politicians. Therefore, it's best to restrict political sortition for laypeople to giving mandatory advice on a single political topic (similar to nominating a court jury for a single case) after hearing a number of delegates and experts selected by the elected parties (similar to a court jury listening to witnesses, the prosecution, and the defense). That way, sortition could not only limit the power of political parties but also the power of opinion polls.

### Autonomous State Simulations

In liberal democracies, pretty much every citizen can become a member of parliament or government. You don't need any proof of qualification and your criminal record can be endless. This is great insofar as it doesn't exclude certain groups of citizens per se from political power—different, for instance, from China, a five-thousand-year-old meritocracy, where even just becoming a simple member of the one state party is a demanding process. This doesn't stop Chinese politics from being corrupt; just the opposite. But the dream of limiting access to political power to highly qualified people doesn't die. In the Western context, a main reference is Plato's concept of an epistocracy—a state run by philosophers as morally superior beings. Today, hardly anybody would believe in such superiority or find it crucial for even qualifying as a good politician. But the underlying concern remains: democratic parties don't select people on the basis of exceptional skills. In the end, it's all about convincing the mediocre masses of party members and voters—and nobody can do this more cogently and passionately than people who are themselves rather mediocre. By contrast, highly intelligent people tend to come across as arrogant, bored, or detached. But what to do about it? Install a ruthless IQ threshold for all political positions? IQ tests are biased, and voters may dislike the politicians who pass the test. A different, nonrestrictive approach could be to incentivize highly intelligent people to get involved solely in the aspects of politics that appeal to them, in particular, the development of innovative governmental tools and the development of virtual simulations to test said tools under various scenarios. Instead of just relying on the studies of a few pleasing think tanks and consultancy firms, governments could initiate open calls on how to improve their politics. Everybody would be invited, in particular, noncitizens without any patriotic inclinations, as people who are personally disengaged with a certain topic are often better at judging it. Participants could also represent the interests of nonhumans. Each year, a renowned and diverse jury could choose several winners who are invited to the respective nation, state, or city to present their proposals for improvement. Contributors would be asked to give open access to their plans to allow others to amend or adapt them. As a further step, different state entities that organize these open calls could organize an international competition between all the winners. However intelligent, the contributions could easily be dismissed as unrealistic. Still, they could help to establish an understanding of politics that doesn't just react to crises but is anticipatory enough to forestall them.

### Informed Voters

Regarding the intelligence of the electorate, it's even worse than that of the elected: When everybody uses their right to vote, how can the outcome be any more than mediocre? To optimize the outcome of elections, capitalists used to be in favor of census suffrage, or, more recently, the libertarian concept of vote markets (e.g., affluent people buying politically disinterested people's votes). Communists have mistrusted their own clientele as blinded by clerical, fascist, or consumerist propaganda, and, following Marx, saw it as inevitable that democracy would be replaced by a "dictatorship of the proletariat."• For fascists and populists, it's legitimate to lie to voters—for their own good. But is there also a way to optimize electoral behavior beyond party lines? A way that doesn't destroy democracy, but stabilizes and energizes it? One approach has been to create state media that's meant to operate in a politically independent and neutral manner. But however honorable the board of directors, it can easily be pushed aside. Moreover, how to ensure that people consume state media? By restricting private media, as Germany did after World War II (in terms of radio and television)? This only appeared plausible in terms of preventing Germany from being quickly renazified. Another option: Voters could be tested to prove that they actually know how democracy works or what different parties stand for. But such tests could be biased and would discriminate against people with certain disabilities or little education. More demanding: Before every election, the electorate could be obliged to participate in further political

• Acknowledge Your Own Oppression
Mutual Enslavements

education. They would listen to representatives of different political parties and discuss the respective platforms among themselves. To ensure that the participants of the workshops aren't partial, they would be selected by lot. The danger of this approach is that many people could find participating so un-attractive that they would rather forbear from voting. But a tax discount or welfare subsidy could work as an incentive. Pro-vided that the workshops are popular among people with little political knowledge, there would be no need for participation to be mandatory.

### Consociationalism

In a monadic society with a multiplicity of identities and interests, the dichotomy of majority rule (often far from repre-senting an absolute majority of citizens) can feel like tyranny. But deliberate, consensual approaches to democracy, as expressed by the Occupy movement and other forms of grassroots assembly, only work in a community that's already pre-harmonized by segregation, expulsion, or intimidation. (Philosopher Jürgen Habermas, an advocate of domination-free discourse, is particularly popular in China.) By contrast, consociationalism is highly pragmatic. The aim is not to deliberate over one way that's best for everybody but to find ways to coexist in difference. Governments are no longer spearheaded by one charismatic (i.e., narcissistic) leader but a diverse council of multiple major political factions. While they can build varying majorities (avoiding the high threshold of a supermajority), this also prevents them from deciding harshly against the interests of any of them, eventually pro-voking a boycott of upcoming decisions. Consociationalism originated in states with adamant ethnic, religious, or linguis-tic divides. In monadic societies, the divides might be subject to quick-changing trends—nonetheless, they can easily outdo any common cause. Switzerland, a highly affluent, quadrilin-gual state with a relatively low state quota and Gini coefficient, serves as an excellent example of how consociationalism can be counterbalanced with a more polarizing direct democracy.[*]

Corona Tribes •
Middle-Class Warriors •

Church of Lots •

Terror's Child Muses •  Society of Games •

### Segregation

With people secluding themselves in identitarian clusters, why still insist on one legislation being applicable to all? Affirmative action already treats people differently with the rationale of promoting equality. In addition, different identitarian clusters could seek a particular legislation regarding affairs within that cluster.• This particular legislation could also include forms of government. While liberal democracy only leaves its citizens the choice between different parties, monadic democracy allows citizens to choose between different forms of government—introducing the next level of freedom, an open competition between political systems: people can decide whether they prefer a substate governed by a grassroots democracy, an oligarchy, or a despot.• Segregation in autonomous substates can happen both with or without territorial division. Zones of territorial exclusivity can also be splattered or temporary. See "Dubai Düsseldorf," in my book *Solution 185-196: Dubai Democracy* (Berlin: Sternberg Press, 2010); and more recently and extensively, Balaji Srinivasan, *The Network State—How to Start a New Country* (n.p.: 1729, 2022). To prevent the substates from evolving into totalitarian sects, members must be able to exit them at any time, and all children must be educated in diverse ideologies and religions.• (This still isn't really the case at most Western schools.) One day a week or several weeks a year, all citizens and residents could be obliged to stay at communities of substates that are fundamentally different from theirs—except for a similar level of tolerance for divergent thoughts and behaviors. People with a high level of tolerance might join substates that are primarily like-minded in encouraging divergent thoughts and behaviors.• People who seek aggressive experiences could join or visit a substate that consents to terror.•

Wanderers
2017

> Due to globalization, borders have been losing importance—
> but not for those left behind by globalization. Instead of
> being discriminated against or criminalized as migrants,
> augmented reality allows Wanderers to collectively
> appropriate a country of their choice.

On May 14, 1948, the state of Israel was founded by virtue of the "natural and historical rights of the Jews." Neighboring Arab countries declared war on it the following night. To this day, many Arab and Muslim countries don't recognize Israel, since its founding involved the disenfranchisement and displacement of Palestinians who were native to the territory. But particularly in Europe and America, after the annihilation of millions of Jews perpetrated by the German Reich, many saw a Jewish state as a safe homeland for the incomparably persecuted Jews. The Federal Republic of Germany, as the successor state to the German Reich, saw itself as having a particular liability in relation to Israel.

In an interview on December 8, 2005, Iran's president Mahmoud Ahmadinejad suggested relocating Israel to Europe. If European states insisted that Hitler had killed millions of Jews, then they should offer Zionists compensation from their own provinces, for instance in Germany and Austria, to set up their state there rather than in Palestine. Iran would aid Europe in this undertaking. Western heads of state as well as the speaker of the Israeli foreign ministry expressed outrage at Ahmadinejad's interview, especially since he again denied the right for the state of Israel to exist. German Chancellor Angela Merkel and Austrian Chancellor Wolfgang Schüssel offered no comment on the proposal to relocate Israel, despite being directly implicated in the plan.

The *Jewish Renaissance in Poland*, initiated by Israeli artist Yael Bartana in 2007, also calls for the return of Jews to Europe, or more precisely to Poland, which alone lost around three million Jewish citizens in the Holocaust. Those called on to return home are all those, non-Jews included, who regard themselves as foreign or other. For the Jews that populate Israel today are, for the most part, no longer refugees or survivors of the Holocaust. Perhaps they aren't even Jews, but only said so to get Israeli citizenship. And the Poland of the *Jewish Renaissance* also need not be located in the state of Poland, which was shifted westward after the Second World War according to the Potsdam Agreement of the Allied powers. A large part of contemporary Poland used to belong to Germany. A large part of what used to be Poland now belongs to Ukraine and Belarus.

National borders often undergo shifts due to war and treaties. Poland has particularly suffered under this phenomenon. With the divisions of 1772, 1793, and 1795, it was entirely robbed of its sovereignty and divided up between Prussia, Austria, and Russia. For over 120 years, there was no independent Polish state in existence. Jewish and Polish fates are therefore related to some extent. Enough, in any case, that Polish nationalists have also come to understand their country as chosen by God, as a "Christ among nations."

Due to the establishment of the UN, sanctions against wars of aggression, and the deterrent of weapons of mass destruction,* there is an effort today to permanently avoid wars and shifts in borders. But while in large parts of the world borders appear to be stable for a historically singular duration,

254 V. INDEPENDENCE, FINALLY

with states at the most splitting up into ever-smaller units, they're also losing their significance. International trade, international communication, and international tourism are constantly on the increase. Lifestyles in different countries and continents are becoming more and more similar.

All the more tragic, then, is the fate of those who are left behind by globalization. Those for whom borders resemble insurmountable walls. Those who can't travel anywhere, with or without a passport. Those who can't even move freely within their own country—whether because they don't have the necessary rights or the financial means.

The existing injustice can be minimized by no longer cementing the borders between and within states, but subjecting them to a constant, peaceful shifting. Then it would no longer be necessary to go to the trouble of emigrating to move to a different state. You could just comfortably stay wherever you are, living in Spain, then Japan, then Malawi. Do you like this state so much that you would even want to follow it?

States don't have to continuously shift over our planet, growing and shrinking. They can also abruptly jump from one place to the next, in the meantime disappearing entirely. When Theodor Herzl founded the Zionist movement in the late nineteenth century, it was unimportant to him whether the new Jewish state would be located in Canaan. He also considered founding a "colony" in other non-Western countries with rather little European immigration, like Argentina or Uganda. Analogously, on October 5, 2007, Ahmadinejad suggested relocating the Israelis to the sparsely populated parts of North America, particularly Canada and Alaska. But there, it's either very cold or the area is under environmental protection.

The real place to consider is in the middle of Europe, in the middle of Germany, which was responsible for the Holocaust and Jewish displacement. Germany is, in fact, quite densely populated as a whole, but the area of the former GDR, which is approximately four times as large as Israel and Palestine, is currently suffering from massive depopulation. Since German reunification in 1990, hundreds of billions of euros

• Pre-AGI Democracy

Rise and Fall of Reich Europa •

have been invested there in modern infrastructure. Nonetheless, it lacks employment options and whole neighborhoods are now threatened with collapse due to underpopulation.• For a long time now, the number of Palestinians living in exile has been so large that Israel-Palestine would be a tight squeeze for all of them, even if all the Jews left. In eastern Germany, however, there would be enough room to duplicate Israel-Palestine to provide additional land not only for new Jewish settlements but also for new Palestinian ones. All the areas that belonged to Israel in the original state would be given to Palestine, and vice versa. Since many Israelis don't even come from Europe, but from Africa, America, and Asia, it would only be consistent for Palestinians to also return home to Europe. I first proposed this in "The Inversion of Palestine-Israel," in *Solution 196–213: United States of Palestine-Israel*, ed. Joshua Simon (Berlin: Sternberg Press, 2011).

But how can this state-shifting begin when historic nation-states vehemently oppose even attempts at independence by individual regions? Resistance could be even more fierce in superstructures like the EU, where a drop in the importance of nation-states is all the more potently felt. In 2014, the population of Scotland was deterred from voting for its independence from the UK, as this would have implied expulsion from the EU.

State-wandering manifests as a concerted citizens' movement: "Wanderers" who already inhabit a certain region or move to it hoist the flag, speak the languages, cook the cuisine, don the traditional clothing, adopt the manners, perform the rituals, celebrate the festivals, live the poverty, simulate the prosperity, and apply makeup to adapt to the predominant ethnic groups in the respective states.

Thanks to augmented reality, not all of these changes have to happen in real life; instead, homes virtually alter their facades, cars their bodies, streets their names, words their sound, faces their color and shape. But there are also strictly analogous Wanderers who insist on doing everything for real and either take clashes with the law for granted or have a vested interest in causing them. They occupy schools and

The inversion of Israel and Palestine within depopulated East Germany, map: Jana Schnell and me, 2011 change their curricula, swap traffic and street signs, and battle militant nationalists who do everything they can to keep—at least certain regions—completely Wanderer-free.

For the Wanderers, it's a matter of opposing both the ethnically and territorially defined national state and traditional cultural diversity-leveling globalization. They're at odds with both de- and reterritorialization. Their xenocentric folklore is a camp Gesamtkunstwerk.•

Some accuse the Wanderers of assuming their national or ethnic identity only superficially and spoofing it. Formerly or still oppressed nationalities and ethnic groups accuse them of neocolonial or racist appropriation that goes far beyond phenomena such as blackface, "Pocahottie" costumes, or "wiggers."

At the same time, there are diasporas that make pacts with the Wanderers to draw attention to their interests, and settlers who infiltrate them with the intent of permanently occupying a territory and preparing it for annexation, similar to radical Zionists on the West Bank. This gives the actual states justification to fight the Wanderers and any form of multiculturalism. Could these states be the ones planting settlers and radicals in the Wanderers' midst?

The situation becomes even more complex with people not just adapting to existing states but to fictional ones that combine playful elements with serious improvements. The host state has to carefully consider what to forbid and what to embrace. If the changes implemented by the Wanderers prove successful, the host state might encourage citizens of the appropriated state, or fans of the state fiction, to immigrate and enforce the community—beyond luring wealthy foreigners with temporary tax exemptions.• Wanderers might also be offered the opportunity to establish an autonomous substate for a reliable number of years—a sort of charter city, but from the bottom up.

Middle-Class Warriors
2015; 2023

> The Western world could gain new, widely acknowledged edge by dividing into numerous substates, which, instead of competing for the lowest taxes for the rich, compete to satisfy the needs of different voluntary tribes.

2015. For more than twenty years, the Western world had been exposed to Islamist attacks, beginning with Al Qaeda's assaults on US targets.° The casualties were one thing—they could easily be retaliated against with advanced technical warfare. But when it came to being radical, the West had lost its cutting edge.

Of course, you could argue that Islamism is a Western phenomenon as well, and that, in the globalized world, the West is everywhere. Still, Islamists made a point of not being part of the modern Western world, while in the last two hundred years, new radicals had basically always been trying to be even more modern, more Western. And while the West stayed radical only on the screen—in violent movies and computer games—Islamists took those aesthetics and made them real.°

Then, the West struck back. In June 2015, the cover of

*Vanity Fair* announced the transition of Olympic Gold winner and reality television star Bruce Jenner into Caitlyn. Jenner is a Republican, sixty-five years old, has been married three times, and is a parent of six kids. With Jenner, gender transition became a mainstream sensation. Here it was again: a romantic radicality of the Western World, and no Islamist would ever be able to adopt it.*

Jenner's transition was proof that you can be radical at any age and not turn into a youth-obsessed maniac. On the *Vanity Fair* cover, Jenner appeared as a prototypical well-maintained lady of her age, with big hair and decent cosmetic surgery. German writer Ernst Jünger's scenario was about to come true: the elderly become the new radicals, since they don't have much left to lose.

Three months after Jenner's *Vanity Fair* cover, another photo took the Western world by storm: the image of Alan Kurdi, a two-year-old Kurdish Syrian boy, washed ashore on the Turkish coast. Again, not that we didn't know about the hundreds of thousands of Middle Eastern refugees before, but this sweet little child with relatives in Canada and a middle-class background felt like an undeniable part of the Western us. And, suddenly, the natural violence of the sea was much more real than the comically exaggerated brutality of the Islamic State. No, the Western world didn't feel responsible for how the Islamic State had turned its own violent games and movies into reality. No, it didn't feel responsible for killing civilians in Afghanistan and Pakistan with drones. But it felt responsible for the death of a small, innocent child that had hoped for refuge in the West.

It wasn't just Alan. Once you mourned his death, you had to mourn all the other children—all the fathers and mothers, all the people who had died and those who were still going to die during their journey to the West. The number of people who risked their lives to escape the Islamic State was many times bigger than the number of people the Islamic State was able to recruit. For every crazy Islamic State boy that executed hostages, there were thousands of boys—and girls and fathers and mothers—who risked their lives to be part of the Western world. They wanted to be nothing but peaceful, normal middle-class citizens, just as Jenner took hormones every day, had cosmetic surgery, and divorced a third time to live the normal life of an elderly middle-class woman. Different from Islamic State warriors, these unarmed warriors of middle-class normalcy hadn't been recruited. They came as an unwanted gift. All the Western world had to do was accept them.

To many Westerners, the transgenic and transnational provenance of the gift was still a problem. Could it be that it turned out to be a Trojan horse? Not in the sense that these warriors were actually fighting for the other side, but that they disturbed the existing middle-class ecosystem? Trans people were mainly trans women, so would women outnumber men in the future? With the refugees, it was the opposite: they were mainly men. But it was unlikely that the trans people would mate with the Arab refugees. The refugees were Muslims, and the trans women could be lesbians or—as seemed to be the case with Jenner—mainly in love with themselves. As Jenner claimed, the transformation into a woman had made her asexual.* · Orcies

In Germany, a large part of the population was quite euphoric about hundreds of thousands of Arabs keen to end up in exactly their country. To welcome them was a chance to outshine Germany's image as Europe's grim, if not sadistic, austerity master. Still, Germany was in particular danger of disastrously repeating two previous welcomes. First, for the millions of Southern European and Turkish *Gastarbeiter* (guest workers) who had helped to sustain the German *Wirtschaftswunder* (economic wonder) through the 1960s and early 1970s, and who, later on, in the 1980s, had been accused of being one of the main reasons for rocketing unemployment numbers. Second, for the East Germans and Russian Germans, and finally for the whole of East Germany, after the end of the Cold War. Euphoria had turned into misery when subsidies for the East had gone into the trillions. Unemployment in the

East had nevertheless stayed high, and Germany had ulti-mately felt forced to start its notorious austerity politics.•

Maybe this time, it will be different. Maybe Middle East-ern refugees are the beginning of a revitalizing *Völkerwanderung* (migration period). Maybe trans people are the avant-garde of a new sexual confidence. But so far, applause for refugees and trans people is very much a matter of *augmented virtuality.* While augmented reality expands the physical environment with virtual elements, augmented virtuality spices up virtual-ity with physical elements,• sustaining a self-perception of the Western middle class as compassionate—even though they're no exception to the sociological rule that affluence and egoism correlate.

The scenario of sealing off refugees and other minor-ities is already in place—and a walled ghetto isn't enough. Egyptian billionaire Naguib Sawiris intends to buy an unin-habited Greek island, rename it Aylan Island, Many media outlets covering Alan Kurdi's death misspelled his first name as "Aylan" and reported his age as three years instead of two years and two months. and invest up to $200 million to give Arab refugees homes and jobs.

But who knows who will end up living in a ghetto: Is it the people on Aylan Island, or the people in the rest of Europe? Spatial separation has lost some of its unconditional power due to technical innovation in telecommunication, transpor-tation, positioning, and military explosives. Yet technologies such as greenhouses, regenerative energies, and 3D printers have also made it easier to live in relative self-reliance with-out loss of comfort. The more densely populated the world becomes, and the more different regions grow dependent on one another's supplies of raw materials, merchandise, and capital, the greater the luxury of isolation.•

Once Aylan Island has become a success, Greece, the economic problem child of the EU, can seize the opportunity to reinvent itself by installing further thematic islands like:

Trans Island

Lazy Island

Fat Island
Vegan Island
Family Island
Children Island
Cat Island
Dog Island
Horse Island
IQ 120+ Island
IQ 130+ Island
IQ 140+ Island
IQ 90- Island
Gothic Island
Steampunk Island
Versace Island
Prada Island
Ad-lib Island
Stripe Island
Apple Island
Hacker Island
Mausoleum Island
Pyramid Island
Last Year Island
Last Day Island
Brothel Island
Gay Island
Lesbo Island
Heterosexual Island
Asexual Island
Pronatalist Island
Anti-natalist Island
Heroin Island
Crystal Meth Island
Ecstasy Island
Cannabis Island
Cigarette Island
Cigar Island
Yoga Island

Pilates Island
Buddhist Island
Horoscope Island
Rockabilly Island
Heavy Metal Island
Straight Edge Island
Antiquity Island
Nudist Island
Love Island
Lovesick Island
Drill Island
Boxing Island
Army Island
Sugar Island
Cuddle Island
Roulette Island
Blackjack Island
Anarchy Island
Monarchy Island
Communism Island
Stone Age Island
Baroque Island
Renaissance Island
Matriarchate Island
Stoa Island
Gossip Island
Mute Island

...

Drastically increasing its attractive coastline, mainland Greece could be cut into hundreds of autonomous islands that are specialized around all sorts of needs and themes. The new Greek archipelago—Greece Archipelago—could become the transgressive future of the Western middle class: its diversification into *voluntary tribes.*

The US already has new cities that specialize in retirees or adherents of a particular religion. These are small spheres of deceleration and dedifferentiation.[*] In Greece Archipelago, by contrast, many come to the island of their choice for no more than an extended vacation. Others design their Greece Archipelago home to showcase an obsession while having another, inconspicuous life elsewhere. Greece Archipelago witnesses the materialization of ingenuous social networks that otherwise take place on the internet.

Every island decides on its openness to visitors and the concessions it expects of them. The island must provide for what are usually civil functions of the state, such as infrastructure, education, and health care, and levy fees and membership dues from its visitors and residents, or sell shares. In order to avoid unleashing a price war among themselves, the islands must prove their uniqueness in ever-new ways.

Each island's distinctiveness may also lie in its form of organization: commercial enterprise, foundation, association, or cooperative. People can decide whether they prefer to be governed by a grassroots democracy, an oligarchy, or a despot.[*] Should the residents themselves provide all necessary services, or do they wish to have a professional administration? Do they want lots of community activities or the greatest possible degree of anonymity? Should the island introduce its own currency in order to emphasize, like a casino, a playful aspect,[*] or should communitarian measures largely obviate the need for a monetized economy? Which form of association is the cheapest for its members? Which is best able to safeguard their interests? What are the benefits or costs of freedom of opinion or censorship? Centralism or self-government? And how much are they worth to members?

While liberal democracy leaves its citizens only the choice between different parties, Greece Archipelago allows them to choose between different forms of government. Some 2,500 years after state democracy began taking shape in Athens, Greece Archipelago introduces the next level of freedom: an open competition between systems of governing.

The people of former Greece who decide not to become citizens of one of the new islands can gather on the remaining non-themed mainland and islands to live off the public revenue raised by general services provided for Greece Archipelago. Police and military services are billed either per inhabitant or per deployment.

> It might sound naive to hope for the creation of substates not to be all about attracting the rich with economic deregulation and little to no taxes—but such substates alone are likely to stir severe social unrest.

2023. Fueled by the success of cryptocurrencies, today it's mainly tech-affiliated libertarians who call for a fragmentation of nation-states into variously governed microstates. Building these microstates not within existing nation-states but on the extraterritorial high seas, as proposed by the Seasteading Institute, isn't feasible yet. They hope for a competitive selection process that will result in the creation of states that overcome "mob rule" and manage to attract the most economically and intellectually successful individuals with a lean government.

There are some basic parameters that are meant to distinguish these states—similar to when buying a car or computer: good price (few taxes), basic functionality (infrastructure), safety (security), speed (few regulations), a bit of design (visual identity, fancy architecture), and maybe some special features (mild climate, beaches). In this context, it has only been tech entrepreneur and investor Balaji Srinivasan who has come up with the idea of further distinguishing these microstates: he argues in his book *The Network State: How to Start a New Country* (2022) that to give autonomous segregations urgency, they would have to introduce "a moral innovation that inverts one of society's core assumptions while keeping all others intact." This premise would be the basis for a committed parallel society that "a more powerful state can't delete, one that justifies its existence as a righteous yet peaceful protest against the powers that be"—though the "One Commandments" Srinivasan gives as examples are mainly health regimes without any communal attachment.

As these libertarian states are expected to be run as owner-led companies, if not patriarchic family businesses (i.e., monarchies), such an approach has also been described as neoreactionary. Its most famous proponents are the internet entrepreneur Curtis Yarvin and the philosopher Nick Land; its most prominent patron is the internet entrepreneur Peter Thiel.

The family-run Emirates give an idea of what states run as owner-led companies would look like: there are the citizens, of which only a few sheikhs, if not one, have a say; there are the customers who have bought themselves into residentship; and there are the busy guest workers who do the servicing and manufacturing, and can be kicked out at any time. All profit in their own terms: the sheikhs (major shareholders) make profit from raw materials and developments, of which they distribute some to the citizens (minor shareholders); the residents (customers) profit from low taxes and affordable services; and the guest workers (employees) profit from getting paid significantly more than in their home countries. Basic rights are limited—except for the ruling sheikh(s)—but the risks of migrating to an Emirate are reinsured by the possibility to return to your home country.

In case all countries turn into companies, your livability, if not your outright survival, depends on your assets staying in demand in several competing states. This will be even more of a problem as robots continue to replace the workforce.* Libertarians might be fine with squeezing the "leftovers" into ghettos, reservations, or rogue states—risking escapes similar to recent refugee crises. Neoreactionaries might also consider incentives to lure—or draconian laws to force—the "leftovers" into sterilization and suicide.° This could lead to a revolution in which the Left and religious fundamentalists join forces—making the Islamic State look like an insignificant joke. In comparison, the current world is a tranquil paradise for the rich. They're equipped with endless opportunities to avoid taxes, can live fearlessly in their niches, or can mingle inconspicuously with the ordinary.

A socially peaceful segmentation of nation-states will have to offer a general welfare scenario. Under this premise, segregating the poor might actually be to their advantage as it would allow them to insulate themselves against the rich and stay safe from their real estate speculation, their monopolies, their drugs. Voluntary tribes and zones exclusively for the poor might help them assist one another, organize, and initiate a new egalitarian movement.°

• Mutual Enslavements •
Acknowledge Your Own Oppression
• Commie

Showing little tolerance for nonconsensual violence,
a monadic society is particularly susceptible to terrorism.

One-Man War
2009

Islamist suicide attacks and Western school rampages inspire and resemble each other. They are narcissistic celebrations of personal agency, not instruments of political change.

Joshua Simon celebrates his thirtieth birthday in Tel Aviv. He's exuberant; the global financial crisis can't bring him down. "Money doesn't exist, money is just an idea," he says, grinning broadly, his pretty eyes sparkling behind his thick horn-rimmed glasses. What isn't, can't be destroyed.

Simon is many things. He's a curator, a filmmaker, the editor of a literary magazine and a film magazine, and he has published a volume of poetry. But above all, Simon is a Communist, organized in party and union. He's currently working on his own talk show on Israeli television, to be called *The Leftists*.

Simon celebrates his birthday at the Riff Raff 2000, a small, cozy club where everyone knows each other. The feeling is similar to the 1990s in Hamburg's Golden Pudel Club or Berlin's Galerie Berlintokyo. They play eurodance, Captain Hollywood, and Ace of Base. At Riff Raff 2000, the new millennium is still waiting.

When I ask Simon why there is no new music in Tel

Aviv's cafés and bars, he explains that for the Western world, the singer Kurt Cobain sealed the faith in a society-changing youth with his suicide in 1994. At the same time, as a "martyr to his own music," he had ensured a level of authenticity that henceforth elevated the suicide attack to being the only authentic counterculture. The end of grunge music was followed by the second intifada.

For the time being, I consider Simon's thesis to be nothing more than cultural-scientific twaddle that's also very much stuck in the 1990s. Even before Kurt Cobain there were romantic musicians who committed suicide and thus increased their posthumous fame. And what should inspire a young Islamist about a whiny American drug wreck?

A few days later, Simon shows me a collection of Palestinian martyrdom videos. With the car bombing of nineteen-year-old Ra'id Zaqarna on April 6, 1994—the day after Kurt Cobain's suicide—Hamas suicide bombers begin to have themselves filmed before the act, and in a moment, it becomes a standardized format. The fighters stand in front of Koranic verses stretched out on the wall. They haven't yet put on the heavy and clunky explosives belt, but hold a Kalashnikov in their hands and assume various more or less well-rehearsed poses. They crouch, shoulder the weapon, and aim in various directions. Some manage a determined facial expression, others stare intimidated into space. These are typical home movies, where the camera operator tries to lighten up the tripod shot with erratic zooms.

In his 2006 Academy Award–nominated feature film *Paradise Now*, director Hany Abu-Assad caricatures the format of martyr videos by having his hero start over several times during the shoot. Abu-Assad thus insinuates that the videos strive for perfection, which they don't need at all, as they're only played to the perpetrator's relatives and the world after the announced act has already taken place. Unlike in politics, here the word follows the deed. Only for technical reasons—dead people can't speak—do the words have to be recorded first.

The Palestinian martyr videos that Simon shows me don't make me think of Kurt Cobain (the idea for the first martyr video certainly came days before his suicide) but of the videos that the Columbine High School rampage killers, Eric Harris and Dylan Klebold, leave for the world on April 20, 1999, showing them in black military pants in front of their collection of pipe bombs and during bumbling shooting exercises in the woods. Or of the video messages and self-portraits that Seung-Hui Cho, the twenty-three-year-old Virginia Tech student, finds time to send off to NBC News on the morning of April 16, 2007, after he has already shot two schoolmates and before he will shoot thirty more people. A chubby-cheeked boy is seen trying to look as grim as possible while holding up two pistols.

Palestinian suicide bombings lack a political target. No Palestinian can believe that Jews would let themselves be driven out of Israel or even just out of the West Bank settlements because of a few thousand dead. The goal of Palestinian suicide bombers is revenge for the humiliations suffered at the hands of Israel. Their motivation is therefore not so different from that of Western students running amok, taking revenge on the regime of their teachers and the humiliation of their schoolmates. Islamist suicide bombers, like school spree killers, are concerned with restoring honor—only that spree killers are ostracized, while suicide bombers are worshipped in large parts of Islamic society. They're placarded on the walls of houses on busy Palestinian streets, and God gifts them with immediate admission to the kingdom of heaven.

Harris's diaries provide information about his enthusiasm for the first-person shooter game *Doom* (1993) and the film *Natural Born Killers* (1994). In *Natural Born Killers*, however, the murders committed by the two protagonists spark an enormous media response, which they themselves still experience. At the end of the film, they escape unpunished. Shooter games, once your avatar has been killed been, can be started over again. Harris and Klebold, however, are certain that they must die in the rampage they've been preparing for months, and they promptly shoot themselves, just as Cho does in Blacksburg, Robert Steinhäuser does in Erfurt, and Tim Kretschmer does in Winnenden.

Eight months before the Columbine High School massacre, the Al Qaeda network starts to commit suicide attacks against the US. In 1993, in the failed attack on New York's World Trade Center, the driver of the truck with the explosives still escaped. In August 1998, however, two martyrs simultaneously ram the US embassies in Nairobi and Dar es Salaam. Two hundred twenty-four people die.

Because Nazis are considered cooler than Islamists in a small American town, Al Qaeda is missing from Harris and Klebold's heroic cosmos ("Religions are gay," they declare in their "basement tapes"). But like Al Qaeda, the two want to go all out. They plan the most devastating attack on American soil to date. Many more people are supposed to die than the 168 in the 1995 Oklahoma City truck bombing. Harris and Klebold plan to detonate two bombs in the school cafeteria and then shoot at the fleeing students instead of fleeing themselves. Only because the bombs don't detonate properly, the death toll remains at thirteen. That's still enough for the first rampage by American teenagers with double-digit deaths in nearly thirty-three years.

What is fundamentally new about the Columbine massacre, however, is the spree killers' self-stylization as heroes. The twenty-five-year-old Charles Joseph Whitman, who in 1966 shot first his mother and his wife and then another sixteen people from the observation deck of the University of Texas at Austin, sees himself as mentally ill and apologizes in his suicide note for the act that seemed unavoidable to him: "If my life insurance policy is valid please pay off my debts [...] donate the rest anonymously to a mental health foundation. Maybe research can prevent further tragedies of this type." Brenda Ann Spencer, who in 1979 at the age of sixteen starts shooting from her parents' house at Cleveland Elementary School in San Diego and fatally hits twice, can only say, when asked who she wanted to hit: "I like red and blue jackets." And when asked why she shot, "I don't like Mondays." In 1991, Gang Lu, a twenty-eight-year-old Beijing native, shot up the University of Iowa campus because he didn't get a prize for his doctoral dissertation and felt ethnically discriminated against. Like so many spree killers, he has good reasons for his revenge, but it remains haphazard.

Harris and Klebold, on the other hand, place themselves above all law from the outset. Their vigilante justice doesn't require any concrete offenses to take effect. Before the crime, Harris writes in his diary: "My belief is that if I say something, it goes. I am the law, if you don't like it, you die. If I don't like you or I don't like what you want me to do, you die. [...] So thats the only way to solve arguments with all you fuckheads out there, I just kill!" Harris wears a T-shirt with the imprint "Natural Selection"—though the two aren't concerned with an intensified fight for survival, because they know that they too will be dead at the end of the day. Harris and Klebold want to live to kill. They don't protect themselves with bulletproof vests or hide. The killing is to become so excessive that it doesn't exclude them themselves. The suicide attack is the absolute act; the perpetrator is completely absorbed in it. Only dust and ashes remain, and memories of those who survived.

Klebold writes: "I know we're gonna have followers because we're so fucking God-like. We're not exactly human—we have human bodies but we've evolved into one step above you, fucking human shit. We actually have fucking self-awareness." Part of this self-styling as an Übermensch* is to ignore that one is also only a follower. Of those who, while not believing themselves to be similar to God, sacrifice themselves for him, like the Japanese kamikaze pilots for a divine emperor. Then, in the war against Iraq, Iran recruits hundreds of thousands of boys from the age of twelve and men over forty-five for the paramilitary Basij brigades, who run against the enemy in closed ranks as cannon fodder or detonate mines. Around their necks, the militiamen wear a small plastic key that's supposed to open the gate to paradise. The graves of the fallen are adorned with softly drawn portrait photos—a break with Islamic tradition.*

Parallel to the Iraq-Iran war, which lasted from 1980 to 1988, the Iranian-financed Shiite Hezbollah begin to carry out suicide attacks with car bombs in Lebanon. Using the "diabolic innovation to marry the IRA's ANFO car bombs to the kamikaze," Mike Davis, "The Poor Man's Air Force," *Harper's Magazine,* October 2006. Hezbollah succeeds in attacking the US embassy in Beirut in 1983, killing over sixty people. An attack on the barracks of the Marine Corps stationed in Lebanon as a peacekeeping force with a Mercedes truck loaded with nearly five and a half tons of explosives kills 241 American soldiers in one fell swoop. US President Reagan sounds the retreat.

From then on, suicide bombing becomes popular with insurgents worldwide. Among the Tamils in Sri Lanka, among the Kurds in Turkey, and above all, among Islamists: in Chechnya, in Palestine, in Iraq, in Afghanistan. Since 2000, there have been hundreds every year.

The suicide attack is an armament measure to somehow counter advanced state control and surveillance techniques. The German Red Army Faction (RAF), active in the 1970s and 1980s, would probably have been unmasked in a matter of hours or days today. Claus Schenk Graf von Stauffenberg would only have had to sacrifice himself, and his assassination attempt on Adolf Hitler on July 20, 1944, would have been a sure success. Today, even suicide bombings usually only target civilians and lower-ranking soldiers. They derive their continuing horror solely from the fact that the tolerance of affluent society toward its own victims is steadily decreasing.*

The lower the tolerance toward victims, the more people are seen as victims in the first place: victims of traffic accidents, victims of discrimination, victims of waves of layoffs, victims of bullying, victims of medical malpractice, victims of cigarette advertising.* Without a political utopia promising a future end to all victimhood, most respond to their victimhood by demanding or suing for compensation.* Others resist social classification as victims: people with disabilities who insist on being considered differently abled, or young people from the lower classes who gather in gangs and show off to place themselves above all "victims." A third group escapes victim-hood by taking revenge and mutating from losers to martyrs.

It's not people who have little to lose anyhow, such as the hopelessly ill, who commit suicide attacks, but people who feel they've been treated particularly unfairly. In Western society, these are inhibited middle-class boys: perhaps a little too fat or too lanky, but not even really ugly. If they fail at school, life is still open to them thanks to their parents' money, connections, and concern—which is why they usually exempt their parents from their massacres. Harris, for example, video-tapes before the act: "I know my mom and dad will be just like...just fucking shocked beyond belief. I'm sorry, all right. I can't help it." Basically no one feels sorry for spree killers. True, there must be quite a few young people who also toy with the idea and just don't dare or can't get their hands on guns, but beyond that there is no Western counterculture that proclaims school spree killers as its heroes.

Western society has more sympathy for terrorists (or even gangsters) who tear others to death and try to escape with impunity than for those who don't exempt themselves from death. Because suicide bombers don't have to act from ambush, their attacks are considered even more devious. Moreover, they may not even experience the eventual benefit of their act.

It's doubtful whether RAF leader Andreas Baader was really concerned with a better world and not primarily with the pleasure of destruction. Osama bin Laden, too, had more exciting things to do when the Soviets were driven out of Af-ghanistan than to help build an Islamist society. But Baader and Bin Laden have at least pretended that their terror aims at a better world.

The Islamist suicide bombings are part of a civil war and at the same time bear the traits of a youth movement. This conflation resembles that in the European freedom move-ments of the nineteenth century or in the 1968 riots. In the latter, attempts to unite students and workers already failed; the differentiation of society was too advanced. The school spree killers are now taking atomization to its logical end.

• Sweetness
Ego Tribes

Middle-Class Warriors
What Comes after Welfare?
•

They're no longer forming a new youth culture, but they're continuing the radicalism that used to be characteristic of Western youth cultures. Youth cultures have imitated the tribe; an individual can't really do that.• In the role of the tribe, all that remains is to wait for your extinction or to carry it out yourself. But instead of dying miserably alone like Kurt Cobain, at least you sweep as many others as possible away to death. For all the ambiguity and unreality of the modern world, dead is dead.

When a timid student decides to commit the biggest massacre possible, it requires extensive preparation and will-power. Today's school spree killers may suffer from depression, delusions, teasing, or internet addiction, but they're not impulsive killers. Like jihadists, they don't see themselves as murderers, but as soldiers of their own blitzkrieg.• Harris writes, "This is just a two-man war against everything else." The spree killers have only one mission left, and they've drilled themselves extensively for it. Horror movies and killer games are training sessions designed to toughen them up and increase their ability to react. But our Western society doesn't want to grasp the obvious: the war on terror has long been a two-front war. The Islamists are at one front, and our own children are at the other.

## Terror's Child Muses
## 2021

> I was fascinated by terrorists as a child. Today, terrorism continues to be inspired by infantile forms of violence. In a pacified society, terrorism will be utterly childish.

The first people I fell in love with were terrorists. The German fear of the communist Red Army Fraction (RAF) peaked in 1977, when I turned eight years old. Every time I accompanied my mother to the post office, I went straight to the wanted poster next to the door and checked it for new faces. The terrorists could be anywhere, and surely we wouldn't notice them as, of course, they would appear very different by now. But I knew they wouldn't attack me or my parents since we weren't rich or powerful.

The first TV news reports I remember were about the RAF kidnapping of Hanns Martin Schleyer, president of the Federation of German Industries and former member of the Nazi SS.° I saw Schleyer with his sad puppy-dog eyes and counted the days of his kidnapping, spellbound. It was the terrorists who had made that ruthless capitalist and anti-Semite so heartily helpless. I didn't want him to ever be free again. It would undo his softness and turn him into a grim, loud man again.

German Federal Criminal Police Office wanted poster, 1972

At school, physical violence was a thing among boys, but in the RAF, the proportion of men and women was pretty equal. These women with long, straight hair and men with beards and big glasses appeared to me as perfect teachers. Their composed, waiting gazes met me from another world, and at any time, they could cross mine. I dreamt of being allowed to stay with them—just me. The war on terror was the new Cowboys and Indians, and I wanted to be with the outnumbered, fearless Indians and their noble cause. Big letters at the bottom of the poster warned, "Watch out, firearms!" But I knew they wouldn't harm me, and the police couldn't harm me either. I was too young. I counted as innocent, no matter what I would do.

Back then I had no idea that the founding members of the RAF had met during their common engagement against authoritarian suppression in juvenile shelters, part of an effort to activate fringe groups as the new revolutionary subject. Soon, in 1980, Iraq would start a war against Iran. Iran would hold against Iraq's military supremacy with thousands of pupils sacrificing themselves as human waves that cleared minefields or drew the enemy's fire. Mohammad Hossein Fahmideh rose to particular fame: at age thirteen, in a desperate military situation, with all his comrades injured or dead, he had supposedly wrapped himself in a grenade belt, pulled the pins out, and jumped underneath an Iraqi tank, killing himself, disabling the tank, and scaring off an Iraqi advance. In the Lebanese Civil War, Hezbollah, financed by Iran, revamped the suicide attack with the car bomb to attack the US embassy and the Marine Corps and make the US back out of the country.*

In the 1970s, terrorism had been at the forefront of globalization. United by anti-capitalism, various terrorist organizations had built international networks. Bank robberies and the Cold War catered them with lots of money. They lived in multiple luxurious flats and drove faster cars than the police. The romantic illegalism of early twentieth-century anarchism had evolved into a James Bond–like parallel jet set. Your life

• One-Man War

was risky, but there seemed to be a reasonable chance of staying undetected for several years and then retiring under-cover in a supportive socialist country. Rapidly progressing computer-based surveillance, DNA profiling, and the fall of the Wall put an end to these golden years. From then on, ter-rorists were best for a single strike. Trying to escape became an unnecessary waste. The suicide attack was terrorism's des-perate optimization, and children were its ideal practicians; their conception of death isn't fully developed, and they're rather easy to manipulate.

Only few terrorist suicide attacks have actually been executed by children. Using them with such cruelty has been too much of a taboo. Instead, fundamentalists have propa-gated suicide attacks as an act of radical manhood and orches-trated them—hyper dramatically up to the irreal—like action movies with supervillains happily anticipating paradise.* For leftist terrorism, the suicide attack has been less appealing, as the Left can't promise paradise. In addition, leftists have to resent the obvious divide between surviving leaders and self-sacrificing assassins. But numerous children around the world have felt inspired to commit their own suicide attacks, usually taking revenge at their most hated personal environ-ment: their school. Diaries left behind explain their motives.*

And again, these children became a main inspiration for the latest evolution of political terrorism: the lone wolf. With computer-based surveillance further evolving, even just the collective planning of a terrorist attack is likely to be de-tected. A successful attack has to happen out of a seemingly instant radicalization. Lone wolves have only limited technical and logistical means. Often, they spontaneously decide about their concrete target. To compensate for their moderate imme-diate impact, they often publish manifestos right before the attack that are meant to inspire others to follow their example. These manifestos resemble diaries of frustrated teenagers.

The distinction between spree killers and terrorists becomes more and more delicate and politically charged. Does the terrorist agenda primarily work as a moral justification

• Middle-Class Warriors
  What Comes after Welfare?

• One-Man War

for an impulsive revenge against the next best? As transformation of a suicide into an act of martyrdom? As the PR stunt of a desperate narcissist to be finally heard?

All these interpretations don't take the terrorist agenda seriously. They regard terrorists as mentally deranged or infantile. Terrorist threats have time and again been used by governments to declare belligerency and suspend certain civil rights. Now, the anti-terrorist agenda is not only meant to protect innocent people but also to protect potential terrorists from themselves.

While capitalism is what liberalizes autocratic regimes (at least on an economic level), anti-terrorism is what makes liberal regimes autocratic. Declaring terrorism the greatest threat to their population, well-established democracies have used the fight against it to break essential human rights like privacy, presumption of innocence, freedom of speech, and freedom of movement. Hundreds of thousands of people have been detained without trial, tortured, or killed. Governments have been secretly igniting terrorism against themselves to legitimatize further anti-terrorist measures.°

With the danger of lone wolves, governments don't need actual terrorism to legitimize draconic anti-terrorist measures. As soon as someone develops the intention of becoming a terrorist, it's already too late. Anti-terrorism has to kill off the root of the problem: people's attraction to terrorism. To imagine what this means, we can look at ways of combating pedophilia, an urge that's commonly condemned to the very core. Measures against terrorism might include the AI-based scanning of all digital—and eventually also nondigital—communication for dubious remarks and patterns, prophylactic medication of the jeopardized, and the ban of any media and communication that could be interpreted as a glorification of terror.

The term *terrorism* was originally coined to denounce governmental massacres and executions during the French Revolution. In the 1970s, the term got appropriated to denounce attacks that were meant to fight terrorist governments. Still, the use of the term seemed justified insofar as these attacks didn't aim at an immediate coup. Rather, they were meant to frighten the government and the ruling classes to a point where they would either give up by themselves or react with draconian measures that would then provoke a proper civil war. Lone wolves today spread terror without any specific plan. The limited impact of their attacks shows an inverse ratio to their global ambition. They would be foremost ridiculous, if anti-terrorism wouldn't have developed a similar inverse ratio between increasing measures and further successes.

But could anti-terrorism finally become so effective that terrorism stops altogether? Or could it become far too obvious that all that keeps terrorism going is the outrageous anti-terror response? To evaluate these scenarios, we have to consider how terrorism and the definition of terrorism might evolve in the future.

### Cyber Terror

The common history of terrorism starts with the Sicarii ("dagger wielders"), a splinter group of the Zealots who were fighting against the Roman occupation of Judea by attacking and kidnapping Romans and their collaborators with small daggers, concealed in their clothes. But around the same time—the first century BC—another group of terrorists was really worrying the Roman empire: pirates. Marcus Tullius Cicero defined them as "communis hostis omnium" ("the common enemy of all"), which later, in the Middle Ages, transformed into "hostis humani generis" ("enemies of humankind"), for they're neither national criminals nor soldiers acting according to the rules of a lawful battle. Disenchanted sailors, they sought revenge against the world. Samuel Bellamy (1689-1717), "Prince of the Pirates," likened himself to Robin Hood and allegedly boasted: "I am a free prince, and I have as much authority to make war on the whole world as he who has a hundred sail of ships at sea and an army of 100,000 men in the field." Captain Samuel Bellamy, quoted in Captain Charles Johnson, *A General History of the Robberies and Murders of the Most Notorious Pyrates* (London: T. Warner, 1724).

Similar to terrorists in the twentieth and twenty-first centuries, pirates found clandestine support from regular states to complement their official politics. It was only when these states realized that they had created an uncontrollable force that most European nations would sign the Declaration of Paris (1856), which abolished privateering.

Today, it's even more difficult to hide on the sea and its myriad shoals and islands than on land. Ships can be observed via satellite, and it's still not possible to stay permanently under water. While at sea every nation has the right to act upon pirates, on land terrorists can find protection in a favorable state.

Cyberspace promised to be the new extraterrestrial. Young, often minor hackers were the first to explore how crypto technology and self-replicating malware allow one to act anonymously, secretly, and remotely. Anonymous, the most famous cyber activist group, has for years been attacking numerous states and companies to oppose censorship and discrimination. The more AI evolves and the more the physical and the digital world entangle, the less cyberterrorism is reduced to disrupting online services and leaking information. Cyberattacks can manipulate elections or the operation of highly risky ventures like nuclear reactors, chemical plants, or airports.

Advancing robot technology (cars, drones, personal assistants, nanobots) and microchip implants might make cyber assassinations more likely than they are today, but so far, cyberterrorism hasn't resulted in immediate murder. The most severe cyberattacks have likely been executed by nation-states. How could that be changed? In 1995, crypto anarchist Jim Bell proposed an "assassination market," where people could donate anonymously to a fund that will be given to whoever predicts the correct date of a certain person's death—inside information that an assassinator could profit from. James Dalton Bell, "Assassination Politics" (1995–96), originally published on the alt. anarchism Usenet newsgroup. Alternatively, a cryptocurrency could be launched whose mined profits go to a terrorist organization. Sympathizers could offer their goods and services in exchange for this terror coin. But still, the killing has to be performed by hand.

Sea Terror
To be successful in the long run, terrorists have to please the law of the mob—attacking persons who large parts of the population detest and want to be punished. Terrorism isn't just a means to a far-fetched end, but a satisfying act of revenge in itself. Sympathies are particularly huge for attacks against occupiers—as performed by the Sicarii. Contemporary terrorist organizations that assassinate common people follow a rhetoric of decolonization. Islamists attack random Westerners as imperialistic spreaders of blasphemy and consumerism; racists attack random Jews as conspiratorial rulers or random migrants as ancestors of a creeping occupation. Leftist terrorists have a more challenging agenda, as their ideology complicates differentiating between the value of certain lives and killing out of revenge. This nobleness is why I, as a child, intuitively fell for the RAF.

In retrospect, however, RAF terrorists don't appear that noble either. In need of self-defense (not of their lives, but against ending up in prison), the actions of the RAF became desperate. Still, they continued to make the rich and the powerful feel vulnerable—to the benefit of social justice. Back then, Germany's Gini coefficient—a number measuring the degree of inequality—was one of the lowest in the Western world.

Today, the ultra-wealthy fear their own AI creations going berserk more than they fear other humans taking revenge on them for paying puny wages, bribing politicians, evading taxes, serving dictatorships, and damaging the environment.[•] Bulletproof cars, defensive architecture, and ubiquitous surveillance have made it far more difficult to attack the rich. All the while, those who feel inclined to terrorism got lazy. Since the suicide attack frees one from the effort to escape and hide, a minimalist approach prevails: just hire a van and ram it against some strangers, or shoot around at a public square and gain a lot of attention anyhow.

Like the Russian nihilist group Narodnaya Volya that used the then-recently invented dynamite to build bombs and throw them at Tsar Alexander II in 1881, for a new wave of well-targeted, awe-inspiring attacks, terrorism would have to adapt the latest technology. From 1911 to 1912, the French anarchist Bande à Bonnot operated with cars and repeating rifles, which were not yet available to the French police. Al Qaeda staged what must have been the most impressive terrorist attack so far, 9/11, by transforming jumbo jets into bombs.

After the discovery of genetic engineering in the 1970s, bioterrorism appeared as a likely new threat. Microbes and viruses could theoretically be manipulated in ways to attack only certain parts of the population, and with the ability to self-replicate, causing millions of casualties from a single attack. Ecoterrorists could threaten to relieve nature by minimizing human overpopulation.

But so far, there have been only few significant bioterrorist attacks—with natural agents like salmonella or anthrax and fatalities falling short of expectations. Most famously, in 1995, the doomsday cult Aum Shinrikyo used sarin in five attacks on three Tokyo subway lines. Thousands of people were injured, but only thirteen died. Bioweapons are rather difficult to manufacture or acquire, and difficult to target. In the future, CRISPR might make it easy to design pathogens that kill people of a certain gender or race. This is appealing to racists and sexists, but not to leftists. What could they do to again spread terror among the bigwigs, like the RAF?

The place where the ultra-wealthy make themselves most vulnerable is at sea. Superyachts allow them to travel to the most remote places without leaving a personally fitted comfort zone. Even more, some ultra-wealthy have a juvenile background in cyber privacy and dream of moving completely offshore to meet their libertarian ideals with their real lives, just as they do with their financial assets. Still, while it's rather easy to hide the identity of your personal devices on the internet, an Automatic Identification System (AIS) is mandatory for international voyaging passenger ships of all sizes. The AIS makes it easy to follow the precise paths of superyachts. They can be protected with potent nonlethal arms like sonic beams, laser beams, pain beams, security smoke, barbed wire, flare guns, and water cannons, but the moment passengers leave the vessel to swim, dive, surf, or jet ski, they become easy targets. Besides, any yacht would be defenseless against a rocket attack or a limpet mine attached by a diver.

Assassinating the ultra-wealthy outside the confines of state legislation would beat them at their own game. Just as the ultra-wealthy profit from small island states that serve as tax havens, terrorists could operate from impoverished island states that allow for the uncontrolled private accumulation of weapons and explosives. To protect their arsenal from air raids, terrorists could hide it undersea. To approach the superyachts without arousing suspicion, they could disguise themselves as Indigenous fishers or artisans. The most villainous could bring children as human shields or distractions.

### Stochastic Terror

Another promising terrorist strategy is to overcome the ambition of immediate killings. The success of the international operations of Al Qaeda and the Islamic State was based on the interaction of a charismatic leadership and autonomous local cells. The direct communication between masterminds and executive force can also be completely cut. Rather than instructing terrorists, the masterminds can incite them with propaganda and instructions that are so vague that their prosecution demands a wide-ranging censorship, like how former US president Donald Trump kept his encouragements for violent uproars allegorical enough to avoid impeachment and prosecution.

More concrete incitements can be formulated anonymously and hidden in games. The author of the popular conspiracy myth QAnon stayed unknown for several years. See Tom Cleary, "Paul Furber: 5 Fast Facts You Need to Know," *Heavy*, November 7,

2022, https://heavy.com/news/2018/08/paul-furber/. Shock sites with horror stories and memes (creepypasta) are particularly appealing to children. In 2014, two twelve-year-old American girls stabbed another twelve-year-old classmate nineteen times to become proxies of the fictional meme character Slender Man. Recent neo-Nazi networks like Atomwaffen Division or The Base propagate their cause with memes, and their known followers are often minors.

Challenges that evolve over several levels and take from several weeks to several years can guide people toward gradual radicalization. Think of the lure of level cults like Scientology or Alcoholics Anonymous. In 2016, the Blue Whale online challenge made headlines—a series of fifty tasks, the last one supposedly being suicide. Alternatively, such a challenge could lead to a terror attack. To make this "riddle terror" utterly unpredictable, the challenge could automatically generate a personalized attack scenario for each participant. Or maybe only some of the participants get chosen to attack—randomly (Russian terror roulette) or according to their merits. Nobody aside from the developers of the challenge would know about its parameters, just as nobody would know how many people are participating in it. If you're chosen, clues could lead to logistical guidance and technical support, like weapons or explosives.

### Deathbed Terror

People who commit suicide can't be punished, but ending your own life can be hard. You can avoid this obstacle by waiting to attack until you have to die anyway.[*] You can start your attack literally from the deathbed: your flatline ignites the bomb. As the bomb has to be installed some time ahead, it's most secure to place it on your own property. The damage can still be significant, if your home is situated in a dense urban area or huge apartment block.

More boldly, you could start your attack some days before your supposed death. Imagine a president whose days alive are counted and who uses the state's nuclear arsenal as

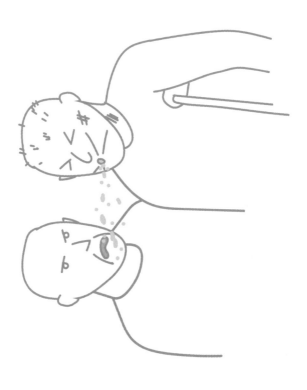

"Old and terminally ill climate activists tried to infect themselves with COVID-19 in order to infect as many other people as possible before death took them anyway." Still from my video series *Deutsch Süd-Ost*, 2020, illustration: Mad Smell

a tool for extortion. Or in case you have a deadly, infectious disease, you can turn it into a slow-motion suicide attack by infecting as many people as possible, only revealing your route of terror posthumously.

If you're old and deathly ill, most people will condemn deathbed terrorism as particularly inglorious. But if you're a child with fatal leukemia and you detonate yourself at the headquarters of the company whose pollution might be responsible for your sickness, it will break people's hearts.

### Speculative Terror

Terrorism works as its own amplifier. The deed is so outrageous that the attention it draws is far greater than its immediate harm. Terrorism is the brute prototype of mass media. Mass media copies the efficacy of terrorism without necessarily doing harm. The disruptive force of mass media is a sublimated form of terrorism (I, for one, lost my enthusiasm for terrorism and became a writer). But a terrorist attack is also the perfect feed for mass media. Mass media further multiplies its force.

In 1991, Don DeLillo's novel *Mao II* juxtaposed the insignificance of a secluded, alcoholic novelist and the momentousness of a Maoist terror organization. As the novelist is an elderly White male alcoholic, while the terrorists are young, vital Arabs, the book anticipated Samuel P. Huntington's 1993 *Foreign Affairs* article "The Clash of Civilizations?" and became quite a success.

DeLillo and his readers didn't know that since 1978, the year after the peak of the RAF, an American man had already been combining secluded writing and terrorism: the Unabomber. Ted Kaczynski lived a primitive life in the forest and sent out a total of sixteen mail bombs, killing three and injuring twenty-three, to oppose technical progress. Then, in 1995, already in his fifties, Kaczynski extorted established US newspapers to publish a book-long rant against the modern world in exchange for ending his attacks.

Kaczynski was unaware that a recent technological

invention was about to make his deal unnecessary. He could have easily communicated to the whole world via the internet, and every further bombing would have added testimonial power. Children, traditionally completely excluded from publishing, understood this—leading to a steep increase in school shootings in the late 1990s.*

Then came the rise of social media and a decrease in mass school shootings committed by their pupils. Adolescents didn't need to spread terror to be heard; they could turn into bloggers, vloggers, influencers, and memers with millions of followers. In the past, closed communities like tribes, churches, sects, or families were needed to terrorize humans just with phantasms and ideas. Children were particularly subject to this indoctrination. But with social media becoming more and more immersive (live streams, HD, 3D), they themselves can turn into manipulators—subjecting other children and inspiring grown-ups.

A common terror among children is bullying: you menace and defame, also openly in front of others, to mark your superior position. Adults usually bully more discreetly to avoid retaliation. On the internet, this isn't necessary, as you can troll people who don't know or won't recognize you. Online rating systems enable one-click bullying.

Even more, children can utterly enjoy teaming up against someone. When adults do this, their individualism and moralism tend to blame it as unfair and scapegoating, unless that someone acted as an obvious tyrant. On the internet, however, everybody can spontaneously or systematically gang up on particular subjects without merging into a mob: sign a petition, boycott someone or something, or bet against them. It doesn't take too much of a personal investment to bankrupt a company or even a state, install a new currency, or shame a person to death.

As children are good at instantly making up stories or delving into one story then another, their synchronizations can be highly unpredictable. On the internet, the algorithms that guide our use of search engines and social media are programmed to keep us on the consumerist track. But sudden or steered events can lead to collective actions that run out of control.

Such actions could spread terror with an explicitly anti-terrorist agenda, like going against people with certain common traits that are supposed to identify them as terrorists, warning of energy vampires that act from a distance and leave no traces, outer space terrorists who intend to kidnap our whole planet, superior beings who will punish us in or out of the future, or identifying accidents or natural disasters as clandestine terror attacks.

To contain decentralized synchronizations of agency, governments can either openly operate autocratically—through censorship and the banning of group formations and assemblies both offline and online—or gently paternalistically, making curiosity and lust for adventure unappealing unless they follow predesigned, risk-free tracks. In the latter case, the state's monopoly on the use of physical force is superseded by a monopoly of mental force.

Many science fictions, from Aldous Huxley's novel *Brave New World* (1932) to Marco Brambilla's film *Demolition Man* (1993), have given an outlook onto the shift from physical force to mental force. Usually, it's understood as new technological possibilities being abused by a powerful elite to lull the masses. But paradoxically, the post-liberal condition of today is consolidated by an expanding understanding of freedom: the more affluent, educated societies condemn as discriminating and abusive, the more unpleasant opinions and information can't just be blamed as stirring terror, but as terror in themselves.*

Stratified societies condemn unwanted remarks as blasphemy or disgrace, while post-liberal societies condemn them to protect the weak. One is about not besmirching the victors, the other about destigmatizing the victims. In a post-liberal world, children are the only humans who are still somewhat tolerated to go wild against others; in particular against grown-ups, as it's they who generally dominate children.

As a child, I loved the RAF terrorists exactly for not acting childish. I loved them for their sense of reality and justice, for their numerical inferiority and their cold-blooded efficiency. They didn't make up stories or rage against the weak. In contrast, the future of terrorism is utterly childish. Whoever exerts terror will be degraded as not really grown-up.

### Confined Terror

Even a radically pacified human society exceeds a tremendous amount of terror, in particular against nonhuman beings. When it comes to nature, we're all terrorists—in the narrow sense of exerting lethal, intimidating violence. And nature is mirroring this terror back on us as global warming, storms, droughts, contaminations, plagues ...*

This makes any fight against human terrorism that suspends general personal freedoms highly disproportional and anthropocentric. If we regard terrorism as childish, the obvious solution is to treat terrorists like dangerous children—not fully responsible for their actions. If they can't be appeased with drugs, therapy, or sublimation, they can be locked up, either temporarily on their own or together with others of their kind; not to punish them but to prevent them from doing harm.

We experience this already today online, though in a privatized, erratic way: mainstream social media is cleaned up of what is considered to be hate speech, overexposure of violence or sexual obscenity, while fringe social media allows for more.* This separation could be implemented with transparent and steady criteria, both online and offline. Whoever feels like speaking or acting more aggressively or having more aggressive experiences would just need to move to special zones of terror. Their harshness ranges from unlimited freedom of speech to certain nonconsensual forms of violence. Leaving these zones is possible at any time, but once you leave, you're put on probation and under special observation for a period that depends on the harshness of the zone.

Terror zones replace safe spaces. With safety being the norm, terror becomes the protected exception. Terror zones

"Nazis were settled on a voluntary basis in Nazi Zoos, where, with didactic contextualization, they were granted unrestricted freedom of expression." Still from my video series *Deutsch Süd-Ost*, 2020, collage: Mad Smell

are the civilizational equivalent to wildlife reserves, protecting both: the wild life inside and the tame life outside. If animals, plants, and terrorists all count as minors, a truly diverse and inclusive society has to protect all of them as its victims and offer them an adequate habitat.*

What Comes after Welfare?
2015

The Islamic State has staged its outrageous acts of violence like video games. In doing so, it follows a Western tradition of romanticizing terrorism as an ultimate act of passion. For the affluent Western world to outdo the Islamic State's radicality, it must reactivate the original Romantic force—love—to not only celebrate longing but to also seek and achieve all-encompassing emotional fulfillment.

Magic aims to make ideas an immediate reality. Enlightened doubts as to magic's feasibility promote an art able to act free from worry that what it portrays will become real. To the extent that "magic" happens after all, responsibility in enlightened societies lies not with the person who came up with an idea, but the person who implemented it. Not only can the person who had the idea not be held accountable, they can't forbid this kind of realization, unlike in the case of a patent. A person who reproduces artworks as such has to ask the creator for permission—but not the person who makes it real. Thus, it's precisely the strict division between fiction and reality that contributes to fiction's continual, unregulated crossing over into real life.

  The coexistence of an enlightened and a magical understanding of the world can lead to concatenations that are as absurd as they are devastating. Last year, the US entered the Syrian civil war because action movie–inspired Islamists in the Syrian desert—introduced by a London rapper—beheaded an American journalist. Soon after, the US regarded the Sony Pictures hack as the second attack by another country on their own soil since Pearl Harbor—as revenge for the fact that the American action comedy *The Interview* (2014) shows North Korea's despot Kim Jong-un getting his head blown off. And again, a short time later, the editors of French satirical newspaper *Charlie Hebdo* were executed for its caricatures of Islam, the attackers acting like players in a first-person shooter game. •

Like in an action movie or first-person shooter game, it seems all too clear who is in the right: here is the prudent West, which knows how to distinguish between fiction and reality; over there are the spoiled young North Korean dictator and the infantile Islamists, who don't accept this line at all. On this end, we have the good West, putting everything into motion as soon as a single innocent person was slain; at that end, a bunch of religious believers who wandered straight from fantasy thrillers to the Middle Ages, and a Stalinism throwback, increasingly *Austin Powers*-esque dictatorship that can't bear to see its leader ridiculed abroad.

But the West also frequently confuses fiction and reality. To make this clear, one doesn't even have to guess how it would feel if an Egyptian film studio run by the Muslim Brotherhood were to produce a blockbuster showing Israel's President Benjamin Netanyahu as a whoremongering idiot blasting away with an army tank—a man two journalists (backed by Egyptian intelligence) were ordered to kill and who is blown up in the end; one need only recall how last year, the actress Scarlett Johansson successfully sued French author Grégoire Delacourt because he published a novel about a woman whose physical resemblance to Johansson is so close that she's constantly being mistaken for her.

It's not just pride and vanity that cause Western societies to take fiction at face value. Ever since the Enlightenment asserted that art is autonomous—groundbreaking in Immanuel Kant's *Kritik der Urtheilskraft* (*Critique of Judgment*) from 1790—there has also been the demand that this autonomy should serve the autonomy of individuals, freeing them from lust and convention. And again, this is most effective when one emulates art in real life.

The Enlightenment can't actually endorse a mechanism like this. Accordingly, what literary critic Harold Bloom deems "the first modern novel," Miguel de Cervantes's *Don Quixote* (part 1, 1605; part 2, 1615), is about a man who mistakes his life for a knightly story. Cervantes's book was meant to undermine the influence of what he referred to as "the slew of vain books on chivalry." And yet the progress of the Enlightenment would be unthinkable without such attempts to emulate art.

This is most striking in the new phenomenon of the youth movement: because the Enlightenment declared existing traditions and myths to be nonbinding, any young generation is free to create its own—most easily with the help of artworks still largely untouched by reception history. From the beginning—meaning since the Romantic period—the hallmark characteristic of youth movements has been that their followers not only identify with literary—and later, film—heroes, but imitate them. It started with Johann Wolfgang von Goethe's *Die Leiden des jungen Werthers* (*The Sorrows of Young Werther,* 1774), where the protagonist's clothing sparked a fashion trend and several fans went so far as to copy his lovelorn suicide. Appropriation like this is generally unintended by the producers of these artifacts (i.e., the writers, directors, actors, and singers), which can only feed the fanaticism of their followers.

In recent decades, this mechanism has lost momentum in the Western world. In the wake of growing commodification, advertising also aggressively works with the promise that qualities attributed to an artifact automatically transfer to the buyer. At the same time, it continually copies and profanes concrete motives of youth movements. Multibillionaires like Richard Branson, Elon Musk, or Jeff Bezos draw on their childhood dreams, not their youth, in the desires that drive them. Often, these are things that existed already back then (space travel, cars with gullwing doors)—just not for them.

In the end, the diminished Romantic suggestion also

• Society of Games • Terror's Child Muses • One-Man War

hits capitalism right in the bottom line. It's not just the critical moment for social change that's lacking. Technological progress suffers as well, since, after all, every great technical venture of the twentieth century—the flight to the moon, the internet, the atom bomb—was initially derived from science fiction and then became a collective vision borne by the state.

In order to evolve, society needs transgressions that either diffuse reality as a fiction or intensify fiction as reality. Childhood learning is based on nothing else.* Anyone who always knows exactly how to separate fiction from reality is doomed to mental ossification. Thanks to postmodernism, Western society is more conscious of this than ever before, only it doesn't seem to help. A number of developing formats such as reality TV, scripted reality, docu-fiction, and mockumentary have the encroaching of fiction into reality as a precondition, but they also tame it. The abolition of the separation between fiction and reality becomes so ordinary that the autonomy of art is called into question. Art thus loses both its innocence and its magical power, which consists precisely in giving presence to something that is *not*.

These days, a truly Romantic transgression is stirring at the one taboo that's intrinsic to the welfare state: violence.* Whoever practices violence can still perceive themselves as being in control—of those they inflict the violence on, but also and especially of their own cowardice and shame. Those who prefer to think of themselves as lone wolves will opt for the rampage, while those searching for connection to the group become hooligans or Islamists.*

Even when Al Qaeda was drawing young men from around the world, it was still difficult to think of it as a youth movement. Attacks like 9/11 were clearly inspired by American films. Yet in his barren hideout, the ailing, gaunt millionaire's son Osama bin Laden looked like a cave hermit who barely knows what a video camera is. His entire self-presentation was designed to claim the greatest possible contrast to the Western world. This is different with the Islamic State. The name recalls the Nation of Islam, an African American freedom movement. The urge to wear a big, bushy beard and banish cropped trousers—any one of today's hipsters could identify with that.* And when you see Islamic State fighters shooting Syrian soldiers from the hip with machine guns or severing their heads on command, they do it as skillfully as at a showy Brooklyn butcher shop.

It's no wonder, the evil Islamists are really only Westerners themselves. No matter where they grew up, be it with Islamic parents or converted, they were shaped by the same shocking, violent productions staged in first-person shooter games and action movies. Execution videos released by the Islamic State copy this aesthetic in both their presentation and special effects; similar to reality TV, they're done to maximize the moment of shock and at the same time to defuse it as unreal.*

Likewise, when a chubby Kim Jong-un sits casually in a chair moved away from a desk—cigarette in his left hand, right hand on his knee, watching the launch of a North Korean long-range missile—it's not a foreign evil we're seeing but a porky little couch potato marked by excessive film and television consumption. Only unlike Homer Simpson, it's not a run-down nuclear power plant he's controlling but an entire run-down country, nuclear weapons production and all.

Where other dictators dabbled in poetry, the Kim Dynasty reveres the cinema. Kim Jong-un's father, Kim Jong-il, was a great cineaste, like his father before him. He wrote the book *The Cinema and Directing* (1987) and ordered the kidnapping of legendary South Korean director Shin Sang-ok and his ex-wife, actress Choi Eun-hee, so that he could produce films with them. The entire country—insofar as it's accessible to foreigners—resembles a massive film set. The Sony Pictures hack would have been the first, frighteningly successful outdoor shot.

But what option is there for those who want to be good but want to avoid being taken for idiots or horrible bores? How can they commit equally drastic offenses that are unequivocally good? Only love can do that. The same, overwhelming

Orcies •    Sweetness •

• Intimate Correctness    Consensual Gift Economy

love that Romantics exalted in the beginning and that has never been fulfilled.° Even if our society understands itself to be hedonistic, psychotropic drugs dim the libido of a large part of the population. Commodities and lighting conditions are referred to as romantic.° People who don't find enough love are told to blame their upbringing, rather than just giving it to them.

Today's welfare states give many people sufficient time and leisure to not only open up to love like the hippies but also to systematically drill into it—a love that applies not only to an individual, family, horde, or nation but to every still-so-hateful sentient being. This means, in effect, that on the street you not only give out "free hugs" but also "free pettings" and gaze at one another in awe. That you extend more than just sympathy to your neighbors, and that your desire for love—including sensual love—is always magically fulfilled, every-where.° Any advertising claim would pale in comparison to this; even the most brutal violence wouldn't seem radical enough. But first we need literature, films, and games showing a new, all-encompassing, overpowering love that we would absolutely want to follow.

# VII. VAST REDISTRIBUTION

Monadism dismisses previous efforts for a just society as
patchy and pleads for their fundamental revision.

## Acknowledge Your Own Oppression
2017

> Democracy is fundamentally unjust. Human rights can moderate majority rule only so much, and identity politics often ends in rivalry. The art world caters to the remorse of the privileged by acting as a temperate agent of the oppressed—widely ignorant of its own oppression.

I have a White, middle-class background. But in Germany, the fact that my parents only went to elementary school was (and still would be) enough to make it pretty unlikely that I would attain a high school diploma and study at university. I'm left-handed, like 10 percent of the population. Still, most gadgets are constructed only for right-handed people, and "left-handed" is a colloquial term for "clumsy." Left-handed people are much more likely to suffer from schizophrenia or to become president of the US—though the latter only applies if you're male, White, and of above-average height.[*]

So far, there has never been a political system that catered equally to all people. By common Western understanding, representative democracy comes closest to such a system. But a democracy is the dictatorship of the majority of voters over the rest of the population: the other voters; the people who don't feel represented by any party or candidate; the people who don't have the right to vote; and the beings who aren't human. Furthermore, parties and candidates are manipulated and bribed.•

We tend to believe in democracy as a guarantor of general—human—rights because democratic constitutions usually include such rights. But this isn't because democracy and human rights are intrinsically linked; rather, it's because they contradict each other. Human rights are supposed to tame democracy. And, as populists would argue, democracy is supposed to tame human rights.

Declaring certain rights isn't enough to put them into effect, as—even though in a more indirect way—judges, too, are selected by the ruling part of the population. Which is why, in the US—whose Bill of Rights was ratified in 1791—it wasn't until 1865 that slavery was forbidden, not until 1920 that women gained the right to vote, not until 1924 that Native Americans gained full citizenship, not until 1962 that all states gave Native Americans the right to vote, and not until 1965 that Black voters were no longer allowed to be discriminated against by poll taxes and literacy tests. Note, 2024: As the current majority of constitutional "originalists" in the US Supreme Court proves, these developments are reversible.

The realization that democracy and constitutional rights alone will never serve everyone to the same degree has led to identity politics.• Proponents of identity politics argue that instead of just pleading for equal rights, the oppressed have to unite to oppress the privileged. The first successful example of identity politics (avant la lettre) was the working class. By organizing themselves into trade unions and thereby monopolizing the supply of labor, members of the working class managed to drastically improve their living conditions. Marxism even called for the abolition of democracy and for its preliminary replacement by a "dictatorship of the proletariat."• It's a concept that—even though you could question whether it was ever truly realized—turned into a major threat for the representative democracies of the Western world. Around 1970, almost half of the world's population was ruled by Marxist-related governments.

Pre-AGI Democracy  •
•  Consensual Gift Economy
•  Mutual Enslavements

It's more than a coincidence that the term "identity politics" started to gain popularity in the 1980s, at a time when the working class lost power, and more and more Marxist governments were defeated. Civil rights movements could no longer rely on support through a socialist struggle. Moreover, one of the main reasons that socialism went downhill was obviously that it was also dominated by White male supremacists and never really cared about all the people who were too oppressed to even hold regular jobs.

Without a powerful and uniting instrument such as trade unions, identity politics focused on affirmative action• and the use of language.• Instead of fighting together, oppressed groups often ended up in open rivalry: the precarious creative class ridiculed the working class as being from the past, while the working class went against migrants and women; in the US, African Americans skirmished with the relatively privileged minorities of Asians and Jews; in Europe, feminists ranted against Arab migrants.•

From a liberal point of view, identity politics embraces oppressed communities for insisting on their identities, not necessarily for their identities as such. Identity politics might even strategically support communities that oppose liberal values. Their identities are supposed to level off once equal rights are achieved. But with the end of the postwar golden era of social welfare, the plea for universal rights appears to be more contaminated than ever with White supremacy. Liberal identity politics is chasing its own tail.

In recent decades, no well-established social subsystem glorified expansive universal rights more than the Western art world. Though this world caters mainly to the White and the rich, it is, at the same time, so irrelevant that it hasn't been able to do much harm to either the privileged or the oppressed. Inclusion became the Western art world's main imperative (whether in terms of gender, race, or even nature) in a thoroughly paternalistic setup, extending from exhibitions at splendid spaces to an artistic practice of unsolicited appropriation. The art world has been all too aware of its

*Itsies  •Intimate Correctness  •Heightism*

abusive nature and has reflected on it so extensively that institutional critique has become its own genre. Permanently
mirroring its own moral failure, the art world has gotten lost
in narcissistic self-correction.

Meanwhile, the era of White supremacy is already waning. So far, only the Far Right seems to realize this, and it
victimizes itself as just another oppressed community that
needs protection.• But to selflessly insist on expansive universal rights makes you even more of an oppressed minority, and,
instead of just eating its own tail, the cause for truly universal
rights could lift itself up by its own bootstraps as well.

Today, most artists and curators have an income that's
below the local average of a regular worker. Many curatorial
positions are temporary and pay like internships. Most artists'
incomes are eaten up by rising studio rents and production
costs, or are hopelessly low to begin with. And the privilege of
meeting rich people in private, and perhaps even being invited
to their homes without having sex with them, doesn't pay
the bills.•

But unlike members of the working class, artists and
curators have never really fought collectively for better working conditions. Artists' unions never gained leverage for proper strikes.
The New York-based activist organization W.A.G.E., which is trying to
establish a moderate minimum payment for freelance work in the nonprofit art sector, has so far been ignored by most major museums and
institutions in the US. Counterfactually, they regard themselves
as privileged (as a kind of courtless court of the rich) and
burden themselves with an immense sense of social responsibility that goes nowhere.

Taking universal rights seriously, the main social
responsibility of artists and curators is not to look upon
oppressed communities, but to acknowledge being one of
them, keen to unite. For the arts, oppression should be less a
theme, more a collective challenge.

• Orcies

• Expanded Sex Work

# Heightism
2021

Identity politics has sensitized us to a wide variety of discriminations. But the most fundamental, intersectional, and obvious discrimination—even beyond the human realm—has been largely overlooked: heightism.

As freely as Donald Trump told the untruth as president of the US, he showed an affinity for autocrats and dictators. But to whom exactly? While Trump's tens of thousands of untruths were carefully counted and sorted by the media, little effort was made to analyze his preferences in this regard more closely.

Brazilian President Jair Bolsonaro was programmatically very close to Trump in his combination of neoliberal economic policies with disregard for ethnic minorities and basic liberal rights. But while Bolsonaro courted Trump again and again, describing himself as "engaged" to him and greeting him with "I love you" at a UN General Assembly meeting, Trump only replied coolly, "Good to see you again," and didn't visit him once. Trump's personal favorites were undoubtedly Vladimir Putin and Kim Jong-un. He praised Putin as "brilliant" and a "terrific person," and with Kim he even hinted at a romance: "He wrote me beautiful letters and they're great letters. We fell in love."

This unequal treatment might have followed strategic considerations. The Russian government had helped Trump get elected, and North Korea was an economically insignificant country. However, when you place Bolsonaro, Putin, and Kim side by side in your mind, another, more banal reason stands out: Bolsonaro is almost as tall as the officially 1.90-meter-tall Trump, while Putin and Kim are at most 1.65 meters tall. Meetings with the latter two gave Trump the opportunity to outdo them by almost a head.

Trump also repeatedly played up his height against political opponents. Among his most popular defamatory adjectives, "little" ranked first, alongside "dopey," "sleepy," "nutty," and "crazy." He called the 1.72-meter-tall Democratic presidential candidate Michael Bloomberg "Mini Mike," and in a televised duel with 1.65-meter-tall Hillary Clinton, Trump repeatedly lined up behind her, clearly towering over her.

You can dismiss Trump's belief that political superiority derives from height as childish and narcissistic, but election research proves him right. Since the advent of television, the taller US presidential candidate has almost always won, except in reelections. Only Gerald Ford and Al Gore lost despite larger bodies—both burdened with the stigma of vice presidency. The fact that Trump failed in his reelection against Joe Biden— former vice president and several centimeters shorter than Trump—could be largely due to the fact that Trump wasn't allowed to stand next to him in televised debates because of the COVID-19 pandemic.

In Europe, height doesn't seem to be that important at first glance. In France, the last presidents—Nicolas Sarkozy (1.66 meters), François Holland (1.70 meters), and Emmanuel Macron (1.72 meters), the latter of whom has also been ensnared by Trump—were all of below-average height. In Germany, the giant Helmut Kohl (1.95 meters) was followed by the small Gerhard Schröder (1.74 meters) and Angela Merkel (1.65 meters). But perhaps this is also because in Europe, tall people tend to be drawn to business rather than politics.

As early as 2004, the German Institute for Economic

Research calculated that in Germany, every additional centimeter of height increases the gross wage of equally qualified men by an average of 0.6 percent. With a difference of ten centimeters, the effect added up to 2,000 euros per year. Studies in the US came to similar results.

The differences are particularly striking on the executive floors of large companies. In his book *Blink*, Malcolm Gladwell calculated that the male CEOs of the five hundred US companies with the highest sales are three inches, or around 7.5 centimeters, taller than average. While 3.9 percent of adult males in the normal population were over six feet tall, the figure was nearly one-third among the top CEOs. Gladwell sums up that "being short is probably as much of a handicap to corporate success as being a woman or an African American." Malcolm Gladwell, *Blink: The Power of Thinking without Thinking* (New York: Little, Brown, 2005).

In the past, a tall stature indicated greater strength and an upscale parental home that had provided better nutrition. In an automated affluent society, it has little practical use anymore. On the contrary, tall people are above all a social burden: they're more likely to develop cancer, require more food and space, and produce (directly and indirectly) more carbon dioxide.

It's true that in the case of women's income, their relative body size is less important—for them, it's rather a low body mass index that matters. But the question remains whether the persistent unequal wages and career opportunities for women and men aren't essentially due to their height difference of fourteen centimeters on average. You might also wonder what would remain of ageism if we grew rather than shrank in old age. Or whether we're more willing to show solidarity with discriminated against African Americans than with discriminated against Latinos, since the former are similar in height to Whites while the latter are significantly smaller.

To most people, "heightism" isn't even a term. Yet heightism runs through all areas of society and everyone's thought patterns. Not even the research of size-dependent behavioral differences is free of it. For a long time, this research was mainly limited to the evaluation of the thesis, known as the Napoleon complex, or small man syndrome, that the feelings of inferiority of small men lead to an increased lust for power and a readiness to use violence. Investigations yielded negative results: men who feel discriminated against for being small are more paranoid, suspicious, and jealous, but they're also more willing to cooperate and don't lose their temper as easily. "Short Men 'Not More Aggressive,'" BBC News, March 28, 2007, http://news.bbc.co.uk/1/hi/uk/6501633.stm. A possible tall man syndrome—an above-average body size leading to overconfidence and increased lust for power—has been ignored by research. Yet it would explain Trump's self-assurance when denying his defeat by Biden.

Perhaps most seriously, heightism is expressed in our relationship with nature. If we're concerned about endangered species, it's primarily regarding large-bodied ones such as trees, elephants, monkeys, bears, dolphins, or whales. In particular, we discriminate by brain size, although small creatures also have amazing intellectual abilities. For example, marine biologist Alex Jordan, who works at the Max Planck Institute for Animal Behavior, recently demonstrated that cleaner wrasses, which are only ten centimeters long, can recognize themselves in a mirror—cats, dogs, and many monkeys can't.•

Since the working class has forfeited its role as the central subject in the struggle for greater social justice, we've witnessed a competition among various marginalized groups to present themselves as particularly discriminated against: women, trans people, Black people, people of color, people with disabilities, the list goes on. Even if intersectional alliances keep emerging, competition for attention prevails in identity politics.•

As early as 1993, Mexican American feminist Elizabeth Martínez warned of "Oppression Olympics." Angela Y. Davis and Elizabeth Martínez, "Coalition Building among People of Color," Inscriptions, vol. 7 (1994), https://culturalstudies.ucsc.edu/inscriptions

• Body with More Organs

• Acknowledge Your Own Oppression

/volume-7/angela-y-davis-elizabeth-martinez/. With the advent of social media, this struggle has become more heated. If you comment on discriminations that you haven't experienced yourself, you make yourself suspect of obscuring the view on those who are actually suffering.

Thus, it can also be criticized that I, as a White man of average height, am writing this text and not my 1.53-meter-tall wife who, despite open stigmatization ("You're tiny!"; "You'd better wear high heels!"), occupies a leading professional position. Why don't I write about my own visual impairment or left-handedness?

I think it's risky to put all the emphasis on your own unequal conditions in the fight for more equality. Consistent political success requires broad alliances. Instead of discriminating against others as less discriminated against, it would be more effective to help as many as possible to also experience themselves as more or less discriminated against and to develop an overarching solidarity on that basis. Corresponding approaches existed in the noughties with Michael Hardt and Antonio Negri's call for a "multitude" united in love, or in 2011 with the Occupy Movement chanting "We are the 99 percent." But they failed to launch concrete political demands and initiatives.

All social groups are affected by heightism; even tall men can experience it from even taller men. Height is undoubtedly measurable, and there is no need for discrete categories such as Black, of color, White, cis, trans, or agender. This is why heightism could become the Archimedean point from which we take a comparative look at all other discrimination—just like how in social democracy and socialism, the exploitation of the worker has been the Archimedean point from which unemployment, homelessness, and poverty in old age have also been fought.

Identity politics has been accused of paying too little attention to material hardships in its media and legal skirmishes. In the fight against heightism, however, you could easily resort to an instrument that directly addresses monetary

Hans Hemmert, *Level (2m groß sein)*, 1997, Styrodur/rubber/velcro (fifty pairs of platform shoes ranging from five to forty-three centimeters in height), © DACS 2024

conditions: a size-based income and wealth tax. Discrimination that goes beyond heightism could be taken into account in the form of favorable coefficients.

It would be similar to Trump's beloved game of golf: the handicap wouldn't be a measure of how far behind some are compared to others, but how much some are given a head start so that everyone has an equal chance to win.

## Consensual Gift Economy
2021

> Whereas aristocratic societies are based on the enslavement of others and bourgeois societies on the enslavement of yourself, monadic societies are based on the re-creation of yourself as distinctly unique. Propelled by the arts, this premise determines the functionality of basic social parameters like governance, money, and charity.

Any society depends on its members giving each other credit, that is, active trust. If everyone were to linger around waiting for others to take the first step, nothing would happen. In oral tribal societies you can give a positive or negative gift (the first is usually simply called a gift; the latter, theft) to other members or tribes, provoking either gratitude or revenge. Giving to others is an investment in bonding and making friends; taking makes a profit you pay for by making enemies. To not respond means to surrender.

Cultures of writing allow societies to reach far beyond what can be inspected by a single person. The tribal principle of solidarity survives within personal relationships, while on a larger scale, the investment in others—as a mutual ownership—is replaced by the investment in personal property.*

The rulers regard their subjects as their property. They enforce both what they give and what they take, and trust that this deal is attractive enough for their subjects not to risk leaving or rebelling. Their subjects have to trust that elsewhere, the rulers' conditions would be even worse, or that risking leaving or rebelling would be punished by taking even more from them. To eradicate any idea of choice, the rulers claim to be chosen by god(s)—owner(s) of the whole world. To set against the rulers, you can claim to follow the commands of the god(s) and risk being demonized.

The rulers unburden themselves from sustaining their subjects by allowing them to trade (i.e., voluntarily agree on an immediate exchange of goods). Here, the subjects compete with others who offer or request similar things. To agree on an exchange, you have to trust in the quality of the others' goods. The judiciary and money can substitute trust in your trading partner with trust in the rulers. You might even agree on only acquiring the right to use a good and return a payment per time called rent (commodities), wage (people), or interest (money). Rather than being enslaved by others, the market enables you to offer yourself as a slave under certain terms. Those who don't manage to sustain themselves through trade might beg, or are offered alms. Alms are gifts that the receivers aren't expected to give back, but that upfront label them as losers. Charity is a degrading act of mercy.

The class that evolves through successful trading, the bourgeoisie, adopts market practices in self-reference: instead of following certain bonds (destinies), you choose between different options. Your enslavement by the ruling aristocracy is replaced by you enslaving yourself.

Monks and nuns are the intermediaries between the aristocracy and the bourgeoisie. They escape the aristocratic command by submitting themselves full-time to transcendental beings and principles (different from shamans, prophets, and priests, who are legitimized as transmitters to ordinary people). The bourgeoisie secularize the monks' and nuns' strategy, create a short circuit, and enslave themselves.

Despite the call for freedom and equality, the range of these self-enslavements is largely restricted, due to social norms and scarcities, with the wealthy male bourgeoisie effectively installing themselves as the new rulers. Only when exploiting the poor workforce to such a degree that it responds with unified strikes, boycotts, and looting, if not revolution, do the rich concede to the demands of the poor. Men, rigidly reducing their wives to the role of mother, make them pamper and emotionally monopolize their male offspring to a degree that ruins their ability to carry on the patriarchal regime. Meanwhile, people's own bodies break rigid regimes of the mind through obsessive behaviors like addiction, OCD, or other neuroses. The self-enslavements of the liberal order are undesirably and asymmetrically intertwined.[•]

What monasteries are in the aristocratic society, the arts are in the bourgeois society: the one legitimate escape. Here, you're allowed to overcome all mutual enslavements, enthrone yourself as your own god or ruler, and perform what would otherwise be inappropriate. But in doing so, you submit to the draconic slavery of originality to prove your godlike genius, only to then be followed by other artists who are forced to be original too. The moment you create a new work of art, it's already history.

In an aristocratic society, the arts express a god's or a ruler's perfection—for the price of not being real. The arts are too good to be true. In a bourgeois society, the arts express human genius—for the price of being too original to be part of everyday culture. In the following individualistic society, striving to be original itself becomes everyday culture. Established artists are no longer idols (laureated outcasts), but ideals. Everybody tries to be an artist, and the arts are no longer protected as the sacred or freaky other—just as asceticism becomes a general principle in a bourgeois society. With masses of other artists around you, it would appear ridiculous to still claim the status of a god—but this only increases the pressure to be original. The artistic focus shifts from fashioning eternal beauty, horror, or truth to distinguishing oneself as unique.

This process gains momentum to the extent that people are replaced by machines as specific means of production—mainly because art still can't be created by machines and because there is more time to consume it. But art can be mass-produced and mass-distributed by machines. And even though the internet allows worldwide distribution for everybody, there is hardly a chance to get through, and even for the few who make it, it's usually with works that can be consumed within seconds.* For most people, it's more promising to work on themselves with the intent of increasing their exchange value within a job, family, friendship, hookup, or romance.* Alternatively, you can work on yourself to make yourself auto-amicably and autoerotically self-sufficient, or to make yourself a gift to the world.* In return, you expect the same sensitivity that the bourgeois society reserves for well-defined artworks for yourself.

A bourgeois society still needs extensive leadership—to ensure everybody's chances in enslaving themselves. Moreover, all leadership has to be checked, contained, and eventually reformed by other levels of leadership: a circular hierarchy between people (both voters and citizens) and different institutions (both elected and governing). The evolution of a bourgeois society corresponds with ever-more bureaucracy, regulations, and taxes.

In a similar fashion, an individualistic society is very much concerned about guidelines. The more individualistic people get, the more they have to coordinate their multiple idiosyncrasies. While a bourgeois society is quick to agree on a humanistic set of universal natural rights and focuses its disputes on how to best guarantee them—leading to a wide range of ideologies from libertarianism to communism—an individualistic society has to navigate between lots of constantly changing priorities.

All substantial discrimination that a bourgeois society allows is supposed to be determined by physiognomy and is thereby deemed natural: race, gender, age. It's a matter of political correctness to also question naturally predetermined discriminations as racism, sexism, ableism, ageism, etc.

Revolting against your naturalized discrimination makes you unify within the frames of an enforced identity.

• Tardies
• Expanded Sex Work

Ego Tribes •
Orcies

Paradoxically, this might make you proud of exactly that identity. Bourgeois society has an ambivalent relationship to identity politics: it's not just that identity politics attacks the blind spots of humanistic universalism but also that it might actually oppose universalism in favor of a fundamentalist backlash.°

The situation gets even more complex when individualism comes into play as it opposes every kind of essentialist identity—also that of humanism. Bourgeois society is cornered between identitarian fundamentalisms and an individualistic radicalization nourished by the arts. The more individualism generalizes the freedom of the arts, the more bourgeois society questions this (often constitutionally protected) freedom and moves toward authoritarianism.

The arts have two options for how to oppose this bourgeois threat: they develop ever-new provocations to test their freedom (and freedom in general), or they use their role as the nucleus of a new, what I call monadic, society to develop new, individualistic modes of togetherness rather than fight existing ones. A combination of both is also possible: new modes might be propagated in acts of aesthetic or symbolic terrorism, if not regarded themselves as such.

Individualism is often confused with egoism.° But it's consumer capitalism that makes individualism antisocial. Even when you meet with people, your attention is dominated by commercial places, services, and fashions, whether in physical space with restaurants (dating), clubs (hooking up), and housing (mating), or on social media. Instead, nonprofit art spaces could offer opportunities to meet far from commercial activities and figure out how to live together in difference— not just in public but also in private; not just politically, but intimately, correct.°

In bourgeois and aristocratic societies, misdeeds are punished—on an ultimate level by the overall institution of the state doing you physical harm. In an aristocratic society, this harm can be irreversible; in a bourgeois society, you're meant to get a second chance; in a monadic society, a criminal is already punished by having been allowed or seduced to

Mutual Enslavements  ·

·  Orcies

·  Intimate Correctness

become one. While humanism assumes that everybody is equipped by birth with an understanding of a set of social rules (or the categorical imperative as a single rule) and the free will to follow them—education merely activating them—in a monadic society, everything is everybody's liability. It comes with being God.

In an aristocratic society, your social status is very much fate, unless violently broken. A bourgeois society outlaws serf-dom and allows for mobility between classes, encourages non-arranged marriages and education outside the family. But you can hardly change your nationality and the family is still a pretty totalitarian unit until you reach the age of consent. Besides, you're expected to live within the naturalized limits of gender, race, and age. A monadic society doesn't just let everyone theoretically develop freely (as in a bourgeois soci-ety) but tries to offer everyone the possibility to actually do so. People can be as different as they like, but no difference—whether in property, intelligence, well-being, or attraction—is a given. It's a society radically devoid of privileges. In case of scarcity, everyone goes without, or a lottery decides.*

In terms of justice, a monadic society is far more am-bitious than communism—and also far more flexible. In a bourgeois society, money has been the ultimate drug, and there is good reason for a monadic society to also treat money like drugs: not to generally forbid it and force it to go under-ground (as in communism) but to contain its use. Money might only be allowed for certain activities, in certain zones, at certain times, or for people who completely commit to it with all its side effects.

A bourgeois society follows majority rule to determine what is right for all. As the choice of the majority might turn out to be wrong, it's important that government and laws can always be reversed. A monadic society has to give up on find-ing one solution or compromise that's best for all. Democracy appears as the terror of the majority over the minority and is therefore not intrinsically better than oligarchy.* While a bourgeois society is constantly balancing between justice and

• Society of Games
Real Estate Porn

• Middle-Class Warriors
Pre-AGI Democracy

freedom within one legislation, a monadic society is balancing between inclusion and segregation. People might not just choose between different political candidates but between different political systems.* The claim of reversibility shifts from your government and laws to your own commitment: everybody must always have the option to exit as well as an abundance of other possibilities to enter. Whether on an intimate or a state level, every interaction requires explicit consent. For a subjectivist monad, its every interaction requires consent. For an objectivist monad, every interaction on Earth requires consent.*

To weigh the needs of all the different personas, communities and substates could easily become very complex and difficult to control. To mitigate this, people could be limited (even more than in a bourgeois society) to deciding about only a few basic parameters, while an executive body of experts and AGI handles the details more or less transparently. If you want to be safe from wrongdoing, you withdraw from society and focus on yourself, or go virtual.*

To still interact directly with others, you can't take anything for granted. Even for basic acts of charity like providing food or shelter, you have to consider numerous ethical, ecological, political, and personal implications. On the other hand, once you dare to be good and help satisfy the needs of others, there is no reason to stop at payable goods and services, if not money, as bourgeois charity does. Why should alms given out of love not include love?* Through teachings and drills, compassion could evolve beyond the scope of traditional charity. Monadic charity has to be intimate as it's based on the very specific needs of the other. Monadic gifts have to be consensual: you can't expect others to respond to your gift in a similar way, nor expect them to be fine with it no matter what. Monadic charity is like trying to please a customer to such a degree that you don't even ask for payment.* No self-enslavement needed. It's your jolly will to help others.

Middle-Class Warriors •
Pre-AGI Democracy

Body with More Organs •
World as Museum

Automatic Privacy •

Intimate Correctness •
Commie •

Commie
2018

> True communism never evolved beyond the size of small
> communities. Is that as far as our genetically determined
> solidarity can reach? Commie is a model for an online
> platform that allows you to give according to your abilities and
> take according to your needs—on a potentially global scale.

### Situation

Automation is about to create a world with an abundance of goods and services and fewer and fewer jobs left to earn them. Traditional capitalism and socialism rely on most people's labor—and it turns out to be quite difficult to replace this foundation with either a general basic income (the socialist answer) or new property concepts that allow you to sell even your personal data, your organs, your right to vote,[*] your citizenship,[*] or your right to live[*] (the capitalist answer). The first appears to be too expensive, the second too cynical.

      Communism could be the answer to this dilemma. People usually regard communism as an extreme form of socialism and therefore in strict opposition to capitalism. But communism is also the ideal market where all offers and demands meet. In real life, socialism is just as far away from communism as it is from capitalism. Both socialism and capitalism stagnate rather than evolve further—neither in a linear progression nor dialectically. The ordinary standard of living of the Western *Lumpenproletariat* exceeds what Marx could have imagined for a communist idyll: central heating, free education, free information, free parks, affordable public transport, affordable fresh fruits and vegetables throughout the year, etc. Still, the welfare state lacks generosity: it offers just enough support to ensure that the unemployed don't revolt. They're still meant to long for a decent job—even if they don't have any chances to get one.

Today, communism mostly exists in the form of small enclaves—communes—that are based on specific bonds like kinship, tradition, love. Communes appear as residues of the prehistoric horde: even smaller in size, and centered around archaic activities like raising children, looting, housing, or modestly industrialized farming. Often they rely on formal or informal force (children are born into a family; marriages are difficult to end; sects and gangs threaten to harm you if you try to leave), or turn out to be pretty fragile. As members who don't seem to fit could always be expelled into the welfare state's safety net, these communes are very sensitive to whether all members are contributing adequately. To make things less complex and more in line with the capitalist exchange economy, the communist maxim "From each according to their abilities, to each according to their needs" is often pushed aside by a simple tit for tat—a nonmonetary credit system of similar favors and sanctions.[*] Privately run charity projects like food banks, giveaway shops, or charity cafés, which offer gratis services to everybody in need without any quid pro quo, come with the flavor of being not really from this world— they're of no significance compared to the amount of wealth generated and moved by the market and the state. In everyday interactions with strangers, selflessness is limited to small symbolic gestures and rare cases of acute emergency.

It's often believed that communal solidarity suffers from genetic limitations: only when you know the others personally might you be committed enough to help them all and not abuse others' generosity; on a large scale, communism

seems to depend on dictates and surveillance, while in capitalism, the invisible hand of the market makes everybody's
egoism serve the common good. But as sociologist Max
Weber first observed, capitalism needs a very specific egoism:
"ascetic Protestantism" makes you reinvest your profits rather
than spend them on your family and friends. In many societies
the adaptation to capitalist morality (often misleadingly called
"amorality") was and is a tedious process. At the same time,
developed capitalist societies were forced to outbalance the
market economy with social welfare and massive subsidies for
certain businesses. Capitalism provoked an unprecedented
public spending ratio of up to 50 percent or more.[*] A core principle of capitalism—to charge or to be charged according to
the service—was never fully implemented. Information technology serves the introduction of ever-new discriminations:
companies rank their customers and individualize their prices
and services due to a set of untransparent algorithmic criteria.
Again, state control is needed to overcome market discrimination based on race, gender, wealth, or age[*]—unless, as in the
case of China's Social Credit System, the state itself facilitates
those discriminations.[*]

    With the internet came hopes of automatically over-
coming capitalism—at least in the sphere of information. The
internet allows everyone to easily share reproducible information in the widest sense (reports, research, comments,
instructions, art) at little or no cost. You can reach out to potentially all humans and nonhumans in the world; to a defined
group of "chat partners," "friends," or "followers"; or to a
specific individual. Indeed, soon, billions of people participated in this practice—only that even before the internet,
information wasn't rare and was often free. Original free content comes with the flavor of advertisements (for products,
beliefs, or yourself) and targeting (for future advertisements or
sociopolitical control). Most free information is cheaply
distributed by spreading (rather than "sharing") unverified
content; properly individualized services like one-to-one

tutorials or investigations on request are rare. Except when it comes to very thin markets, we're flooded with unwanted and unreliable content. Instead of gaining knowledge, we lose interest in knowledge altogether—though not enough to actually drop out and get offline. We never stop looking for ever-more options, which we hardly pursue (except when it comes to shopping).•

The internet also offers new opportunities for non-virtual charity, as it no longer depends on a fixed space and regular opening hours or persistently going through hundreds and thousands of offers until you accidentally stumble upon one that fits you. But platforms specializing in giveaways didn't really take off, as comparable services got incorporated into dominant corporate platforms; for the sake of expansion, trading platforms often let people offer and request items for free. Crowdfunding asks you to fund projects just out of enthusiasm; what funders get in return usually isn't much more than symbolic recognition. It's begging, but for exceptional needs, and with the platform receiving a share of all alms. Couchsurfing offers free travel accommodation, though it promotes itself more like a non-romantic dating service. Dating apps offer free opportunities for romantic encounters but are designed in ways that make you continue to be on the lookout for new matches rather than actually meeting and then exiting the app for a relationship.• Blockchains allow you to cheaply finalize agreements in a trustworthy way, without governmental approval, in order to make their own currency credible and applicable.

### Challenge

To become a common reality, communism has to give up on merely objecting to the existing political and economic system. See *Solution 275–294: Communists Anonymous* (Berlin: Sternberg Press, 2017), which I edited with Joshua Simon. But thanks to autocratic socialism, communism lost too much credibility to make a democratic transition to communism likely. An advantage of

• Church of Lots

• Orcies

the world of finance is that you don't need to win over the majority to introduce a highly lucrative investment asset. But while it might be worth speculating on the rise of a dictator, the outcome of a successful bet on communism would be the confiscation of your win.

Meanwhile, information technology is rapidly developing. Even though it's currently serving an ever-greater accumulation of money and power, people still don't give away their attention spans via exclusive contracts. Power and money can be accumulated rather safely but our attention has to be won anew every day. So why not give initiating communism through information technology a proper try? Programming, promoting, and maintaining an online platform would be less risky and effortful than a violent revolution or tiring politics. Maybe the only reason it hasn't really been tried yet is that after a century of brutal struggles to overcome capitalism, it doesn't appear to be heroic enough.

A significant communist online platform would have to:
- be self-sufficient
- inspire the will to help
- privilege those most in need
- allow for a complex division of labor
- provide costly means of production
- expand beyond its territorial vicinity without staying purely virtual
- ensure a certain quality without following strict hierarchies, preselecting members, or spying on members
- actually help people and not just overwhelm them with options
- gradually grow the number of users and the intensity of user engagement

Concept

Different from a communist enclave, the communist online platform Commie doesn't expect you to live a completely communist life. You can dedicate as much or as little to the communist commune as you like. Commie operates as a nonprofit

DAO. Major decisions are subject of referenda while honorary delegates are responsible for day-to-day decisions and tasks.

Commie could start with a fixed number of people. In case there are more applicants than places, a lottery would determine the initial members.[*] Only a very small portion of members could buy into Commie, either for a fixed high minimum price or through an auction. To propel speculation, these members could have the right to resell their NFT-based membership at a different price, of which 50 percent or more goes to Commie. You could also donate part of your savings or earnings. This income is used for operational costs and to finance nonprofit companies that offer complex gratis services to Commie's members. The members decide about investments per referendum, and the delegates supervise them to avoid abstraction of funds.

Commie's basic function is to allow its members to publish all kinds of unilateral offers and requests. The platform isn't a swap meet but rather works like a giveaway shop. To avoid discrimination, it doesn't follow a "first come, first served" logic. In case of excess demand, drawing lots decides. Offers and requests are made completely anonymously, unless certain information (location, age, gender, etc.) is of particular relevance. To protect the platform from state interference, complete encryption is mandatory.

To avoid internal moral pressure, members don't know about others' commitment to the group. But to keep them motivated, members know about their personal commitment ranking based on the number of times they've submitted something and the votes by its beneficiaries.[*] In the transitional phase from capitalism to proper communism, a higher ranking could increase your chances in the distribution lottery. Hardships allow you to go for a lower handicap in the lottery. Like all major settings of the platform, ranking and lottery algorithms are subject to a regular debate and vote.

Offerers and requesters are encouraged to share their experiences anonymously with the community or in a mutual debriefing. In case there is a claim of abuse, volunteers hear both sides and offer mediation and advice. In the event that this effort doesn't succeed, the case is brought to the elected authority to investigate and eventually impose measurements that facilitate safe interactions.

Commie can grow indefinitely or also fork into smaller divisions that each cater to specific mentalities or identities. To avoid discrimination between the different divisions, every request or offer that isn't met within a division is automatically forwarded to the others.

Still, doesn't Commie stabilize capitalism rather than pushing it back? True, poor people tend to be more generous than rich people, so instead of insisting on taking from the rich, Commie makes the poor help each other instead. But helping each other is a legal method to avoid taxation and to at least not actively feed the rich.[*]

Intimate Correctness
2018

The call for spontaneity results in indifference toward
strangers. Artist Dora García's performance series
*The Romeos* enforces male flirting and works as a pre-study
on how to extend affirmative action to the intimate sphere
and redistribute love.

Libertine Chastity

Who are you to approach a stranger? Then again, your looks
and movements are constantly sending signals anyhow.
Modern urban life came hand in hand with a set of bourgeois
rules, in particular manners and dress codes, which were
supposed to if not minimize, then at least homogenize, this
constant signaling. Increasing individualization made such
codes appear random or oppressive, and it became a matter of
personal freedom to shake them off. At the peak of this development, the hippies combined the search for their own
expressions with an effort to communicate as uninhibitedly
with strangers as they did with friends. To act spontaneously
was regarded as a matter of truth (i.e., authenticity). Once
people overcame social restrictions, all their aggressions,
frustrations, and neuroses would evaporate or could be acted
out in primal scream and encounter group therapy to finally
realize that all beings on Earth are connected and dependent

on each other.[*] New theoretical schools like cybernetics or ecology seemed to have the same essence as old schools of mysticism: we're all one gigantic entity. No need to love your neighbor as though they were yourself—your neighbor is yourself! The more you relate to and release your own impulses, the more you will overcome your egoism and submit to global, if not cosmic, harmony.[*]

This concept of a general (re)union came with two apparent problems. First: if others weren't ready to find themselves in you, they could be repelled by your openness and generosity or exploit it. Second, as the different mystic schools already knew: the only reliable way for us humans to realize that we and everything or everyone around us are the same is in communal ecstasy or meditation (i.e., when we overcome concrete manifestations of ourselves and the world). Paradoxically, opening up to the world leads to a double de-limitation: from those who don't open up sufficiently or from the world and ourselves altogether. Hippie-infused technology, in particular social media, didn't make it any better: starting with the promise of turning the whole globe into one great village, social media actually fractured it into countless different community particles that are hostile or, at best, indifferent to each other with lots of loneliness in between.[*]

Meanwhile, our presence in public space (the physical one where you meet strangers involuntarily and can't turn them off) morphed into a sort of limbo. Our freedom to appear however we like and therefore not give a damn about what others think goes hand in hand with an indifference about others' appearance. To be able to bear each other, both sides play it cool (like mutual servants)—which, then again, doesn't make it that attractive to appear extravagant, as people won't really express how much they're impressed or repelled. And what would our one true expression be anyway, when we moderate ourselves according to different communities? As a result, we rather dress down, in a casual way.[*] If we mark ourselves permanently with tattoos, we usually do it in a camp, ostentatiously nonessential manner and in places that we can

Sweetness  •

Body with More Organs  •

•  Automatic Privacy

•  Tardies

hide under our usual clothing.* We might dress revealingly but shy away from active seduction and being seduced by strangers. Even people who are already intimate with each other shy away from making out in public.

To initiate an intimate encounter, you have to overcome initial ignorance and doubt. Different from pre-hippie times, there is no script to follow, and when making a move, you have the complex task of being surprising (original), fun (playful), sincere (authentic), and serious (trustworthy) all at once. This is particularly the case with men approaching women. As it's traditionally up to men to court, and as men are at the same time the more aggressive and violent gender, it makes women twofold reserved. To avoid making fools of themselves, most men don't hit on female strangers in public. Those who try nonetheless easily appear even more idiotic, and their likely failure tends to make them aggressive, that is, if their mating rituals don't already show aggressive undertones from the beginning—aggression being the only way they seem to be able to make an impression on female strangers.

### Enforced Flirting

To break this tainted dynamic (which could eventually lead to a ban on flirting in public) and to again turn public space into a promise of mutual desire, artist Dora García developed the performance series *The Romeos* (2008–ongoing). She cast young, mostly heterosexual men (according to common standards, attractive, and, according to a poster announcement, equipped with an "impeccably respectful and polite" demeanor) to spend all day flirting and eventually getting intimate with strangers.

In a heterosexual context, it's usually women who are paid to flirt (hostesses, bartenders, waitresses) and seduce (strippers, escorts, mistresses), as men are supposed to do it anyhow—even though they do it less and less and, if they still do it, despite a shrinking tolerance, more and more inappropriately. Recently, García explained in an email to me: "There was the idea of a vengeance, since we're always presented with women's desire and desirability seen through the lens of men—this was the opposite."

The fact that the Romeos act secretively and on their own terms releases you from the shame of accepting a paid service (in line with the decency of gigolos and mistresses to offer their services not explicitly as such and to expect gifts rather than a fee). The fact that the Romeos are on another woman's mission and payroll spices up the encounter with some James Bondish flair—with García as Miss Moneypenny: "I had images in mind going from Socrates to Gilles de Rais to Wall Street–eager apprentices ready to do anything to progress in life, young male ambition at its top excitement."

García's first two *Romeos* performances were limited to a few days and had the character of nonscientific experiments. Except for some random photos, the performances weren't observed by the artist, and she explicitly didn't ask the performers to report back to her about their experiences. Quoting from the instructions García sent to the performers of the first Romeo performance at the Frieze Art Fair in London in 2008: "I trust you completely and believe you will carry out the performance as agreed, but you could go home and sleep and I would never know. This trust I place on you liberates you from any 'results,' I will never ask you what happened and therefore you will betray no one's feelings by telling what happened."

Even though the term Romeo refers to the code word for East German Cold War spies who used their seductive powers to get their hands on the capitalist enemy's confidential information, García didn't expect her Romeos to spy. She even announced a time and area where her Romeos were supposed to be active. What intrigues García about spies is how knowledge about their deployment accumulates uncertainty—serving contemporary art's epistemological cause to question and subvert. The Romeos bring back flirting as a casual joyful encounter but at the price of deceit. Quoting again from García's instructions to the performers: "The important thing is that the poster placed at the art fair explaining the project makes everyone at the fair suspicious of every young, attractive, and kind man around, and there will be a lot more of them than you five; every conversation will be under suspicion, and this will be independent of anything you do; even if you are at home sleeping, the suspicion will be there." And while with spies, the uncertainty is usually limited to those who might be spied on, in the case of the Romeos, even they themselves are left in doubt about what their mission is actually about: Which person should they approach next? Should they always tell the truth, or at what level of intimacy should they reveal their true identity? At what point is it time to say goodbye? Should they instead stay at home and get paid anyway?

In the last weeks, I managed to interview seven of the nine former Romeos about their experiences, and each of them had a different take on the challenge. It had been nine years (London) and six years (Paris) since their performances, and memory itself had become pretty deceitful. But distance also helped to emphasize and contextualize some key experiences. Back then, most Romeos had been in their early or mid-twenties and had just finished or were about to finish their studies in theater or performance. For many, it had been one of their very first proper engagements (according to varying memories, rewarded with around 150 pounds per day in London and around 300 euros in Paris), and being left alone for a couple of days with enormous freedom made them extremely aware of their strengths and weaknesses—as a performer and as a person. This was even more the case as both performances had the spatial limitations of an art fair (Frieze London and Paris Photo, respectively)—an environment most of the performers weren't familiar with and none had spent that much time in.

While some felt intimidated by the audience at the fair (in particular, the audience's disinterest, if not annoyance, about the presence of young men without any apparent assets), others felt empowered by an official, though secretive, mission within an environment of power. Some suffered from an unclear agenda, while others enjoyed getting paid decently for doing whatever. Some enjoyed acting without an audience; others felt observed by people who supposedly recognized them as Romeos (particularly when these people were the ones who initiated an encounter). For some, the performance came naturally, as to them, flirting was a daily "pansexual" routine and part of every conversation; others felt uncomfortable ("stalkerish," "creepy") about their task, hid behind a masquerade (a hat, a flamboyant suit), and felt even more exposed. Some were fine with using a standard pretext (asking for directions, inquiring about a certain topic) to make contact; others felt embarrassed and bored by themselves. Some encountered people strictly by chance (whoever would make eye contact with them, whoever would start to contemplate the same artwork); others followed personal preferences (even looking for an actual partner in life) or specific challenges (flirting with an elderly woman, approaching a famous artist). Some kept their conversations casual; others actually tried to act sort of like spies and get a hold of intimate information. Some would have been up for continuing certain encounters beyond the fair and making out; others would have found it disturbing if someone would have really hit on them.

Sometimes phone numbers were exchanged or the conversation continued via email and social media, but even though some Romeos had heard of other Romeos getting intimate, the ones I spoke with (all heterosexual) told me that they never made out with someone or dated someone outside the fair. None of them were really tested in their ability to make someone fall in love with them and to make them believe themselves to be in love. The only women who became (platonically) involved with the Romeos for more than an hour (one even throughout all the days of the performance) seemed to know about their role and to actively play with it. None of the Romeos I spoke with remembered having ended up in an ethically delicate situation, and I wonder if being all too aware of that risk made them play it safe from the beginning: no one made up a fake identity (except not mentioning their deployment as a Romeo); no one proposed kissing, hugging, or snuggling; and no one invited someone to dinner or a drink outside the fair. Some tried for more but didn't succeed. And those who might have succeeded might have had good reasons not to tell me or not to speak with me at all. Had there actually been cases in which people felt betrayed? This begs the question: How or under which circumstances could the Romeos actually seduce and avoid moral pitfalls?

### Love Redistribution

The aristocracy act as though they're the natural masters of humankind. Monks and nuns escape their command by submitting to a transcendental being (God) or principle (nirvana). The bourgeoisie secularize this strategy, create a short circuit, and enslave themselves.[*] To, at least in (liberal) theory, not suppress others, they focus on the accumulation of entities like money or knowledge, which, unlike territory or natural resources, aren't naturally limited but can be produced: there is enough for everyone who tries hard (i.e., enslaves themselves). But as bourgeois production nonetheless depends on others' human labor, others' consumption, territory, and natural resources, it hasn't just accumulated wealth but also reached unique proportions of exploitation (colonialism, imperialism, racism, patriarchalism, pollution).[*]

The internalized slavery of the bourgeoisie is totalitarian against others and oneself. Early on, this provoked Romanticism to proclaim the complete freedom of the individual, celebrating enthusiasm and spontaneity. This liberation was contained privately as love marriage and expressed socially as nationalism, both utterly totalitarian concepts. In the case of nationalism, your fate is to act like permanently mobilized soldiers; in the case of love marriage, like mutually enchained prisoners.[*]

Only when bourgeois society managed to provide general affluence while looting at an ever-greater scale did a large number of citizens make a new effort to fundamentally liberate themselves and society: the hippies. The bourgeoisie had discredited the aristocracy as vain (i.e., unproductive and pretentious): important matters beg straightforward measures; otherwise, you shouldn't shove your weight around, that is, neither lie nor tell the truth, neither obey nor disobey— just shut your mouth and endure, or seek distance. The hippies understood even that form of passive politeness as dishonest and enslaving. If only all people would be true to themselves and others, it would produce enough generosity and understanding to render politeness no longer necessary.

But just like love, truth can't simply be revealed. And even if it could, why should all different loves and truths get along in harmony? After the defining moment of hippie culture passed, political correctness worked as a new etiquette—one that explicitly expands liberal respect to those the bourgeoisie discriminated against in the first place as less productive, such as people with disabilities, racial minorities, and women. Affirmative action adds policies to mere words and gestures.[*]

Only why should affirmative action be limited to the public sphere? Even though making out in public is rare, at least talking about intimate matters in public has become common.[*] Where to draw the line? Why fight against discrimination based on race, gender, age, height, etc. and not apply affirmative action to intimate relationships?

From a liberal understanding, intimacy is supposed to be authentic: we like and desire what we like and desire. So, once we realize the discriminatory social implications of our very own feelings, what can we do? Blame capitalism, nationalism, and other dirty isms for having polluted our minds with disgust, neglect, and superficiality, and return to hippie naivety? Or accept that our discriminatory tendencies are rooted in our very nature and that all we can do is try to overcome intimacy altogether as an inevitable source of injustice and pain? Our society is moving in the latter direction anyhow: both the frequency of sexual intercourse and the percentage of people living in a relationship are declining, while we're overrun by tools and media for optimizing masturbation.[*] People who are mad, old, or depressive and therefore likely to have particular difficulties in finding sex or a partner receive

• Heightism    Acknowledge Your Own Oppression

Automatic Privacy •

• Orcies    Ego Tribes

medication that as the main purpose or a side effect reduces their libido.* All we have to do is pathologize ever-more personal conditions.

The liberal alternative is to hold ourselves responsible for being lonely and optimize ourselves to become more attractive and remain so longer—both physically and mentally. We have to constantly enhance ourselves while at the same time being positive about who we currently are. That's a difficult task, and as with every liberal agenda, it runs the risk of instead increasing inequalities.

But just as we can work on ourselves to become more attractive, we can work on finding people attractive whom we usually overlook or avoid. This might be an even more difficult task, but while liberal self-improvement puts the most pressure on those who are considered less beautiful, such an *intimate correctness* holds the privileged particularly liable. Intimate correctness completes political correctness by making feelings, just like words and gestures, part of our etiquette. Political correctness denies the dichotomy of normal/right and abnormal/wrong; intimate correctness denies the dichotomy of true/authentic and false/fake.

Who and how we love are the result of myriads of changing and changeable factors. One crucial factor that all established forms of intimate relationships (from the arranged marriage to the romantic affair) used to have in common is a balancing of the partners' assets. There might be more or less tolerance about what counts as an asset (love, beauty, age, wealth, education, character, social rank), about who is evaluating these assets (the lovers themselves, their families, their friends, their peers, their religious leaders), and to what degree different kinds of assets are convertible. The inherent principle is always that of a market in which the value of the different assets is determined by supply and demand. Whoever ignores this logic is considered to be insane or idiotic.*

Except for its mystic interpretation, free love didn't question the love market but tried to radically liberate it. Free love applied the trickle-down theory to love—with similarly disastrous effects of growing inequality. To utterly liberate love (also from restricting it to humans and domesticated nonhumans), we have to overcome the market principle.* Our responsibility is no longer just to love as much or as little as our counterpart but to give the love that we're good at giving and receive the love that we need. The communist maxim "From each according to their abilities, to each according to their needs" is finally applied to what—once our basic material supplies are secured—most people regard as most important in life: love. While political correctness can intimidate us in our private encounters by making us more sensitive to others' and our own wrongdoings, intimate correctness boosts our love on every level (courtship, care, sex) by empowering us with a new willingness to give and to receive. Making this effort, we can train ourselves to regard all sorts of humans (and other beings) as beautiful and desirable.

Intimate correctness has already been anticipated by Utopian Socialist Charles Fourier. In his book *Le nouveau monde amoureux* (The new amorous world, 1816–18), people live in collectives that regularly come together for meticulously planned orgies. "Angels of virtue" ensure that even the unattractive and infirm receive their "sexual minimum." Ursula K. Le Guin's short story "The Ones Who Walk Away from Omelas" (1973) sketches an utterly harmonious anarchy where "the beautiful nudes can just wander about, offering themselves like divine soufflés to the hunger of the needy and the rapture of the flesh."

Fourier's and Le Guin's utopias come with a price: in *Le nouveau monde amoureux*, private intimacy is strictly forbidden, and in "The Ones Who Walk Away from Omelas," the social idyll depends on detaining at least one pitiful member of society, a random child, in horrible misery. Both limitations might not be substantial: Fourier still fell for the romantic legend that true intimacy trumps any social contract. But love can be both socially committed and private. Le Guin's story ends with people leaving Omelas to eventually find or build a society whose grandeur isn't propelled by guilt.

Still from my video with Alexa Karolinski, *Army of Love*, 2016, commissioned by the 9th Berlin Biennale

García's *Romeos* can be seen in the tradition of these two concepts and can help demonstrate the actual challenges that intimate correctness is facing. The most obvious one is betrayal. Even if the Romeos were to act openly (communicating their agenda at the beginning of every encounter) and even though nothing like a true self exists, the question remains about how much the Romeos only *perform* their interest in the other and how much they really feel it. But every intimate encounter with strangers (and often even with long-term partners and friends) is troubled by that concern. The Romeos could contain it by working on a voluntary basis, not accepting any gifts, and vowing honesty. Exaggerations and lies would be performed only upon request.

The second challenge applies to any affirmative action: How to avoid paternalism and not end up reaffirming discriminatory divisions? But people who lack love can belong to all social groups; the challenge might rather be to also act intimately correct with people who otherwise appear as privileged. To avoid annoying and disturbing others, intimately correct Romeos should act only upon request. A badge could indicate their services.

The third and final challenge: Are we (or at least some of us) actually able to perform intimate correctness in the full sense? This is what my recent project with García and others, *Army of Love*, draws on. Spies can act in disguise and are never to be trusted completely. Soldiers are marked with a uniform and are fully accountable for their actions. Soldiers are armed with a dangerous device (in this case, love) and are drilled to use it under specific circumstances. Armies have been used to enforce what we today call a fascist ideal of beauty: tall, slim, muscular, spotless bodies. It was a romantic mobilization that made this ideal ubiquitous, and it might take a ubiquitous army to overcome it.

Thanks to everyone who discussed the texts and ideas in this book with me, especially Julieta Aranda, Christian Bayerlein, Lauren Boyle, Staci Bu Shea, Ekaterina Degot, Sonia Fernández Pan, Rosa Ferré, Dora García, Mathias Gatza, Ine Gevers, Martin Hammer, Marah J. Hardt, Ingeborg Harms, Nikolaus Hirsch, Hanspeter Hofmann, Elfriede Jelinek, Alex Jordan, Martti Kalliala, Alexa Karolinski, Rem Koolhaas, Maria Magdalena Ludewig (†), Tom McCarthy, Michelangelo Miccolis, Erik Niedling, Kyong Park, David Pearce, Hila Peleg, Filipa Ramos, Markus Reymann, David Riff, Marco Roso, Alessandro Schiattarella, Emily Segal, Joshua Simon, Mirjana Smolic, Jenna Sutela, Alexander Tarakhovsky, Francesca Thyssen-Bornemisza, Matthias Vernaldi(†), Ignacio Vidal-Folch, Luuk van Middelaar, Jeronimo Voss, and Dana Yahalomi. Thanks to all my students at the Institute Art Gender Nature, HGK Basel FHNW, for sharing and discussing their views with me. Thanks to Niklas Luhmann(†), who sparked my interest in social configurations and critically commented on my first efforts to fathom them in my own terms. Thanks to Caroline Schneider for her long-standing trust in my take on the world, Anita Iannacchione for her exceedingly engaged edits, and Boah Kim for her graphic vision of this book. Thanks to the editors who worked with me on previous versions of these essays, in particular, Nick Axel, Max Bach, and Alexander Scrimgeour. Finally, I thank Chus Martínez for being my partner in life and ideas, and our son, Viggo Napoléon, for challenging me in ever-new, joyful ways.

Earlier versions or parts of the following essays have been previously published:

"Acknowledge Your Own Oppression"—*Mousse*, no. 60 (October–November 2017)

"Automatic Privacy"—*e-flux Architecture* (June 2020), as part of *Housing*, a collaboration with the Karlsruhe Institute of Technology Chair for Theory of Architecture

"Body with More Organs"—as "How Can the Trees Stand Us Any Longer," in *Spike*, no. 65 (Autumn 2020)

"Comic Purgatory"—*ISSUE*, no. 9 (2021), the annual art journal of LASALLE College of the Arts, Singapore

"Consensual Gift Economy"—as "Jolly Compassion," in Marie de Brugerolle, ed., *Post-performance Future: Method/e* (Monlet: T&P Publishing, 2023)

"Expanded Sex Work"—*Spike*, no. 37 (Autumn 2013), translated from the German by Gerrit Jackson

"Heightism"—as "Die älteste Diskriminierung der Welt," in *Das Magazin*, no. 41 (2020)

"A House of Her Own"—*Kradvat Interwoven* (2017)

"Intimate Correctness"—*Dora García: Love Comes from the Most Unexpected Places* (Trondheim: Trondheim Kunstmuseum, 2018)

"Middle-Class Warriors"—*032c*, no. 29 (Winter 2015/16), furthermore, the chapter is based on an excerpt from "Theme Communities," in my book *Solution 186–195: Dubai Democracy* (Berlin: Sternberg Press, 2010), and on "Solution 262—∞: Greece Archipelago," in *South as a State of Mind*, no. 3 (Fall/Winter 2013)

"Posthuman Test Grounds"—*Spike*, no. 67 (Spring 2021)

"Real Estate Porn"—*e-flux Architecture* (November 2016), as part of *Superhumanity*, a project at the 3rd Istanbul Design Biennial, produced in cooperation with the Istanbul Design Biennial; the National Museum of Modern and Contemporary Art, Korea; the Govett-Brewster Art Gallery, New Zealand; and the Ernst Schering Foundation

"Terror's Child Muses"—*e-flux Architecture* (June 2021), as part of *Cascades*, a collaboration with MAAT—Museum of Art, Architecture, and Technology, Lisbon

"Wanderers"—*Obieg*, no. 3 (2017), translated from the German by Amy Patton

"What Comes after Welfare?"—*Mousse*, no. 47 (February–March 2015)

"Wishful Death"—as "Mein Wille geschehe," in *Das Magazin*, no. 16 (2020)

"World as Museum"—an excerpt from "Wet Gods," in my book *Solution 295-304: Mare Amoris* (Berlin: Sternberg Press, 2020)

"World as Program"—as "World Program," in Hanspeter Hofmann, *NEON TYPEN*INNEN*, 2022, inkjet and tape on newsprint, edition

Ingo Niermann is a speculative writer and the editor of the Solutions Series at Sternberg Press. Recent books include *Solution 295-304: Mare Amoris* (2020), *Burial of the White Man* (with Erik Niedling, 2019), and *Solution 275-294: Communists Anonymous* (coedited with Joshua Simon, 2017). Based on his novel *Solution 257: Complete Love* (2016), Niermann initiated the Army of Love, a project that tests and promotes a need-oriented redistribution of sensual love. His work has been featured at the Berlin Biennale; the Istanbul Biennale; documenta, Kassel; the Venice Biennale; ZKM | Center for Art and Media, Karlsruhe; and the Solomon R. Guggenheim Museum, New York. Niermann is a lecturer at the Institute Art Gender Nature, HGK Basel FHNW.

Ingo Niermann
The Monadic Age
Notes on the Coming Social Order

Editor: Anita Iannacchione
Proofreading: Danielle N. Carter
Design: Boah Kim
Typefaces: JA RS (Boah Kim, Jacopo Atzori),
Lyon (Commercial Type)
Printing: Tallinn Book Printers, Estonia

ISBN 978-1-915609-24-3

Distributed by The MIT Press, Art Data,
Les presses du réel, and Idea Books

Cover: Boah Kim

Published by Sternberg Press
71–75 Shelton Street
UK–London WC2H 9JQ
www.sternberg-press.com